Strengthening Experiential Education within Your Institution

by

Jane C. Kendall, John S. Duley,
Thomas C. Little, Jane S. Permaul, Sharon Rubin

A sourcebook for faculty, deans, presidents, and program directors who want to see their institutions utilize the full value of learning through experience. A collection of advice and models from U.S. colleges and universities that have worked to integrate experiential education into their institutional missions, campus values, curricula, faculty roles, financial and administrative structures, and evaluation systems. For those who want to offer their students carefully monitored opportunities for active learning through internships, field studies, cooperative education, community service-learning, practica, cross-cultural programs, and other forms of experiential education.

**National Society for Internships
and Experiential Education**
Raleigh, North Carolina
1986

Jane C. Kendall, John S. Duley, Thomas C. Little, Jane S. Permaul, and Sharon Rubin, *Strengthening Experiential Education within Your Institution.*
Raleigh, North Carolina: National Society for Internships and Experiential Education, 1986.

Library of Congress Catalogue Card Number: LC 86-060472
International Standard Book Number: ISBN 0-937883-00-X

Illustrations and Design by Carol F. Majors
Production by PUBLICATIONS UNLIMITED, Raleigh, North Carolina
Printed in the United States of America

Table of Contents

About the
National Society
for Internships and
Experiential Education

(919) 834-7536   122 St. Mary's Street
Raleigh, N.C. 27605

NSIEE is a professional association that brings together the many types of people involved in providing the diverse array of experiential learning opportunities — internships, field experiences, service-learning, cooperative education, intercultural experiences, and others — for the exchange of ideas, professional support, training, research, state-of-the-art discussions, and help for institutions and programs.

NSIEE has many voices — NSIEE members cross the usual professional and educational lines — presidents, deans, faculty in all fields, internship and cooperative education directors, career development and service-learning professionals, personnel managers, supervisors, students, corporate executives, nonprofit groups, government officials, and others. NSIEE was founded in 1971 as the Society for Field Experience Education and the National Center for Public Service Internship Programs. These two groups joined in 1978 under the current name of the association.

NSIEE'S MISSION — to support the use of experiential learning as an integral part of a quality education. NSIEE is concerned with the integration of intellectual, ethical, affective, career, and personal development of learners through experiential education in all its forms. Goals:

ADVOCACY - promoting experiential learning throughout the educational system and the workplace,

PROFESSIONAL DEVELOPMENT - providing opportunities for the professional growth of experiential educators, employers, and students,

QUALITY - identifying, developing, and disseminating principles of good practice, and

INNOVATIONS AND RESEARCH - encouraging leadership and experimentation with innovative uses of experiential learning, identifying and disseminating results of innovative projects and research.

What Does NSIEE Offer?

Experiential Education newsletter - current issues, new publications, research results, legislation, program developments, opportunities for professional development, student views, NSIEE activities, funding sources. Published bimonthly September through June. Sent only to NSIEE Members.

National and regional conferences - newcomers and veterans in experiential education gather for professional development and exchange at intensive national and regional forums.

Publications - papers and books examining key issues in experiential education, a collection of syllabi for courses with experiential components, guides to designing or improving a program for internships or other types of experiential education, a national directory of internship opportunities for students, "how to" guides for students who want to find and make the most of a field experience or internship, and more. See the full list and order form at the back of this book.

National talent bank and referral network - a computerized talent bank of 1,200 faculty in all fields and administrators in all types of positions who are experienced with field programs and courses and who have volunteered to provide free assistance by phone and mail. Helpful for those who want to develop or improve a course or program. Request description and order form for the "Peer Assistance Network in Experiential Education" (PANEL).

Information and technical assistance materials - a rich collection of materials on successful programs, research studies, conference presentations (audio, video, and print), conceptual papers, and other resources. NSIEE is the national depository for information on experiential education concepts, programs, policies, and practices. Request "PANEL" information for details.

Consulting services - assistance in clarifying your needs regarding program development or the strengthening of experiential education within the entire institution. NSIEE provides materials to help in an institutional assessment, recommendations of consultants who can meet the particular needs identified, and follow-up services. The cost of the consultant's time and travel is paid by the recipient institution.

Special Interest Groups - opportunities for professional contacts and leadership. NSIEE committees and special interest groups include publications, research, faculty interests, service-learning, cross-cultural and international learning, secondary education, cooperative education, media resources, learning theories, career development, community colleges, secondary education, educational reform, employers/field sponsors, student concerns, conference planning, and membership development. Participation for NSIEE members only.

Special projects and services - NSIEE members are invited to participate in national pilot projects and other services funded by grants to NSIEE for innovative activities.

How to Join NSIEE

You and your institution will benefit. NSIEE provides a national and regional support system for faculty, program directors and staffs, deans, counselors, advisors, supervisors, students, and others who are involved in experiential education at any level. The membership categories are:

Institutional/Organizational Membership ($200) - for colleges, universities, departments, established programs, secondary schools and systems, nonprofit organizations, and corporations. One Institutional/Organizational Membership covers up to 5 individuals for full membership benefits and provides some benefits to others in the member program, department, or institution also. A one-year subscription to the *Experiential Education* newsletter and copies of other informational updates for up to 5 individuals. Discounts on conference registration fees and eligibility for election to the NSIEE Board of Directors for up to 5 representatives. Complimentary copies of selected publications, a membership directory, information and clearinghouse services. Anyone from the member program or department can receive discounts on NSIEE publications and participate in NSIEE committees and special interest groups. This is the membership category for presidents, deans, administrators, departmental coordinators, and directors of established programs for internships, cooperative education, or other types of experiential education. Includes full voting privileges and national recognition.

Individual Membership ($60) - Individual Members receive a one-year subscription to the *Experiential Education* newsletter, a discount on NSIEE conference registration fees and publications, information and clearinghouse services, eligibility for election to the NSIEE Board of Directors and participation in NSIEE committees and special interest groups, full voting privileges, and the opportunity to participate in the future of experiential education.

Student Membership ($35) - For individuals engaged *primarily* as a student and currently enrolled in an educational institution. Includes same benefits as for Individual Members. Proof of enrollment may be requested.

Sustaining Membership ($500) - For individuals, corporations, philanthropic organizations, and institutions committed to the value of experiential education. Includes full benefits of membership and additional national recognition if desired.

To become a member of NSIEE and utilize the services offered, complete the membership form on the opposite page.

National Society for Internships and Experiential Education
122 Saint Mary's Street • Raleigh, North Carolina 27605 • (919) 834-7536

Membership Enrollment

(for one year following enrollment)

___ New membership ___Renewal

Membership category:
Sustaining Membership .... $ 500____
Institutional Membership .... $ 200____
Individual Membership .... $ 60____
Student Membership .... $ 35____

Total due for membership $ _____

I believe the work of NSIEE is valuable and warrants a special contribution. I am enclosing an additional amount of:
___$1000   ___$500   ___$100
___$50   ___$20   ___ other
Total contribution ($ _____)

Contributions to NSIEE are tax deductible. NSIEE is a nonprofit organization under Sec. 501(c)(3) of the IRS code. Thank you for your support.

How did you hear of NSIEE?_____

Why did you join NSIEE?_____

_____

Name _____ **Title**_____

Program/Department _____

Institution _____

Address_____

_____

_____ **Zip**_____ **Phone (   )**_____

Complete the credit card section below or enclose check or money order payable to NSIEE. Foreign orders must be paid in U. S. funds. Mail to NSIEE at the address above.

Credit Cards

VISA _____   Mastercard _____

Card No. _____

Expiration Date _____

Account name_____

Acknowledgments

This sourcebook reflects the collective ideas and work of literally hundreds of people across the country. It draws on the successes and failures of many people engaged in strengthening the role of experiential learning as an integral part of the way colleges and universities teach their students. To all of these colleagues, friends, and leaders, I extend deep appreciation for their work and for their refreshing openness to sharing their ideas and expertise with others through the National Society for Internships and Experiential Education (NSIEE).

To the four "Peer Consultants" who served the colleges and universities represented in the NSIEE National Pilot Project and who co-authored this sourcebook goes a special thanks. John Duley challenged us all with probing questions and an unfaltering concern for the welfare of students and communities. Tom Little's analytical abilities and quiet intellect offered behind-the-scenes leadership throughout the project. Jane Permaul's constant attention to the needs of practitioners of experiential education kept us on the track. Sharon Rubin often helped people put together the right words to communicate what they were learning on their own campuses. Her sharp, colorful mind and commitment to the liberal arts make a real contribution to higher education and experiential education.

Thanks to the Fund for the Improvement of Postsecondary Education (FIPSE), U.S. Department of Education, for its support of the National Pilot Project. Lynn DeMeester of the FIPSE staff served as a constant link with others engaged in the process of institutional change to improve teaching and learning. Besides serving as "poet-in-residence," she was a rigorous, supportive Program Officer and a substantive contributor to the entire project. Thanks also to Rusty Garth, Joanne MacDonald Grason, and the other FIPSE staff and grantees whose suggestions added to the project and sourcebook.

Thanks to the representatives from the NSIEE/FIPSE Pilot Institutions in 1983-85 (see Introduction) who shared their insights, reviewed draft chapters of the sourcebook, and made important changes on their home campuses. You can see their ideas quoted throughout this sourcebook.

Thanks to Morris Keeton and Walter Sikes for permission to reprint their writings. Thanks to Tom Little and the Council for Adult and Experiential Learning for support of the writing phase. Thanks to Jim Heffernan for his interviews of the pilot institutions' representatives and for his photographs. The following NSIEE members also kindly assisted with photographs: John Berg, Dick Couto, Elliott Gabriel, Peter Gotlieb, Millie Katz, Fran Koenigsburg, Barbara Lanckton-Connors, Marlyn Lawrentz, Joe Ann Lever, Marilyn Perry, Ed Potts, Patricia Ruh, Margaret Schramm, Sandy Sosnik, Rose Marie Springer, and Hal Woods.

For particular ideas in the project, thanks to Rich Ungerer, Jim Case, Joan Macala, Bob Sigmon, Dick Couto, Michele Whitham, Tim Stanton, Susan Stroud, Zelda Gamson, Harold Hodgkinson, and Ran Coble.

Thanks to Annette Wofford for her tireless production of the manuscript through several rounds of editing. Claudette Moore transcribed tapes from two years' worth of workshops and discussions so that the comments of the campus leaders quoted here could get to you firsthand and fresh. Thanks to Sally Migliore for her careful proofreading and her work in compiling a thorough index to help this sourcebook serve the field as a continuing reference and catalyst. Thanks to Matonia Day for her assistance, to Carol Majors, Publications Unlimited, for the production and laser typesetting, and to Peter Krusa of PBM Graphics, Inc., for the final printing.

Jane C. Kendall

Charts, Tables, and Special Features

Introduction

Strengthening Experiential Education within Your Institution

*T*his sourcebook is both an institutional planning book and a national diary. It is a strategy handbook for those who value experiential education and who want to strengthen its role in the way their colleges and universities teach. It is also a distilled collection of the experiences of hundreds of faculty and administrators who have struggled with what the role of experiential education should be in their institutions. It was written to help other colleges and universities be aware of the patterns that have emerged through NSIEE's first fifteen years of work with faculty and administrators across the country who are engaged in this process of "institutionalizing" experiential education on their campuses. We offer you the collective learnings of faculty, deans, counselors, advisors, department chairpersons, and others whose experiences point to principles that your institution can use.

What is Experiential Education?

*"E*xperiential education" refers to learning activities that engage the learner directly in the phenomena being studied. This learning can be in all types of work or service settings by undergraduate and graduate students of all ages. This sourcebook focuses on experiential education as a pedagogy that may be manifested in many different forms — internships, field experiences, cooperative education, practica, cross-cultural and international learning, community and public service, and other forms of carefully monitored, experience-based learning. The experiences can be part-time or full-time, paid or unpaid, and evaluated for credit or not credited. As you will see as you read, however, we take the position that credit *should* be given for appropriately documented, college-level learning. This book emphasizes policies and practices for experiential learning by students while they are enrolled rather than the assessment of learning that occurred prior to matriculation. Nevertheless, the principles and advice offered here can also be useful to those who work with non-credit programs, the assessment of prior learning, outdoor education, experiential learning in the classroom, and any type of educational innovation or improvement.

Who Should Use this Sourcebook?

*T*his sourcebook is for those involved in teaching, developing curricula, administering experiential education programs, evaluating educational programs, long-range planning, or overseeing any of these functions. It is for anyone who values active learning and who wants to see its full potential utilized in his or her program, department, division, or institution. This book can be used by any person or committee smart enough to flip on the switches that other schools have provided here to shed light on the common pitfalls in establishing a coherent approach to experiential education. A lighted path is quicker, safer, and less expensive than one full of dark pits.

This book is intended for:
- college and university presidents and vice presidents,
- academic deans, assistant deans, and provosts,
- faculty on curriculum committees,
- department chairpersons,
- faculty responsible for departmental programs for field experiences, internships, coop-

erative education, cross-cultural and international learning, community service, practica, etc.,
- faculty who utilize experiential learning in their courses,
- directors and staffs for any type of experiential education program (see list above),
- career counselors and academic advisors,
- student development professionals,
- directors of institutional development, alumni affairs, community service, and public relations,
- those interested in institutional change, innovation, and improvement in higher education,
- those interested in how a national association can stimulate and support improvements in local policy and practice, and
- leaders in high schools who

want to strengthen experiential education within their schools or school systems (and who are willing to translate the terminology and examples to fit their own settings).

While this book generally refers to the whole institution as the organizational unit under consideration, the same principles apply to smaller units, such as a department, division, or school within a college or university.

This book is *not* intended for those who want specific advice about how to design a program. For help in establishing or revising a particular program or course, please see the front of the book for information about the publications, talent bank, conferences, and other services provided by the National Society for Internships and Experiential Education.

Why This Sourcebook?

1. *Because experiential education needs to be institutionalized in higher education -*

"There is now a good deal of research evidence to suggest that the more time and effort students invest in the learning process and the more intensely they engage in their own education, the greater will be their own growth and achievement, their satisfaction with their educational experiences, and their persistence in college, and the more likely they are to continue their learning. . . .

While one can ask what a chemist knows, for example, one is not involved in that knowledge until one does what a chemist does."

-"Involvement in Learning: Realizing the Potential of American Higher Education," National Institute of Education[1]

With this introduction, the National Institute of Education's Study Group on the Conditions of Excellence in American Higher Education recommends that college faculty increase their use of "internships and other forms of carefully monitored

experiential learning. . . . [Such] active modes of teaching require that students be inquirers — creators, as well as receivers, of knowledge. . . . Students are more apt to learn content if they are engaged with it."[2] NIE also advises students to "make sure that you take at least one independent study course and one internship during your college career, and that these experiences involve research and an opportunity to apply theory to problems in the world beyond the campus. Insist that your institution provide these opportunities."[3]

In the past decade, great strides have been made in the effective use of experiential education. Chapter 1 explains why it has proven a valuable and necessary partner to classroom instruction in attaining educational goals. As report after report calls for better writing and thinking skills, better citizenship skills, better cross-cultural awareness, and more for each tuition dollar for college graduates, experiential education has much to offer to enhance the quality of higher education and the outcomes of the curriculum, particularly in the liberal arts.

Questions of quality, accounta-

bility, and access to opportunity are already paramount in commission reports and national studies as higher education moves into the hotseat of public scrutiny. *Because experiential education is an extremely effective means of teaching and learning, its place in the debates about quality is essential.* Its benefits address several of the expectations that the public will continue to hold for colleges and universities which are supported by taxes and hard-earned tuition funds: quality of learning, an educated workforce, employable graduates ready for responsible citizenship, leadership, access for nontraditional learners, and positive partnerships with business and the community. When college presidents and deans engage in the upcoming public debates about the quality and cost-effectiveness of higher education, they will need to understand the positive role experiential learning can play. And experiential learning will need to be a recognized part of institutional policies and values in order to reap its full benefits for educational improvement.

The threatened cutbacks in federal financial aid programs heighten the accountability question (as students and parents have to dig deeper into their pockets) and the timeliness of the need to integrate experiential learning into the curriculum. Cutbacks in student aid also enhance the importance of working during school; experiential education can increase the likelihood that work hours are planned with learning goals in mind. With the "back to basics" movement toward liberal education and traditional disciplines, experiential learning must make its case now that it is an essential part of the mission of liberal arts education.

The problem is that experiential education is still not integrated into the ongoing structure and curriculum of higher education ("institutionalized") in such a way as to ensure its availability and quality for a majority of future students. At most colleges and universities, experiential education is not yet part of the five-year plan, the *expectations* for how faculty members regularly teach, and the accepted systems for work load and compensation. It does not get attention as part of the regular educational program receiving periodic evaluation and the type of institutional scrutiny that helps to ensure quality. In this sourcebook, the term *"institution-alization"* will be used to refer to the integration of experiential learning into the school's ongoing system of values, its mission, curriculum, academic policies, degree requirements, administrative structure, faculty compensation system, budget, and evaluation system.

It is still "unlikely that a history major, a sociology major, or even a business major at the undergraduate level will be urged, much less required, to experience the discipline or profession in practice as essential to degree studies. The idea that a liberal education can be consummated only with a substantial infusion of supervised experiences of contemporary society and institutions is rarely entertained in curriculum design."[4] Some professional and applied fields — medicine, architecture, clinical and counseling psychology, social work, and elementary and secondary education — have accepted experiential learning as a regular part of professional preparation. This book focuses

significant, sponsorship of learning outside the classroom is still not built into the reward structure for salaries, promotions, and tenure. For example, it may be a junior faculty member who "gets stuck with the intern program this year" while trying to publish and do research. Or, when the dedicated professor who sees the value of experiential learning leaves, the "program" too often folds. In *Preparing Humanists for Work: A National Study of Undergraduate Internships in the Humanities*, the Washington Center found that among the 600+ institutions responding, "most programs have no funds specifically allocated for internship activity," and "most faculty who sponsor internships receive no compensation for their involvement."[6]

Some programs are still marginal in part because of the way they were conceived and carefully nurtured by one faculty or staff member. There may be no structure to sustain the program when that person leaves or runs out of contributed time. When there is this *lack of continuity and compensation by the institution's reward system*, experiential education is highly vulnerable. As long as experiential education is "extra" and done on volunteer time, the institution cannot hold its supporters accountable for any standards of quality. Often

experiential education.

Lack of institutional funding is also a continuing problem. The largest single source of funds for one model of experiential education, Title VIII of the Higher Education Act of 1965 (as amended), has provided programmatic support for over 900 cooperative education programs nationwide. Despite an effective lobby by the co-op community, each year a number of programs are in jeopardy because of their dependence on federal grants rather than hard institutional funds.

2. *Because institution-alizing any educational improvement is a slow, complex process* - Integrating something as broad as a pedagogy like experiential education across an institution that is as diverse as a college or university is by definition an ongoing, yet dynamic process. It is more than ensuring that one program or course is well supported. It means seeing experiential education as a method of teaching and learning and building this approach into the institution's system of values and the regular way that faculty teach. It means infusing experiential education into the curriculum across the campus rather than developing one or two field courses. Experiential education is a means to an end rather than an end in itself.

This type of institutionalization requires the involvement of leaders at all levels within the college or university. It is nearly impossible for a single faculty member or a director of a single program or office to have the time, perspective, or power to institutionalize experiential education. The process must involve a number of people in different roles over an extended period of time. Ideas and proposals need time to percolate on a campus. A further challenge is that few campuses have a proven model for this type of sustained planning for strengthening the use of a particular style of teaching and learning. This sourcebook provides suggestions for how to begin and can serve as a reference book throughout the process for all the individuals and committees involved on your campus.

When college presidents and deans engage in the upcoming public debates about the quality and cost-effectiveness of higher education, they will need to understand the positive role experiential learning can play.

---

on the institutions and disciplines (especially the liberal arts) in which experiential learning is still viewed by some as "only an adornment or even a digression."[5]

Too many internships and other field experiences are still sponsored by faculty only as an extra assignment or out of personal commitment to this mode of learning. While the personal rewards of teaching in this of teaching in this way can be very

experiential education is tacked onto the already loaded job of the director of career planning and placement. On the surface, this can relieve faculty of an administrative burden, but it can also remove experiential education even further from the academic enterprise which can sustain it. See the chapter on administrative structures for ideas about a balance between the roles of various campus offices and the faculty involved in

3. *Because of these needs, the National Society for Internships and Experiential Education (NSIEE) launched a two-year national pilot project* in the fall of 1983 to work intensively with twenty selected colleges and universities that were at critical junctures in institutionalizing experiential education. Support was provided by the Fund for the Improvement of Postsecondary Education (FIPSE), U.S. Department of Education, and by the pilot institutions themselves. The original pilot schools are listed in this introduction.

National Pilot Schools 1983-85

NSIEE/FIPSE Project to Institutionalize Experiential Education

Adrian College, Adrian, Michigan
Bradford College, Haverhill, Massachusetts
University of California, Santa Barbara
Coker College, Hartford, South Carolina
University of Colorado, Boulder
Guilford College, Greensboro, North Carolina
Hartwick College, Oneonta, New York
Illinois State University, Normal
Kennesaw College, Marietta, Georgia
King College, Bristol, Tennessee
Manhattan College, Bronx, New York
University of Massachusetts, Boston
Neumann College, Aston, Pennsylvania
University of New Hampshire, Durham
Otterbein College, Otterbein, Ohio
Rhode Island College, Providence
Skidmore College, Saratoga Springs, New York
Westmont College, Santa Barbara, California
University of Virginia, Charlottesville
College of Wooster, Wooster, Ohio

NSIEE "Peer Experts" (advanced consultants) worked with each of these schools for one or two years to help clarify and address the issues regarding the institutionalization of experiential education on each campus. Through this NSIEE/FIPSE Pilot Project, a team of leaders at each pilot school conducted institutional assessments, convened interested faculty to discuss ideas and concerns, formed or strengthened faculty committees, wrote strategic plans, organized faculty and staff workshops, shared their problems and progress with representatives of the other pilot institutions at national seminars, evaluated their progress regularly, and revised their strategies as needed along the way.

We wanted to find out what was unique about experiential education as an academic improvement. Does it follow the same patterns as other innovations? Do all the usual principles of organizational change also so fit the institutional changes needed to incorporate experiential education? We decided to practice what we preach as experiential educators and draw on our own collective experiences at real institutions facing real concerns. *What we found was that the same issues came up everywhere.* Several clear patterns emerged, and some approaches worked better than others for institutionalizing experiential education. Originally we had planned to do ten brief case studies at the end of our FIPSE grant. As the significance of the emerging patterns and principles became evident, however, we decided to do this sourcebook to try to communicate the wealth of valuable learnings that came out of the experiences of the pilot institutions. See "NSIEE Resources and Services" for information on further consultation services available as part of a 1985-88 NSIEE national project. Unless otherwise obvious, "we" throughout this sourcebook refers to the five NSIEE Peer Experts who are also the authors of the book.

Too many internships and other field experiences are still sponsored by faculty only as an extra assignment or out of personal commitment to this mode of learning.

How to Use This Sourcebook

*E*ach chapter represents one of the "critical issues" that came up at all of the twenty pilot institutions — integrating experiential education into the institutional mission, curriculum, faculty role, quality controls, administrative structures, and economic system. The issues are intricately interrelated. They appear in order from the most basic and overriding — "Building Experiential Education into the Mission of Your Institution" — to the more specific issues of adopting administrative and financial structures that support experiential education. The book is also designed as a continuing reference book; each chapter can stand alone, and the heavy indexing can help you find relevant sections as the institutionalization process brings you and your colleagues to new issues. A coherent approach to experiential education requires attention to all six of the critical issues.

Each chapter includes the reasons the issue is important, quotes from the representatives of the pilot schools about what they learned as they addressed this issue on their own campuses, case studies, checklists and charts to help you diagnose your own status and next steps, and recommended resources for further reading. Feel free to photocopy any of the exercises or other parts of the sourcebook, but full credit (sourcebook title, publishing organization, authors, date, and page number) is required by law. We encourage you to *use* the sourcebook freely to clarify the issues for your institution, diagnose your needs, and develop a strategy for addressing these needs. If you need assistance during any stage in this process, contact the National Society for Internships and Experiential Education for help.

Before You Begin

*B*efore you begin, you may find the following questions helpful in clarifying your institution's strong and weak points regarding experiential education:

FOOTNOTES

[1] National Institute of Education, *Involvement in Learning: Realizing the Potential of American Higher Education*, U.S. Government Printing Office, Washington, D.C., October 1984, pp. 17 and 28.

[2] *Ibid*, pp. 27-28.

[3] *Ibid*, p. 78.

[4] Thomas C. Little, Editor, *Making Sponsored Experiential Learning Standard Practice*, New Directions for Experiential Learning, No. 20, Jossey-Bass, San Francisco, California, 1983, p. 1.

[5] *Ibid*, p.1.

[6] Carren O. Kaston with James M. Heffernan, *Preparing Humanists for Work: A National Study of Undergraduate Internships in the Humanities*, the Washington Center and National Endowment for the Humanities, Washington, D.C., November 1984, "Executive Summary," p. 3. Study and Summary available from NSIEE.

WHERE DOES YOUR INSTITUTION STAND?

For each question listed below, circle the number that indicates the degree to which that condition has been established on your campus (or in your department, division, or school):

To what degree. . .	None					Very much
a. ...is there evidence that experiential education is valued and recognized as contributing to the mission of the institution?	0	1	2	3	4	5
b. ...is experiential education integrated into the curriculum and recognized as a legitimate part of degree requirements?	0	1	2	3	4	5
c. ...are faculty actively involved in offering experiential learning opportunities?	0	1	2	3	4	5
d. ...are there intentional quality controls for experiential education in the institution?	0	1	2	3	4	5
e. ...is experiential education part of the institution's ongoing system for quality assurance and evaluation?	0	1	2	3	4	5
f. ...are experiential education activities fully recognized in the economic system of the institution (faculty compensation, work load, and promotion; allocation of resources; etc.)?	0	1	2	3	4	5
g. ...do the administrative structures established for experiential education support its goals in the institution?	0	1	2	3	4	5

1

Building Experiential Education into the Mission and Values of Your Institution

*M*any of us — most of us — enter experiential learning through the back door rather than through the study of pedagogy. We are faculty who are asked by an interested student to supervise an independent study course incorporating field experience. We are student affairs professionals who receive a request from an employer to help locate a few good students to work part-time. We are administrators in church-related colleges who struggle with the vision of our students' moral growth through service. We are former Peace Corps volunteers who want to introduce students to the challenges of understanding another culture. We are academic advisors or career counselors who are concerned about our students' despair over the usefulness of their educational choices. We are deans who want to break through our students' passivity and make them feel the wonderful excitement we have felt as we have learned.

One day we take a fateful step. We say yes to the student, to the employer, to the idea, to the plan. Before we know it, we are doing something quite different from our colleagues. We are intellectually excited, but we may be quite isolated.

As we struggle to master the theory behind our day-to-day activities, we may be misunderstood, ignored, or even confronted by those with other ideas about education. Sometimes we feel inspired, sometimes we feel burned out, but rarely do we feel disengaged. That engagement is the source of our energy but often the root of our dilemma. We sometimes care so much that we forget to step back to see ourselves, our programs, and our mission in the context of our departments and our institutions. This chapter is therefore intended to help faculty and administrators involved in experiential education to analyze the present status of experiential learning within their institutions as well as to assess their own roles. Several diagnostic instruments presented here will approach the issue of "value" to the institution in different ways. The examples and suggestions offered are based on a number of different types of schools.

Why Is It Important for Experiential Education to Be Connected to the Values and Missions of Your Institution?

*I*n the past few years, a number of books on the business world, from *Theory Z* to *In Search of Excellence* to *Corporate Culture*, have stressed the idea that individual companies have specific, and readily perceivable, cultures. The notion that the shared values of a particular organization define it, not only to the outside world, but to itself, may not be an exceptional idea to an anthropologist or to a sociologist, but it is one that most participants in organizations tend to ignore. By tapping into the rich meanings evoked by the symbols, ideologies, language, beliefs, rituals, and myths that define the organizational culture, participants can see much more clearly in what way their goals are consistent with organizational goals. Ignoring the culture dooms one to the periphery. Deviants may hold a few specialized roles in any society or culture, but

7

We sometimes care so much that we forget to step back to see ourselves, our programs, and our mission in the context of our departments and our institutions.

they are not important for its central functioning.

Businesses are not the only organizations with specific and defined cultures. We tend to generalize about "higher education" as we would about Fortune 500 companies, but we know that community colleges are not like research universities, and neither one is like a church-related liberal arts college. Moreover, two community colleges may have very little in common in terms of their value systems. When you understand the cultural values of your own institution, you can understand not only how to help experiential learning become better institutionalized, but also how to express your own values about experiential learning more effectively.

The issue of values is a complex one. In an article on "Values as the Core of Institutional Commitment: Finding a Common Ground," Jane Kendall points out that in addition to historic and administrative values, the institutional culture also incorporates the particular values of the faculty, the students, and in the case of experiential learning, the values of the field site supervisors as well.[1] Although there are a number of ways in which these interested parties may seek a working balance among their values, there is no magic administrative structure, no magic model that will solve the problems of match between the values of experiential learning programs and the institution.

Even when some consensus is reached, it does not necessarily hold. Organizations evolve through time as conditions change, and so must our values. A new president, a change in

student demographics, a new business environment in the state, or a new Watergate can all result in a change of direction for a campus. Experiential learning, if it is to stay vital and responsive to institutional needs and priorities, must always be seen in this complex cultural context.

What Are the Most Common Values and Missions of Colleges and Universities, and What Does Experiential Education Contribute to Them?

"Know all you can about the rationales for experiential education. Because ours is a church-related college, I learned all I could about the liberal arts rationale and the theological rationale."
—Douglas Boyce,
Dean
King College
Bristol, Tennessee

Despite the notion of a cultural context specific to each institution, we can generalize somewhat about the values that colleges and universities typically hold. The three-legged stool of teaching, research, and community service is a familiar metaphor in higher education, although the varying lengths of the legs may make sitting on such a

Daniel Beaudoin, from Suffolk University, conducts research at the New England Aquarium in Boston.

stool extremely precarious! A fourth and often unspoken value for any school is institutional stability and status. Any organization aims to maintain its own existence, and most colleges and universities are also aware of how they are perceived by the general public and by peer institutions in terms of their quality and overall prestige. The four priorities of teaching, research, community service, and institutional stability and status vary, of course, from college to college. Yet there *are* ways in which experiential learning relates quite readily to each of these values.

1. Teaching — If we think of what most colleges and universities say they reward, we find teaching at or near the top of the list. The transmission of knowledge to a new generation is such an important value that faculty often give up opportunities for much more lucrative employment to spend their lives at it. Experiential learning is a pedagogy that expresses this value in many different ways.

First, experiential learning is complete learning. As David Kolb points out, when students start with concrete experience and then have the opportunity to step back and reflect upon the experience, to form generalizations and conceptual models in relation to prior learning, and to test the implications of this conceptualization through new experiences, they can achieve the mastery of both theory and practice.[2]

Second, experiential learning is student-centered. Although some faculty teach as if students were empty vessels to be filled with content, most good teachers know that student motivation and active *engagement* in the subject matter are crucial to learning. Because experiential learning is individualized and incorporates student interests and needs, it enhances students' active involvement in their learning.

Third, experiential learning helps students develop multiple competencies. As Kolb has shown,[3] each of the aspects of experiential learning enhances different types of competencies:

• Concrete experience develops affective competencies such as dealing with people, being sensitive to people's feelings, being sensitive

INSTITUTIONAL INTERESTS:	+	CONTRIBUTIONS OF EXPERIENTIAL EDUCATION:	=	INSTITUTIONAL SUPPORT OF EXPERIENTIAL EDUCATION
Effective curriculum		Academic knowledge		
Research		Generic liberal arts competence		
Public service		Moral-ethical development		
Effective student development programs		Career development		
Stability and status (enrollments, public and alumni relations, development)		Student empowerment, self-confidence, and motivation		
		Public service		
		Institutional stability and status (admissions, retention, community and alumni relations, development)		
		Research opportunities		

When you understand the cultural values of your own institution, you can understand not only how to help experiential learning become better institutionalized, but also how to express your own values about experiential learning more effectively.

to values, and being personally involved.

• Reflection enhances perceptual competencies such as gathering and organizing information, listening with an open mind, seeing how things fit into the big picture, and developing comprehensive plans.

• Practice in conceptualization develops symbolic competencies such as analyzing quantitative data, building conceptual models, and generating alternatives.

• Testing concepts in practice enlarges students' behavioral abilities as they learn to set goals, commit themselves to objectives, adapt to changing circumstances, make decisions, and lead others.

While some of these competencies are related quite specifically to success on the job, all of them are necessary for intellectual maturity and mastery of an academic discipline.

2. **Research** — While research is an important value at large universities, it also remains significant at small liberal arts colleges because the generation of new knowledge goes hand in hand with its transmission to students. Students' experiential learning activities present faculty with a steady stream of relevant research problems. Faculty contacts with field supervisors offer a rich source of professional expertise, collaborative research opportunities, funding sources, and up-to-date resources and technology.

"If the main purpose of the university is to advance knowledge for the general society, then one way that experiential education at UCLA contributes to that purpose is that the students provide a linkage between the faculty and what is happening in the outside community. They help faculty both in terms of identifying problems and bringing back questions

to consider. So there is a direct contribution toward that mission of the university."
  -Jane Permaul
   NSIEE Consultant
   and Director
   Field Studies Development,
   UCLA

"It does happen, either directly through student and faculty involvement or indirectly through our office dealing with a business. We have a consulting center on campus. I can call the director of the consulting center and say, 'I've just been to XYZ company and they would like to ask the university to help solve problem A.' Now if the university asks a faculty member and possibly grad students to research problem A, this may result in research that can be used for publication or for some joint, patentable activity."
  -Robert McCaffery, Manager
   Field Experience Programs
   University of New
    Hampshire

"Manhattan College has a Small Business Institute which offers seniors the opportunity to analyze the management of small business enterprises and develop consulting skills through field work. Working in teams under faculty supervision, the students provide assistance to the small business community."
  -Kristen Murtaugh, Director
   Cooperative Education
   Manhattan College,
   New York

3. **Community Service** — Community service has very different manifestations at land-grant universities and at denomination-based colleges, but experiential learning is consistent with a diverse range of public service activities. At most state universities, a significant mission is very practical service on behalf of the industries, government, and citizens of the state. At the University of New Hampshire, for instance, the new President's interest in making the campus more respon-

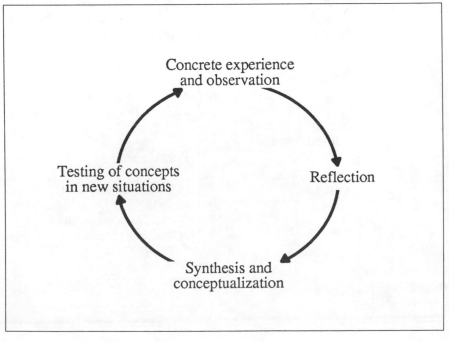

sive to new high technology businesses mirrors the efforts of the state government to welcome and support the growth of such industry. The work of students in internships and cooperative education can be a crucial link in serving the needs of these industries and in making their needs known to the University. For instance, site visits by faculty to these students could result in information about regional needs that can be met by the University in informal and formal consultation and in collaborative research projects.

At other colleges and universities, community service emphasizes an ethical component — service in the traditional sense of service to society, or service in the sense of training students to be responsible and ethical citizens. Strong examples of such "service-learning" programs include Vanderbilt University's Center for Health Services, the University of Vermont's Vermont Internship Program, Michigan State University's Service-Learning Center, Dartmouth College's Internship Program, Brown University's College Venture Program, and Stanford University's Public

Sandra Watson, an environmental chemist at Southern Wood Piedmont, obtained her job because of experience gained as an undergraduate student intern at Converse College in South Carolina. She has since had three Converse College students work as interns for her.

WHY EXPERIENTIAL LEARNING?

"The experiential approach is a powerful motivator for learning because it is positive, and meaningful, and real. The learning environment is success-oriented rather than competitive. It offers opportunities for real-life problem solving in which feedback is uncontrived and immediate, and in which results are real-life physical and emotional consequences. Because the learners participate in the design, implementation and management of their own learning, they are invested in the goal, hence internally motivated. That motivation frequently transfers back to the traditional classroom as students recognize the need for more theoretical background, as they try to draw inferences and conclusions from their experiences, or as they find reasons to improve their basic skills. The need for theoretical understanding of human relations becomes important if one is helping in a crisis intervention

center. Understanding of motivation is important when marketing a new product.

"Additionally, by providing for integration of ideas and actions into the large community, experiential learning facilitates the transition to adulthood and develops skills for responsible citizenship. Documented outcomes of experiential learning include concern for fellow human

---

"We must teach students how to reflect on their experiences, define their learning goals, and independently manage their own learning."

---

beings; the ability to get things done and work with others; self-motivation to learn, participate and achieve; an improved self-concept, confidence, competence and awareness; responsibility to the group or class; openness to new experiences; and a sense of usefulness to the community.

"Finally, experiential education contributes to the preparation of a well-educated and productive workforce. If our goal were merely to

beat the Japanese in the high-tech race, we could train our students to be crack technicians through classroom experiences in math, science and computer technology. If our goal is to prepare an enlightened citizenry to lead productive and purposeful lives and to contribute to the growth and development of society, then we must insure that they learn how to learn, how to grow and adjust to change.

"Workers of the future need both generalized competence and specific job skills which may not apply to their future job requirements. Future jobs will require different skills, and workers must be prepared to meet the changing needs. We must teach students how to reflect on their experiences, define their learning goals, and independently manage their own learning. These outcomes require an education which combines experiential learning with abstract learning."

-Reprinted from "A Nation at Risk: Another View," *Experiential Education* newsletter, NSIEE, March-April, 1984

Service Center. As an example, a model University of Kentucky program which placed students in government internships was designed to help them think through the ethical implications of decision-making about public policy and about their own decision-making as well. As the director described the program:

"The students involved in the program, while spending a full-time internship in a public agency of their choice, are involved in an interdisciplinary humanities seminar taught by faculty members in political science, philosophy, and the philosophy of education. The seminar is an attempt to develop the 'partici-

pant/observer' approach to an integrated experience. Drawing upon the experiences of the students themselves, weekly journals, and extensive readings, the seminar considers such issues as the limits, potential, and demise of citizenship; the value structure of public agencies; alienation; constitutionalism in the political process; and human development as it affects the way individuals resolve personal values and conflicting pressures in a political situation. Through weekly meetings it is hoped that students will come to some personal reconciliation, not as judges of the community, but of their own role as actors in a situation requiring

"The experiential approach is a powerful motivator for learning because it is positive, and meaningful, and real."

insight, the application of human knowledge, and personal reconciliation of serious ethical concerns." [4]

At religious institutions in particular, experiential learning through community service can powerfully support the institutional value of students' moral development.

4. Institutional Stability and Status — All schools attempt to define qualities that make them unique, and experiential learning can enhance this uniqueness in many ways. For instance, many students attend schools such as Antioch, Northeastern, and the University of Cincinnati specifically because of their cooperative education programs. Skidmore College is typical in reporting that its internship program is frequently mentioned by applicants as a desirable characteristic of the school. Technical institutions can make special use of experiential learning in undergraduate research. At the Massachusetts Institute of Technology, for example, undergraduates are matched with faculty members involved in research projects. Such collaboration not only enhances student learning in content areas, but it also helps students understand the nature of scientific problem-solving in more complex and realistic ways than laboratory experiments could. The program is so popular that more than 75% of the undergraduates at M.I.T. participate in it, so it is part of what is unique about this institution. Experiential honors programs and semester-long programs that give students the opportunity to live and work in another city or country offer colleges additional ways to enhance their status and define their uniqueness.

The Public Service Center
Stanford University

"You Can Make A Difference"

"Contrary to the popular myth of student apathy toward public service, there is a very real sense of responsibility and yearning to serve -- and we are only beginning to tap it."

Donald Kennedy
President
Stanford University

In addition to status and uniqueness in the higher education community, institutional stability is a priority for most colleges and universities. Experiential education can contribute in significant ways to the following factors in institutional stability:

a. *Admissions* — Parents and students are becoming more aware of the importance of experiential learning as part of a complete education. As tuitions rise and students become more discerning consumers of education, they are asking more questions about the experiential offerings of the institutions they are considering. Colleges and universities that are able to articulate the role of internships and other types of experiential education in their institutional mission and curricula will fare better in admissions than institutions that do not articulate this role.

b. *Retention* — Students gain increased motivation and persistence after they participate in experiential learning. Others redefine their aspirations. Although more research needs to be done on benefits to students, most practitioners identify experiential learning as important in helping students make sense of their studies and renew their commitment to educational goals.

c. *Institutional Development* — Experiential education provides avenues for constructive, active involvement of alumni and community and business leaders in the central educational goals of the institution. As these people and their organizations interact in substantive ways with students and faculty, the alumni and community leaders who sponsor students on internships become a partner in the educational enterprise. Besides supporting the teaching function of the school, these partnerships can also lead to increased alum-

Volunteers Kathleen Matheson and Rafael Perez (standing) deliver surplus food to the elderly through the FOOD MARCH program in New York City. This is part of the City Volunteer Corps, which places students aged 17-20 in volunteer positions throughout the city.

ni giving; corporate contributions for scholarships, professorships, and programs; research grants; access to corporate and governmental research facilities and contracts; bequests; and other sources of institutional funding and related opportunities.

d. *Public relations* — In addition to supporting the institution's goals for community service, experiential education can enhance the college's public relations. For example:

"The Field Experience Program is a crucial link with the community around Durham, the state of New Hampshire, and the entire country. It is clear that most faculty and administrators understand the first link, but are less aware of the potential for regional and national recognition that might result from the placement of students with large regional and national employers. First, the competence of University of New Hamp-

shire students would be recognized in a larger arena than is now the case. Site visits by faculty would result in information about regional needs that can be met by the University in consultation, both informal and formal, and in potential collaborative working relationships and grants to the institution. The hesitance of faculty to sponsor students might be alleviated by their recognition of the potential benefits of such sponsorship to their own departments; the hesitance of the University to fund the Field Experience Program separately from tuition generated might be alleviated by its understanding of the value of good community interaction to furthering the goals of the institution. Whether or not some formal actions are taken to [foster] collaboration between the Field Experience Program and the development functions of the University, University of New Hampshire students will continue to represent the institution to the local, regional, and national communities. It is certainly in the best interests of the University to help them represent it very well."
  -Sharon Rubin, NSIEE
    Consultant,
  Report to the University of
    New Hampshire

These partnerships can also lead to increased alumni giving, corporate contributions, research grants, bequests, and other sources of institutional funding and related opportunities.

Analyzing the Values of Your Institution

*B*efore you can articulate how experiential education fits into the values and mission of your institution, you must look carefully at what these values are for your school. A simple way to start is to assess for your institution the importance of each of the most common values of higher education as discussed earlier in this chapter. Begin by completing the chart at right, "Values of my Institution: Part 1." Put an "X" on each line to indicate the relative importance of each mission or value for your institution. You may find that you need to talk with other key individuals on campus to get a clearer picture of what the underlying values really are. If you are focusing on a particular department or division, you may want to consider separately the institutional values and the prevalent values of your unit.

A second — and more revealing — exercise to help you analyze the mission and values of your institution looks at particular factors that reflect the underlying goals. Complete the chart "Values of my Institution: Part 2" at right. On each continuum, put an "X" on the line to show where your institution falls. The two ends of each continuum do not necessarily represent opposite approaches. In fact, some are mutually supportive and intricately interrelated. But it is helpful to consider the relative impor-

From *Strengthening Experiential Education in Your Institution*, National Society for Internships and Experiential Education, Raleigh, North Carolina, 1986

VALUES OF MY INSTITUTION: PART 1

Put an "X" on each line below to indicate the relative importance of each value or mission to your institution:

	Not important at all	Very important
a. Teaching:	<--->
b. Research:	<--->
c. Community Service:	<--->
d. Institutional Stability:	<--->
e. Institutional Status:	<--->

VALUES OF MY INSTITUTION: PART 2

Put an "X" on the line below to indicate where your institution falls on the following continua:

Institutional factor	*Where does your institution fall on this line?*		
Faculty reward system:	Research	<-------------------->	Teaching
Emphasis for undergraduate student outcomes:	Preparation for work	<-------------------->	Liberal learning
Learning focus:	Practical application	<-------------------->	Theoretical concepts
Reaction to change:	Focus on historic goals	<-------------------->	Respond to current market
Focus for planning:	Short-term	<-------------------->	Long-term
Image:	Elite	<-------------------->	Open
Curricular focus:	Competency-based	<-------------------->	Content-based

SAMPLE VALUES OF A COMMUNITY COLLEGE

Put an "X" on each line below to indicate where your institution falls on the following continua:

Faculty reward system:	Research	<------------------X--> Teaching
Emphasis for undergraduate student outcomes:	Preparation for work	<--X------------------> Liberal learning
Learning focus:	Practical application	<---X------------------> Theoretical concepts
Reaction to change:	Focus on historic goals	<-X-------------------> Respond to current market
Focus for planning:	Short-term	<--------------X------> Long-term
Image:	Elite	<-------------------X-> Open
Curricular focus:	Competency-based	<-----------X---------> Content-based

SAMPLE VALUES OF A PRIVATE LIBERAL ARTS COLLEGE

Put an "X" on each line below to indicate where your institution falls on the following continua:

Faculty reward system:	Research	<---------------X----> Teaching
Emphasis for undergraduate student outcomes:	Preparation for work	<------------------X--> Liberal learning
Learning focus:	Practical application	<-------------------X-> Theoretical concepts
Reaction to change:	Focus on historic goals	<-----------------X---> Respond to current market
Focus for planning:	Short-term	<------X-------------> Long-term
Image:	Elite	<-------X------------> Open
Curricular focus:	Competency-based	<-------------------X-> Content-based

tance of the different values they reflect. Again, you may want to complete this chart for *both* your unit and for your institution as a whole.

If we consider many of the colleges in this country, especially the larger ones, it is not always easy to figure out exactly where on each continuum the institution lies. Different departments may vary quite fundamentally on their focus on learning, for instance, but there is usually some general institutional ball park that you can identify.

For example, see the chart to the left entitled "Sample Values of a Community College" for the values that might be common for a two-year institution.

A small, private, liberal arts college, on the other hand, might look more like the sample chart entitled "Sample Values of a Private, Liberal Arts College" on the bottom left side of this page.

Even if experiential education contributes significantly, its place in the ongoing curriculum, administrative structure, and economic system of the college or university will not be strongly established until its contributions are clearly articulated and recognized across the campus.

From *Strengthening Experiential Education in Your Institution*, National Society for Internships and Experiential Education, Raleigh, North Carolina, 1986

Is Experiential Education Consistent with the Values of Your Institution?

*T*he next step is to assess the extent to which experiential education supports the mission and values of your institution. Now complete the accompanying charts regarding the particular values and goals of experiential education as you use it.

You may find that while a particular value is not important for experiential education *per se*, experiential education still *contributes* to that goal in the school. For example, research may not be an explicit or primary goal of the experiential learning program, but the program may support the research mission by helping to identify problems for research, funding sources, business or community facilities for research, and faculty consulting opportunities. Similarly, you may not be directly concerned about institutional stability or status, but your program or course may provide benefits for admissions, retention, alumni and public relations, institutional fundraising, or the general visibility of the school. On the chart above, put a "C" on each of the five lines to indicate where experiential education *contributes* in these direct or indirect ways.

Now compare your responses here to the responses you gave on the "Values of My Institution" charts (Parts 1 and 2). Are the values of your institution and those of experiential education congruent? Where do they overlap, and where do they conflict? How

From *Strengthening Experiential Education in Your Institution*, National Society for Internships and Experiential Education, Raleigh, North Carolina, 1986

VALUES OF EXPERIENTIAL EDUCATION: PART 1

Put an "X" on each line below to indicate the relative importance of each value or mission to your experiential education program or course:

	Not important at all	Very important
a. Teaching:	<-->
b. Research:	<-->
c. Community Service:	<-->
d. Institutional Stability:	<-->
e. Institutional Status:	<-->

VALUES OF EXPERIENTIAL EDUCATION: PART 2

Put an "X" on the line below to indicate where your experiential education program or course falls on the following continua:

Program factor	*Where does your experiential education program fall on this line?*		
Faculty rewards:	Research	<--------------------->	Teaching
Emphasis for undergraduate student outcomes:	Preparation for work	<--------------------->	Liberal learning
Learning focus:	Practical application	<--------------------->	Theoretical concepts
Reaction to change:	Focus on historic goals	<--------------------->	Respond to current market
Focus for planning:	Short-term	<--------------------->	Long-term
Image:	Elite	<--------------------->	Open
Curricular focus:	Competency-based	<--------------------->	Content-based

can you get closer to where the college is on these lines? What would you change? What are some strategies for rethinking how you are organized, what you are doing, how you spend your time, and whom you involve?

Colleges and universities differ significantly on the relationships between the two sets of charts. For instance, a cooperative education program at a small liberal arts college might emphasize preparation for work while the college emphasizes liberal learning. On the other hand, a state college attempting to be responsive to the current needs of area businesses and the internship program at the colleges might both emphasize practical applications of learning. In many colleges that come out of a religious orientation, there is a clearly articulated service mission; moral maturation through service to others is an expected part of students' education. Service-learning programs may therefore be more welcomed than programs that emphasize career exploration.

"I think you have to look for evidence *that experiential education is valued and recognized as contributing to the institution's goals. Its inclusion in the mission statement is one piece of evidence. At the departmental level, you need another type of evidence. For example, is it part of the regular teaching load?"*
-Lynn DeMeester
Program Officer
Fund for the Improvement of Postsecondary Education

If your college emphasizes its historic goals and prides itself on not jumping into "fads," it might be necessary for you to think about the kind of administrative structure and reporting line that looks most traditional. The academic vice president, especially if he or she has been around for many years, may be able to identify most closely with the historic mission of the institution. On the other hand, a new president who has a mandate to transform the mission of the institution and to search out innovation might be

Academic Deans discuss how experiential education fits into the missions of their institutions. From left, James Bierden of Rhode Island College, Doug Boyce of King College, Al Hamilton of Manhattan College, and Ed Potts of Westmont College.

interested in a new way of organizing experiential learning within the college. At Kennesaw College, the installation of a new president gave impetus to the creation of a cooperative education program.

If the values of the institution are articulated primarily in terms of the academic curriculum, experiential learning programs which are closely connected with the curricula of particular departments and programs will fare much better than programs which do not. For instance, one large state university offers field experiences through the Division of Continuing Education due to an unusual historical circumstance. Therefore, credits are continuing education credits rather than departmental credits. They can be used by students in only the most limited ways as general electives toward graduation. Students and

As tuitions rise and students become more discerning consumers of education, they are asking more questions about the experiential offerings of the institutions they are considering.

faculty alike are often frustrated by the crediting system, which seems to ignore both the educational goals of particular students and the curricular goals of departments. On the other hand, at Illinois State University, all experiential learning credits are offered through cooperating departments, all are sponsored by regular faculty in those departments, and all may be used as elective credits within those departments. Therefore, faculty can take ownership of what they credit, and students can incorporate experiential learning at appropriate points in their major programs.

"I think the key to this whole thing is to think of this as a long-term educational process. And I think if you're going to convince faculty and administrators of the value of experiential learning, you've got to shape the program and shape your goals along the same lines that their goals are stated. So, I think you have to talk about intellectual development and cognitive learning methods and so forth when you talk about the benefits of an internship program. That's the only way ours can exist."
-Mary Jo White
Assistant Director for Cooperative Education
Career Services
University of Colorado

If the values of your institution and your experiential program or course differ, it is important to ask if the college culture appreciates diversity enough to support your differing goals, or whether you should bring your program practices more in line with institutional values. It might be particularly useful to have faculty, students, and administrators all fill out these charts to determine whether there is agreement about institutional and program values, or whether different constituencies within the institution perceive them in different ways.

TEACHING AND EXPERIENTIAL LEARNING VALUES. Teaching is a particularly complex value to try to define. Even at

Most practitioners identify experiential learning as important in helping students make sense of their studies and renew their commitment to educational goals.

schools which value teaching in the reward structure for faculty, pedagogical practice generally remains undefined. The idea of student involvement in learning, or student-centeredness, which is so crucial to experiential learning, may or may not be a

value within your institution. Are students encouraged to be active, self-directed learners, or is passivity expected? Do students understand the potential in experiential learning? Do they demand it? Are they encouraged to use it, or are there institutional barriers in their way? The "Identifying Student-Centeredness in Learning" inventory below is a quick way to begin an analysis of whether your school, classroom, and campus environment fosters a student-centered approach to learning. It should provide the basis for a lively discussion among the students, faculty, and administrators. You may want to answer the questions separately for graduate and undergraduate students.

IDENTIFYING STUDENT-CENTEREDNESS IN LEARNING

In the institution as a whole:

1. Is there a history or philosophy of student-centeredness? Is this history or philosophy represented in the college catalog, the mission statement, and administrative policies?

2. Is there a supportive environment on campus for students' active involvement in learning through coursework or the co-curriculum?

3. Do curricular improvement and faculty development activities focus on student-centeredness?

4. Does academic advising help students understand how to take responsibility for their own learning?

5. Is student demand a motivating force for the provision of experiential learning opportunities?

6. Is the proportion of experiential learning to traditional learning in and out of the classroom substantial?

7. Are students encouraged to plan and carry out experiential learning activities?

In the classroom:

1. Do students have opportunities to engage in discussion, or are most courses based on a lecture format?

2. Do students become involved in short-term role-playing or simulations?

3. Do students carry out laboratory experiments or merely watch them being performed?

4. Do students engage in group activities, such as learning projects?

5. Are students encouraged to reflect on their own experiences to enrich their learning?

6. Do students have the opportunity to become involved in short-term, out-of-class experiential assignments, such as volunteer activities, to enhance learning?

7. Are students helped to connect theory to application through field trips, interviews, shadowing, or analysis of applied examples from the field?

8. How many different active learning opportunities do students have in the average course?

9. What proportion of class time is devoted to such activities?

Out of the classroom:

1. Do students have the opportunity to engage in long-term, intensive learning activities for credit, supervised and monitored by faculty?

2. Do students have the opportunity to engage in independent research or study?

3. Can students participate in learning through experiencing another culture?

4. Do co-curricular activities emphasize active learning?

5. Do faculty encourage students to extend their learning styles through structured, challenging involvement in all aspects of the learning cycle?

6. Do academic advisors and faculty encourage students to become aware of the ways in which experiential learning fits into their own educational goals?

Is Experiential Education Valued and Recognized at Your Institution?

*N*ow you have analyzed the mission and values of your institution and of your experiential learning programs and courses. You have identified areas in which experiential education is very congruent with the institution's goals and areas where the two differ. The next step is to determine whether the contributions of experiential education to the institution's mission and values are *recognized*. Even if experiential education contributes significantly, its place in the ongoing curriculum, administrative structure, and economic system of the college or university will not be strongly established until its contributions are clearly articulated and recognized across the campus. How can you tell if it is recognized and valued? Begin with these seven questions:

1. How much is experiential learning used at your institution?

2. Is it integrated fully into the curriculum?

3. Are faculty committed to it?

4. Do the administrative structures for experiential programs and courses support the goals of experiential education?

5. Is it built clearly and adequately into the financial system of the institution?

6. Is it recognized as an issue for ongoing quality controls within the institution?

7. Are the faculty and staff who administer experiential learning courses and programs valued?

The other chapters of this sourcebook focus on Questions 2-6 above. Please read these chapters and

John Gazewood, a medical student at Vanderbilt University, works with teenagers in a community health education program in Nashville through Vanderbilt's Center for Health Services.

do the recommended exercises to get a more complete answer to these questions for your institution. We will discuss Questions 1 and 7 here.

HOW MUCH IS EXPERIENTIAL LEARNING USED AT YOUR INSTITUTION? Most of us who might call ourselves experiential educators run internship or cooperative education programs, sponsor students engaged in field experiences, advise students who volunteer within the community, or counsel students about the role of experience in career development. Although we are aware that experiential learning can take place in any environment, we are used to thinking about experiential learning as quite distinct from classroom learning. Most colleges agree, defining experience as something that happens off campus, often in a work site. Since this conception is quite limited by the number of students able to participate and the number of times they are able to participate, experiential learning may initially be put in the same category on campus as travel abroad,

involvement in extracurricular activities, or participation in an honors program — excellent frosting on the cake of traditional classroom learning.

The "Inventory of Experiential Education Programs and Courses" in Chapter 2 will give you some sense of what is being done at your institution, and how much of it is being done, with respect to short-term and long-term, out-of-class experiential learning. At your college, are:

* your seniors in education going out as student teachers?

* your law students doing supervised clinical training?

* your computer science students creating games?

* your economics students trying out the effects of different data on the same economic model or the same data on different economic models?

* your psychology classes involved in role-playing?

* your American Studies students doing oral history interviews with people who have lived through the Depression?

* your physics majors doing laboratory experiments?

* your French majors developing an original dialogue?

* your sociology students taking a poll on campus?

* your journalism students putting out the campus newspaper?

Does your campus currently perceive these activities as experiential learning? Can it come to recognize such activities as experiential learning?

Does your campus currently perceive these activities as experiential learning? Can it come to recognize such activities as experiential learning?

IS THE ROLE OF THE EXPERIENTIAL EDUCATOR VALUED WITHIN THE INSTITUTION? There does not seem to be a "correct" place for experiential educators on the organizational charts of their institutions. At a recent workshop for some of the participants in the NSIEE/FIPSE Pilot Project, a group of six college representatives noted that their organizational homes are: an office of off-campus programs, two particular departments, a campus internship office, an interdepartmental program, and the career development office. In their respective institutions, these

---

It is possible to help those on campus to see the contributions that experiential learning makes.

---

six people report to an academic vice president, the dean of the college, the dean of arts and sciences, the director of arts and sciences, the director of student affairs, and a department chairperson. We *have* found that at most colleges, programs reporting to academic administrators rather than student service administrators have the capability to move toward integrating into the curriculum more easily, but there is no magic location. The "Assessing the Value of the Experiential Educator to the Department or Institution" inventory to the right might shed some light on where you as an experiential educator are now within the value system of the institution, and where you might like to be.

ASSESSING THE VALUE OF THE EXPERIENTIAL EDUCATOR TO THE DEPARTMENT OR INSTITUTION

1. Do you have a defined status within your department or college, i.e., position title and position description? Is your involvement with experiential education seen as a legitimate role, or is it something which is above and beyond your normal full-time duties? Is it risky to your position to be involved with experiential education?

2. Do you have job security? That is, if your position is now funded by a grant and the grant ends, is it likely that your position will be maintained by your department or college? Is your pay comparable to the pay of other professionals of similar background and experience within your college or in similar colleges?

3. Are your working conditions adequate? If you are coordinating a campus-wide program, do you have an office? Adequate supplies? Support staff? Are you listed in various catalogs and directories so students and faculty can find you easily? If you run a departmental program, do you have secretarial support? Access to a long-distance telephone line? Privacy for consultation?

4. Do you operate as part of some larger unit? Does your dean or department chair take an interest in what you do and give you critical feedback on your performance? Do you have co-workers to give you both challenge and support, or a group of peers within your unit?

5. Are there campus or departmental policies that define a role for your position or program? If not, are you able to work toward establishing such policies?

6. Are you encouraged to take responsibility for program development and implementation, and are you given sufficient authority and funding to carry out your responsibilities?

7. Is the work you do rewarding in itself? Have you or can you make a commitment to it? Do you feel you can reasonably accomplish the amount and kind of work you are asked to do or that you see needs to be done?

8. Are you seen as a spokesperson within your department or institution for experiential learning, and are you invited to sit on committees, to give presentations, and to provide information based on that position?

9. Is there the possibility for advancement within your college or department, i.e., does supervision of students and management of the program count in decisions about tenure, promotion, and merit pay increases?

10. Do you get recognition from your superior and from your peers for good work? Are your achievements in your profession acknowledged by the campus by notices in the faculty newsletter, by congratulatory letters from administrators, and by other members of the campus community?

11. If your position were in danger of being eliminated, would your department or the campus community notice and try to prevent that from occurring?

12. If you left, would the program be continued? Would it be able to thrive? Grow? Change?

If you have the potential to change your role, and to strengthen your position in terms of the values and mission of the institution, you might consider what Tom Little has humorously defined as the ABC's — the three primary roles of the experiential educator:

A • In the role of **advocate**, the experiential educator assumes a proactive stance on the value of experiential learning to students, faculty, administrators, employers, and the greater community. For example, the Director of Professional Practice at Illinois State University takes this role by developing plans for experiential learning with each department, giving grants to departments for partial funding of their activities, giving consultation to departmental and college coordinators, helping departments develop handbooks and other materials, giving workshops for local employers, and in all ways representing experiential learning to and for the institution.

B • The **broker** role can involve a number of different activities. For instance, the broker can help interested students find faculty and academic units willing to sponsor students, can develop placements and interest students and faculty in particular host organizations, or can introduce faculty and work site supervisors interested in developing joint research projects. As an example, the Cooperative Education Director at Manhattan College operates primarily as a broker for the entire School of Arts and Sciences.

C • The **coordinator** might provide information on internship placements, maintain student records, organize publicity, develop handbooks for participants, and generally make sure that order is maintained. The director of internships at the University of Colorado has coordination as a primary function. Other primary coordinating functions — faculty communications, evaluation, research, professional development, etc. — are discussed in the chapter of this book entitled "Establishing Administrative Structures that Support the Goals of Experiential Education."

Whatever your primary role, you will have to protect against the tendency of all other participants in the experiential learning process to heave a sigh of relief at your expertise and expect you to take charge of everything. At a number of schools in the NSIEE/FIPSE Project, faculty told us that the internship coordinator was irreplaceable. "We don't know what we would do without her," they would say, or "We could never do what he does." It is important to share your expertise, train others to do what you do, collaborate with faculty and staff across campus, and hold on to your long-range goals.

Articulating the Contribution of Experiential Education to the Mission and Values of Your Institution

"You must be able to make a case for experiential education in terms of the 'coin of the realm,' which means articulating the educational value of your particular program or course for your institution. It means being able to communicate the unique and distinctive contribution that experiential education makes — because nobody else is going to do that for you. The results of a survey done at Michigan State University provide an example. When asked why they used experiential education, faculty responded that it provides unique opportunities for students to: (1) gain confidence in the upper levels of the cognitive domain [application, integration, and synthesis]; (2) acquire specific skills that are more easily acquired in the field than in the classroom; (3) acquire specific knowledge about an institution or an agency; (4) learn how to learn on their own; and (5) enhance their personal growth and development."

-John Duley, Professor Emeritus
Michigan State University

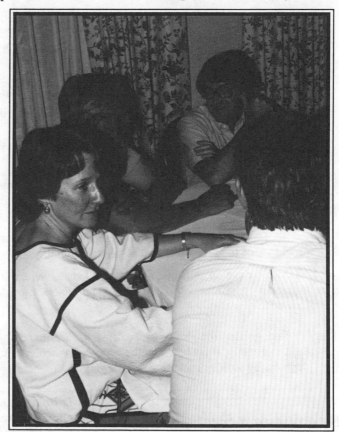

Sally Snodgrass, a faculty member in psychology and member of Skidmore College's Committee on Educational Policy and Planning, listens as faculty from other liberal arts colleges discuss their schools' missions in relationship to experiential learning.

If you have not found congruence between institutional values and experiential learning values within your college, you must consider strategies for changing the role of your program and the role you play within your college. However, even if you have found a close relationship between these values, it is important to articulate that relationship continually. For example, in relating the internship program's goals at Hartwick College to the mission statement of the institution, the Hartwick Internship Advisory Committee became clearer in its perception of its tasks and more steadfast in its commitment to them. The faculty committee at this small liberal arts college in upstate New York articulated the relationship as follows:

This goals statement at Hartwick has become a standard against which decisions and an ideal against which reality can be measured. The goals statement may be revised in time, and should be, but its development provides a framework of shared values that encourages the committee to take on many difficult tasks.

Skidmore College, another liberal arts institution in upstate New York, took a slightly different tack in defining experiential education in relation to its intellectual mission:

"Skidmore's long experience in combining career preparation and liberal arts education has established strong connections between the life of the mind and the life of practicality and action. Students participating in Skidmore's new curriculum will

observation, the modes of self-expression, and the quantitative and technical skills which make intelligent, effective action possible. The internship program will confirm the success of this partnership."

If there is some agreement that there is a campus environment supportive of experiential learning but not in an overt or organized way, it is possible to help those on campus to see the contributions that experiential learning makes. Here are several ideas for raising the overall awareness of experiential education:

1. Organize a consortium of faculty, administrators, and even students interested in experiential learning. Most campuses have interest groups that meet occasionally over a brown-bag lunch. If a mailing list is too difficult or too expensive, arrange a free notice in the campus newspaper. George Mason University had an experiential learning consortium for several years, and a number of constructive policies came out of very informal discussions.

2. If a newsletter takes too much time, try regular features in the campus newspaper, faculty newsletter, and alumni bulletin. Students who want writing experience will often do the legwork if they get a byline. Hartwick College now has an article in the campus paper each month, written by a peer advisor from the Internship Office, to give students and faculty an opportunity to find out about interesting student internships.

3. Be a constant catalyst for awareness of experiential education. When you see a good article about sociology field work, copy it and send to to people in your sociology department who might be interested. NSIEE has plenty of such resources. Introduce the French professor who teaches through drama to the history professor who likes to have students act out some of the great debates in European history so they can trade hints. Let the students interested in computer modeling know about the research project the professor in

---

GOALS OF HARTWICK COLLEGE'S INTERNSHIP PROGRAM

Consistent with the educational objectives of the College, which emphasize intellectual excellence, ethical values, and effective and responsible participation in a democratic society, the Hartwick Internship Program provides opportunities for students:

1. To expand their awareness of the world beyond the campus by exposure to a variety of careers, disciplines, life styles, and environments.

2. To develop and expand their knowledge and/or skills in a work setting.

3. To gain experience in the disciplined and discriminating use of evidence in making decisions and solving problems in a work setting.

4. To gain an appreciation of creative and decision-making processes of the arts and sciences, as carried out in a work setting.

5. To develop self-reliance, personal style, values, and beliefs in a manner consistent with becoming responsible and productive individuals.

Recognizing the individuality of each student and unique nature of each internship, it is clear that these goals are achieved to varying degrees, by various means, and with varying emphases.

Be a constant catalyst for awareness of experiential education.

benefit from this twofold understanding of 'higher education.' They will learn the contemporary and historical perspectives, the methods of inquiry and analysis, the critical flexibility, the strategies of precise

geography is conducting. Let people on campus know about professional meetings in experiential education, especially regional ones which do not cost much in travel funds. The Field Studies staff at UCLA, for example, makes a point of inviting professors to meetings of experiential educators.

4. Collect information about the diversity of experiential learning that occurs on your campus, and make it available to the president, dean, faculty, and the director of alumni relations. Your research can demonstrate the ways that experiential education contributes to their goals for your college or university.

5. Offer to co-sponsor a workshop with the faculty development or teaching improvement staff, and invite faculty who encourage experiential learning in a variety of ways to share their approaches with others.

"When I first got this position I thought, 'In the preparation of our materials I ought to consult what the college says in the catalog about the mission of the college.' And it all
seemed so great, it fit right in -- 'the preparation of students for careers which touch the community wherein they will live.' So there did seem to be a concern that we prepare students for life after college. But now I've been listening more carefully to the President's addresses and to the themes that keep coming up in what he says. He focuses on 'liberal learning,' which is to produce students who have good critical thinking skills and good communications skills. On the other hand, in many departments in the institution, faculty who do research and who publish are the ones who are being rewarded, not necessarily the ones who may be turning out students with these critical thinking skills. So I guess I really would like to have some help in showing the President how this program fits his conception of the mission of the institution. For program growth in the future, I think I need to have the upper-level administration feel that whatever it is they're talking about, whether it be liberal learning or 'refinement of
morals and tastes,' cooperative education and internships do that. I will have to learn myself how to do this better."
-Kristen Murtaugh, Director
Cooperative Education
Manhattan College, New York

6. Be sure students communicate their support for experiential learning as part of the curriculum.

"Much of the pressure for keeping internships at Skidmore has come from students. When we moved away from a 4-1-4 system when internships were done primarily during the January term, students were extremely concerned that internships might be lost. They fought hard. They presented a formal petition at a faculty meeting. They wrote articles in The Skidmore News. It generated a real furor."
-Barbara Hubert, Director
Career Planning and
Field Experience
Skidmore College
Saratoga Springs, New York

Gregory Williams is a Teacher Education major doing his co-op experience at the Bethlehem Community Center in Winston-Salem, North Carolina. He is a student at Winston-Salem State University.

It is only through understanding and expressing experiential learning values in relation to the culture of your college that true institutionalization will be possible.

7. Work with student groups that want to relate extracurricular activity to classroom learning. At the University of Maryland College Park, for example, a special section of a course on leadership is reserved for officers of student organizations who want to use their own experiences to understand the theoretical foundations of leadership.

Articulating clearly the contributions experiential learning makes to your college or university is not an exercise in rhetoric, but a significant intellectual process. As many people as possible should participate in its work. It is only through understanding and expressing experiential learning values in relation to the culture of your college that true institutionalization will be possible. ❏

FOOTNOTES

1 Jane C. Kendall, "Values as the Core of Institutional Commitment: Finding a Common Ground," in *Making Sponsored Experiential Learning Standard Practice*, ed. by Thomas C. Little, New Directions for Experiential Learning, No. 20, Jossey-Bass, San Francisco, California, 1983, pp. 27-42.

2 David Kolb, *Experiential Learning: Experience as the Source of Learning and Development*, Prentice-Hall, Englewood Cliffs, New Jersey, 1984.

3 *Ibid.*

4 Robert F. Sexton, "The Promise of Experiential Education for the Liberal Arts," *Dimensions of Experiential Education*, ed. by Robert F. Sexton, National Center for Public Service Internship Programs (now NSIEE), Raleigh, North Carolina, 1976, p. 35.

RECOMMENDED RESOURCES

Dewey, John, *Experience and Education*, 1938, available in paperback through Collier Books. The best classical theory on experiential learning.

Gross, Edward, and Paul V. Grambsch, *University Goals and Academic Power*, American Council on Education, Washington, D.C., 1968. Chapter 2 presents the results of a study of what the goals of American universities are and what they ought to be. This chapter offers a good overview for understanding the differences in the perceived and the preferred goals of universities.

Kendall, Jane C., "Values as the Core of Institutional Commitment: Finding a Common Ground," in *Making Sponsored Experiential Learning Standard Practice*, ed. by Thomas C. Little, New Directions for Experiential Learning, No. 20, Jossey-Bass, San Francisco, California, 1983. The critical issue of values in relation to the institutionalization of experiential learning is explored in a comprehensive way.

Kolb, David, *Experiential Learning: Experience as the Source of Learning and Development*, Prentice-Hall, Englewood Cliffs, New Jersey, 1984, and *The Learning Style Inventory*, McBer and Company, Boston, Massachusetts, 1976. The best contemporary theoretical background on experiential education.

Mentokowski, Marcia, "Can the Concept of Human Development Supply a Unifying Purpose for Higher Education?," Alverno College, Milwaukee, Wisconsin, 1983. An example of how experiential learning fits the mission of an outcome-oriented liberal arts curriculum.

Newman, Frank, Catherine Milton, and Susan Stroud, "Community Service and Higher Education: Obligations and Opportunities," *AAHE Bulletin*, Washington, D.C., June, 1985. The latest rediscovery of experiential learning in relation to the goals of higher education.

2

Integrating Experiential Education into the Curriculum

"*At Westmont College, we have taken three steps in integrating field experiences into the curriculum. First, we got each department to list the internship as a legitimate course offering in the catalogue. Then we helped the departments to build it in as a legitimate part of the major. Of course this took longer in some majors than others. Now our Curriculum Committee is considering a proposal for some type of experiential learning to be required for graduation.*"

> -Edwin Potts
> Assistant to the President
> Director of Off-Campus
> Programs
> Westmont College
> Santa Barbara, California

"*The faculty may be willing to concede that sociology students can learn a great deal in what they would regard as applied sociology. But I don't have a very good answer for the classics skeptic or the philosophy skeptic, or for that matter the history skeptic.*"

> -H.C. Erik Midelfort
> Associate Dean, College of
> Arts and Sciences, and
> Professor of History
> University of Virginia

"*Courses or programs are included because faculty believe certain knowledge and skills are necessary. They will be convinced to use experiential education if they think it is the most effective and efficient way to learn that knowledge and those skills.*"

> -John Duley
> NSIEE Peer Consultant
> and Professor Emeritus
> Michigan State University

"*Integration of experiential education into the curriculum is an acknowledgment of its legitimacy at the institution. But of equal importance, what is experiential education's real currency value? Is it encouraged or required for all students ... or are students indirectly punished for engaging in experiential education?*"

> -NSIEE Peer Consultants

Even among the many institutions where experiential education enjoys academic credits, the question on truly integrating experiential education into the curriculum still seems to persist. Why? The comments made above by various deans and faculty reflect some of the critical issues.

What Does "Integration into the Curriculum" Mean?

Before looking more closely at the critical issues in building experiential education into the curriculum, focus for a moment on the various degrees of potential integration into the ongoing academic program of the institution. What does it mean to be "part" of the curriculum? Are a few courses enough? Listen as the NSIEE Peer Consultants struggle with these questions:

Jane Kendall: Originally we talked about "the integration of experiential education into the curriculum of the institution so it is available to all students." Now we are saying that availability is not enough.

Sharon Rubin: It's really a matter of whether experiential education is recognized as a

Lynn DeMeester, Program Officer, Fund for the Improvement of Postsecondary Education, U.S. Department of Education

John Duley, Professor Emeritus, Michigan State University, and Tom Little, CAEL

legitimate part of degree requirements. I'll give you an example. Bob McCaffery's office is part of Continuing Education, and the only credits he can give are Continuing Ed. credits, which can be used as electives. They can't be used for departmental electives; they are free-floating electives. In one college the credits really cannot be used to satisfy any requirements, while students in the other colleges have electives and can use them as electives, but there seems to be a perception that they are not valuable credits.

Tom Little: It's not just the fact that experiential education is available, because at most places, if students want to find it, they can find it. The question is whether it is important enough that it becomes a part of their primary educational planning. The question is *"What's the value? What's its real currency?"*

Jane Permaul: Some schools do use experiential education only for general electives. In the degree program you are allowed to take perhaps 12 units of general electives. You could take an internship or you could take some other things. But you can't take everything as general electives. So experiential education is "legitimate" because it does count toward your degree program, but not to the level of importance as a major requirement.

John Duley: Then it's a legitimate *part* of the educational program, but it isn't really encouraged.

Jane Kendall: Well, you have different levels. Some are general education

requirements, some are major requirements, some are general electives. Often when you can get general electives, they are of no real use to the students in terms of their degree programs.

John Duley: It needs to be part of the package that an institution plans for students to complete.

Jane Kendall: So it's not enough to say that it's a "legitimate part of the curriculum" because Sharon's example from UNH is legitimate. They can get credit. It's just not very valuable credit.

Sharon Rubin: Yes, I've been to some schools that have these funny "co-op credits" that can't even be used toward degree requirements.

Tom Little: It's got to be somehow expected or encouraged — not just for the exceptional student with a lot of initiative who seeks it out and perseveres.

Jane Permaul: But at some schools where there are a lot of options, nothing is encouraged.

Jane Kendall: Would we conclude that it does have to be a legitimate part of degree *requirements*? If it's not recognized as part of the degree requirements, then there is a real problem.

Tom Little: *The value of the currency is the issue.* At Rhode Island College, the credits are there and the students are encouraged to do experiential learning, but now as you see the curriculum tightening up everywhere, there are fewer and fewer places left to do anything. The pressure to get jobs is so great that students take most of their electives in the major. That's a pressure on students. So I think the question is the value of the currency — the currency value of this learning.

Lynn DeMeester: It sounds as if students are sometimes inadvertantly punished for participating.

Sharon Rubin: I'd like us to take a fairly strict stand on this because it is really irritating to me to hear faculty say "We believe our students should do it, but they can't have credit from this department. We don't recognize the credit they get as part of their degree requirements for this degree." Students have to use internship credits as electives outside their departments. Faculty say, "Well, we'll let them do an internship instead of taking a course in statistics" or something like that. That to me is hedging about whether this is a legitimate educational activity or not. Is an internship accepted by the department as something that a student would normally do as a major in that department? It doesn't have to be a requirement, but as long as everyone says "Yes, you can do it, but you have to go somewhere else," then that's not integration into the curriculum.

Tom Little: The other question is who grants the credit and for what.

Jane Kendall: Another aspect of curriculum integration is how experiential educators view what they do as distinct or as part of a larger effort. I have always seen experiential learning as a methodology of teaching and learning. Then it is something that should pervade the way the institution teaches, whereas so much of what we talk about is "programs." Do you just add on internship courses, or do you teach faculty how to use experiences as part of the way they teach students? Often

experiential educators see the curriculum as something "over there" that can't be touched, so we have to go all around it. Rather than seeing that *that's* the issue.

Tom Little: We have a dual problem. Many administrators of experiential education programs do not think about teaching; they think about administering a program. Then many faculty in higher education do not think about pedagogy; they think about content. The two reinforce each other to avoid the educational issues in experiential learning.

John Duley: Experiential educators need to work with faculty to advocate for field components — even when faculty are not thinking about pedagogy *per se.*

For schools where experiential education is not yet integrated into the curriculum at all, a few examples may help in understanding what this incorporation might mean. First, a typical way of integrating experiential learning with traditional, classroom-based learning is a seminar that links the two. At the University of Virginia, for instance, students doing internships in social service agencies come together weekly for a seminar to explore issues related to sociological and psychological theory, interpersonal relations on the job, research methodology, and other topics. At Bradford College, a seminar on the nature of work has been designed to complement internships. At other schools, seminars preceding the internship experience allow faculty to ground students both theoretically and practically. Michele Whitham and Tim

Sharon Rubin, Assistant Dean for Undergraduate Studies, University of Maryland

Jane Kendall, Executive Director of the National Society for Internships and Experiential Education, and Jane Permaul, Director of Field Studies Development, UCLA

Tom Little, Regional Manager, Council for Adult and Experiential Learning

Whether the goal of curricular integration is students' improved understanding of content, enhanced cognitive development, expanded repertoire of generic liberal arts skills, or empowerment as independent learners, there are simple and complex models to fit those goals.

Stanton have described the extensive and intensive pre-field preparation that students in Cornell's College of Human Ecology internship program undergo.[1] At Berea College, on the other hand, debriefings after students complete work assignments are the norm.

Intensive but short internships, used by many schools which have adopted a 4-1-4 school year schedule, have presented special challenges to faculty who wish to integrate experiential learning more closely with the traditional curriculum. At Skidmore College, a faculty committee carefully screens students' proposals for field study to make sure that the experience they expect to have will allow them to fulfill the learning objectives they plan. At Hartwick College, the internship coordinator and several faculty members visit students at their internship sites to assess the quality of the students' learning opportunities. Other schools bridge internships with both prefield preparation and postfield debriefing.

Schools with strong science programs might want to emulate the Undergraduate Research Opportunities Program (UROP) offered by the Massachusetts Institute of Technology, which matches undergraduates with faculty members involved in research projects. Such collaborative research not only enhances student learning in content areas but helps students under-

stand the nature of scientific problem-solving in more complex and realistic ways than laboratory experiments could. The program is so popular that more than 75% of the undergraduates at M.I.T. participate.

The National Collegiate Honors Council sponsors a similarly intense learning experience for students, but one very different in design. Honors Semesters give students from across the country an opportunity to come together to explore a theme through living in a particular environment, taking courses, and participating in a wide variety of experiences for learning. For instance, in a San Antonio Border semester, students examined the nature of borders generally, and a political border in particular, through living in San Antonio. They frequently crossed the border to Mexico to interview those with a different border perspective, and they participated in internships and short-term,

out-of-class learning experiences, as well as taking traditional courses. Semesters at the United Nations, in Washington, D.C., and in Puerto Rico have given gifted students additional contexts into which they can fit their learning.

Whether the goal of curricular integration is students' improved understanding of content, enhanced cognitive development, expanded repertoire of generic liberal arts skills, or empowerment as independent learners, there are simple and complex models to fit those goals. Faculty in the same discipline at other institutions, faculty from "traditional" field experience programs such as social work or teacher education, national organizations such as the National Society for Internships and Experiential Education, and books such as *Preparing Humanists for Work*,[2] can all provide a wealth of models worthy of sharing.

PREPARING HUMANISTS FOR WORK:

A NATIONAL STUDY OF UNDERGRADUATE INTERNSHIPS IN THE HUMANITIES

CARREN O. KASTON

WITH

JAMES M. HEFFERNAN

THE WASHINGTON CENTER

Why is Integrating Experiential Education into the Curriculum Important?

"If it's not part of the school's curriculum, what do you have? We are talking about a method of learning. If it's not part of the curriculum, it's missing the main boat."

Simply stated, the curriculum is the primary expression of the institution's view of what needs to be learned. If experiential learning is not built into the curriculum, it will not be part of the way the faculty teaches and the way the institution approaches education. A college or department either recognizes all four parts of the complete learning cycle (Kolb, 1984), or it does not. There are many levels of curriculum integration and many different approaches that schools can take, but commitment to experiential education as reflected in the curriculum is *the* primary factor in the long-term institutionalization of any educational innovation.

What Are the Critical Issues?

*O*nly a portion of the educational value of experiential education has been widely acknowledged and accepted. Everyone — faculty, students, administrators, field sponsors and experiential educators — have praised the value of experience as an effective means of exploring career goals and preparing for specific careers. The federal cooperative education program, with $14.4 million appropriated last year, is a clear acknowledgment of this type of education. Over 900 colleges and universities have this form of experiential education. But the faculty resist, rightfully, concluding that while career preparation is important for their students, it is not an objective of the academic curriculum and hence should not be a part of the curriculum. It belongs in career planning and placement services and, in fact, many experiential education programs are administered through those offices. Says a dean, "It's got to be more than career education . . . if it is to gain faculty approval." THE OBJECTIVES OF EXPERIENTIAL EDUCATION PROGRAMS MUST CONTRIBUTE TO AND BE COMPATIBLE WITH THOSE OF THE ACADEMIC CURRICULUM. See the next section of this chapter entitled "Academic Validity and Acceptance" for some of the criteria.

Only recently has the potential contribution of experiential education to the academic curriculum been explored and discussed. And perhaps the academic deans and faculty who most need to be informed in this area are currently the least informed. One academic dean reflected the frustration by saying, "I don't have a very good answer for the philosophy professor who is a skeptic." This suggests that

For faculty to adopt the use of experiential education, such programs and courses must provide faculty with incentives and rewards which are at least comparable to those gained from teaching through lectures, seminars, and laboratories.

FACULTY AND DEANS NEED OPPORTUNITIES TO LEARN ABOUT WAYS EXPERIENTIAL EDUCATION HAS CONTRIBUTED TO VARIOUS DISCIPLINES AND OTHER ACADEMIC PROGRAMS.

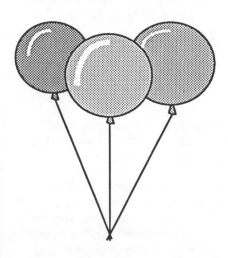

"I see liberal arts education as a bunch of colorful helium balloons, all floating up to the ceiling and with all these funny things written on them — like HISTORY and PHILOSOPHY and SOCIOLOGY. And if the roof weren't there, they'd just fly right on out. Each one has a little string on it. What experiential learning does is to tie the strings down so that there's something anchoring them and tying them together. This is important because life does not come to us in five 3-hour courses a week. It comes in one big swirl of psychology and literature and philosophy and history, with a little economics and government thrown in."

-Nancy Gansneder, Director
Undergraduate Internship
Program
Departments of Sociology
and Psychology
University of Virginia

Not only do faculty need to be informed about the many contributions experiential education can make to both liberal arts and disciplinary curricula. They also need to be convinced that experiential education is an effective and efficient teaching method. Given the prevailing counseling model used in experiential

Experiential education must be recognized through credits that count toward the major and degree requirements if it is going to be a legitimate, supported partner to classroom learning.

education, faculty sometimes feel burdened, rather than relieved. (See Chapter 5 of this sourcebook for a discussion of the counseling model and some alternatives.) Further discouragement comes from the tradition that sponsoring students on "independent study" or off-campus study is not usually compensated at the same level as teaching a class. FOR FACULTY TO ADOPT THE USE OF EXPERIENTIAL EDUCATION, SUCH PROGRAMS AND COURSES MUST PROVIDE FACULTY WITH INCENTIVES AND REWARDS WHICH ARE AT LEAST COMPARABLE TO THOSE GAINED FROM TEACHING THROUGH LECTURES, SEMINARS AND LABORATORIES.

Finally, there is the question of legitimacy and status. Seldom does anyone — a student, faculty, administrator or fieldwork sponsor — enjoy participating in activities which are considered peripheral, second class, or outright useless. Activities perceived to be in these categories have little value beyond the immediate pleasure of doing them. Yet, most experiential education falls into extracurricular activities (as part of career development or community service), restricted electives which do not count towards anything, or general electives which count towards the degree, but not toward major or general education requirements. The most valued academic currencies are in the form of credits that count toward the major or toward general education or degree requirements.

On the other hand, reluctant

faculty are most likely to grant experiential activities at least peripheral academic status when pressured to include experiential education in the curriculum. The challenge then becomes whether to accept a lesser status just to get in the door or to insist on a more substantive status. If the program gets into the institution with a lesser status, does it have a chance to move up the ladder? EXPERIENTIAL EDUCATION MUST BE RECOGNIZED THROUGH CREDITS THAT COUNT TOWARD THE MAJOR AND DEGREE REQUIREMENTS IF IT IS GOING TO BE A LEGITIMATE, SUPPORTED PARTNER TO CLASSROOM LEARNING.

Implied in these four critical issues is the dominant position which faculty play in matters regarding curriculum. Regardless of the campus size and differences in governance, the one area in which faculty are consistently most involved and influential is curriculum. A review of literature on curriculum development will quickly reveal that little is written specifically for higher education. The final analysis is that the faculty decides. Courses and programs are included because faculty believe certain knowledge and skills are necessary. How anything is taught is also the prerogative of the faculty, frequently solely the decision of the individual instructor. Conse-

quently, IF EXPERIENTIAL EDUCATION IS TO BE INTEGRATED INTO THE CURRICULUM, FACULTY INVOLVED IN THAT CURRICULUM MUST BE FULLY CONSULTED AND INVOLVED IN THE INTEGRATION PROCESS.

"Departmental autonomy is strong and highly prized. The impetus for courses or curricular changes originates in the various departments. Thus, if other departments are going to offer experiential learning opportunities, that action must come from those departments."
-Nancy Gansneder, Director
Undergraduate Internship
Program
Departments of Sociology
and Psychology
University of Virginia

To summarize, the challenges in integrating experiential education into the curriculum involve the following:

1. The objectives of any and all experiential education courses and programs must be clearly articulated, and if these are to be included into the curriculum, the objectives must contribute in a qualitative way to the goals of the curriculum.

2. Faculty need opportunities to know more about the value of experiential education and how it can be used as a teaching tool.

3. The use of experiential edu-

Jeff Chinn, Assistant Provost at Illinois State University, discusses curriculum issues with Jane Permaul, UCLA, and Nancy Gansneder, University of Virginia

cation by faculty must be a positive experience. The experience must at least be as meaningful and rewarding as teaching via more traditional means.

4. The credit earned for learning that is achieved experientially must have equal status as credit earned through lecture and seminar formats.

5. Faculty must be fully con-sulted and involved in the integration effort and have full control over its use as they would over any other course or program in the curriculum.

Ultimately, experiential education must gain equal status with other approaches to the teaching/learning process. If these five challenges are met, it has a good chance of doing just that.

Where Does Experiential Education Stand in Your Curriculum?

*B*efore jumping into a campaign to integrate experiential education into the curriculum of your institution, look around and see what is already in place and where these programs and courses are on campus. Chances are that there is more "experiential education" going on than one would ever have imagined. In part, faculty practice experiential education but do not identify it as such, simply because they are unfamiliar with the concept per se. Further, experiential education comes in so many forms and shapes and satisfies so many possible purposes that it is most likely scattered all over campus without any one focal point. Therefore, in assessing what is available on campus, be sure to leave no stone unturned. If you are concerned about only one department or division, the same assessment approach is an important starting point. These are the first steps toward assessing where you are:

1. Begin by making a simple list of all the experiential education activities offered. Figure A lists the most common types and forms of experiential education; it may remind you of more stones to turn as you inventory what your institution or department is already doing. Figure B lists examples of the goals of experiential education courses and programs. It can help you think of other activities to consider for the inventory.

2. For each course or program that uses experiential learning, complete the Inventory of Experiential

The acceptability of experiential education (and thereby its integration into the curriculum) is largely dependent on how the faculty and administration perceive the process of assuring that college-level learning is taking place and that it is worthy of the credit being granted.

Programs and Courses (Figure C). Ask the faculty and administrators involved in these activities to complete their own profiles or review what you write.

3. Tally the responses from the inventory to determine how much experiential education is being used, what objectives it is fulfilling, and the status of these activities in the curriculum. More specific questions are provided to help you with this analysis.

4. Consider the strengths and weaknesses of the current offerings. See the questions provided to help you with this assessment.

Figure A

TYPES AND FORMS OF EXPERIENTIAL EDUCATION

1. *Discrete Experiential Education Courses or Programs*	2. *Experiential Education as One or More Components of a Course or Program*	3. *Other Experiential Techniques Incorporated into a Course or Program*
cooperative education	field projects	role playing
field study, fieldwork, field research	field trips	laboratory work
independent study	participatory observations	simulation games and exercises
internships	oral interviews	student-led class sessions
practica	site visits/field observations	(presentations or discussions)
service-learning	use of primary source or raw data	group learning activities
work-learn	others	other active forms of learning
others		

Figure B

EXAMPLES OF GOALS OF EXPERIENTIAL EDUCATION COURSES AND PROGRAMS

Experiential education can be a powerful educational tool contributing to the accomplishment of many important educational goals. The examples noted in Figure B are divided into six areas, some with overlap. They are separated to help clarify the potential contribution of experiential education to various concerns of higher education.

1. *Academic Discipline-Related Knowledge and Skills*
   — To acquire knowledge in an academic discipline (e.g., learning about the history of a particular type of industry or corporate configuration and its impact on the economy by interning in a corporation of a particular industry)
   — To test and apply theories developed in a particular discipline (e.g., to determine if the theory of spatialization learned in geography is indeed useful in urban planning and to what extent, by interning in a city planning office)
   — To apply, integrate and evaluate a body of knowledge and method of inquiry of an academic discipline (e.g., are the knowledge and method of critical analysis in history and literature transferable to the evaluation of scripts for media entertainment or to a manual for the use of complex equipment?)

2. *Generic, Cognitive, Liberal Arts Skills*
   — To acquire general functional skills and attitudes for productive adult life (e.g., interpersonal and communication skills, problem-solving, critical thinking)
   — To become responsible citizens by understanding issues of social concern and developing skills for citizen participation
   — To develop and practice the ability to learn in a self-directed manner from daily life experiences as well as from formal structured instruction

3. *Ethical and Moral Values*
   — To develop and apply moral reasoning or judgment (e.g., values clarification and testing)

4. *Career Development*
   — To explore career options
   — To develop and demonstrate competencies needed in a career

5. *Personal Development*
   — To gain self-understanding and self-reliance
   — To gain self-confidence and a sense of self-worth

6. *Other Educational Outcomes*
   — To increase motivation to learn in both the academic and personal arenas
   — To gain a sense of empowerment about one's education
   — To have access to knowledge or equipment not available or easily attainable through on-campus instruction.

Pat Cunliffe, standing, Supervisor at Square Industries in Jersey City, New Jersey, teaches accounting procedures to Helen Bilyj, Maria Hatzelis, and Eileen Monahan. All three students are in the Cooperative Education Program at Saint Peter's College.

Figure C

INVENTORY OF EXPERIENTIAL EDUCATION PROGRAMS AND COURSES

Ask each faculty or staff member responsible for a program or course with components for experiential learning to complete a separate inventory form.

Academic or administrative unit_____

Program or course title_____

Name of faculty sponsor(s)_____

Name of staff coordinator_____

Year program or course began_____

Program Goals — *An experiential learning program or course typically has multiple goals. For this program or course, put a "1" beside the most important goal below, a "2" beside the second most important, and a "3" beside the third most important:*

____ To apply, integrate and evaluate a body of knowledge and the methods of inquiry of an academic discipline

____ To develop work competencies for specific professions or occupations

____ To develop social awareness and habits of responsible citizenship by direct involvement in community concerns

____ To enhance understanding of different cultures and environments

____ To develop and apply moral judgment

____ To explore career options and gain general work experience

____ To foster personal growth and maturation, e.g., self-understanding, self-confidence, interpersonal skills, coping with ambiguity

____ To improve the ability to learn in a self-directed manner

____ To gain access to knowledge or equipment not easily attainable on campus

Academic Status

		Yes	No
1.	Does the program or course have the respect of the other faculty or staff in your unit?	__	__
2.	Does it have the respect of students (or is it seen as an easy way to earn credit)?	__	__
3.	Is the program recognized outside your unit by administrators, faculty, and/or students?	__	__
4.	Is the program required in a course of study or as a graduation requirement?	__	__
5.	Does it provide academic credit?	__	__
6.	Are letter grades provided?	__	__

(continued on page 34)

From *Strengthening Experiential Education in Your Institution*, National Society for Internships and Experiential Education, Raleigh, North Carolina, 1986

7. If credit is awarded, how is it recognized?
   ____ for general education requirements
   ____ in the academic major
   ____ as an elective outside the major
   ____ credited but does not apply toward degree requirement

8. What is the average number of academic credits earned in one academic period?
   ____ semester hours   ____ quarter hours

9. If letter grades are provided, who makes the final recommendation for credit and the grade?
   ____ faculty sponsor   ____ faculty committee
   ____ program or course coordinator   ____ site supervisor
   ____ other, specify:_____

10. How is the learning recorded on student transcripts?
    ____ not recorded
    ____ course labels and credits that cannot be distinguished from those obtained from classroom learning
    ____ course labels and credits that are designated as experiential learning
    ____ credits labeled by subject area with no specific course label or title
    ____ credits aggregated and labeled in a block as experiential learning with no course title or subject area
    ____ competency statements
    ____ narrative description of work performed or other achievements
    ____ other, specify:_____

Program Participants

1. How many students participated in the program during the past academic year? _____
   In the summer? _____

2. What was the total number of academic credits generated by the program in the past year, including the summer? _____

3. What is the predominant academic classification of participating students?
   ____ Lower Division
   ____ Upper Division
   ____ Graduate

4. What are the minimum requirements for participation?

5. Is the program restricted to particular majors?   Yes ____   No ____

6. If the program is not restricted to particular majors, what are the predominant majors of participants?

Program Staffing

		Yes	*No*
1.	Does the program have a faculty sponsor?	___	___
2.	Does the program have a coordinator?	___	___

From *Strengthening Experiential Education in Your Institution*, National Society for Internships and Experiential Education, Raleigh, North Carolina, 1986

3. How are these roles recognized? Check the appropriate level for each column below:

	For faculty sponsor	*For program coordinator*
No institutional recognition	_____	_____
Institutional recognition but with no reduction in other responsibilities such as advising or committee work	_____	_____
Institutional recognition through overload compensation	_____	_____
Institutional recognition as part of regular work load	_____	_____

4. What is the percentage of time allocated for program responsibilities for the period the program or course is being offered?

    _____% for faculty sponsor   _____% for program coordinator

Program Operation

1. How do students generally find out about the course or program?
    ___ listing in catalog   ___ publicity materials (brochures, etc.)
    ___ listing in class schedule   ___ class announcements or presentations
    ___ campus newspaper   ___ other, specify:_____

	Yes	No
2. Are formal learning plans used in the program?	__	__
3. If yes, are they required?	__	__
4. Are handbooks available for students, faculty, and field supervisors?	__	__

5. Who arranges the field site for experiential learning?
    ____ student
    ____ administrative personnel
    ____ faculty
    ____ other, specify: _____

6. How many hours a week does a student typically spend in the experiential, non-classroom component during the academic term? _____ hours

7. How many weeks is the usual experience? _____ weeks

(continued on page 36)

From *Strengthening Experiential Education in Your Institution*, National Society for Internships and Experiential Education, Raleigh, North Carolina, 1986

8. What procedures are used to prepare students prior to program participation?
    ____ no specific preparation required
    ____ required course for credit
    ____ optional course for credit
    ____ required non-credit seminar
    ____ optional non-credit seminar
    ____ required workshop
    ____ optional workshop
    ____ one-to-one advising or tutorial
    ____ self-instructional materials or software
    ____ other, specify:_____

9. Which of the following are typically used to monitor students' progress?
    ____ telephone conversations with students
    ____ telephone conversations with field supervisors
    ____ on-site visits
    ____ individual conferences with students on campus
    ____ seminars concurrent with the experience
    ____ papers, journals, or reports submitted periodically by the student
    ____ written reports by field supervisor
    ____ other, specify:_____

10. Which methods are commonly used to evaluate students' learning?
    ____performance tests (such as work samples, observations of students in the work setting)
    ____simulations or situational tests (such as academic games, role playing, case students, in-basket exercises)
    ____product assessment (such as evaluation of paintings, poetry, proposals, writing samples, interview tapes, special projects)
    ____student self-assessment (such as job inventory checklists, self-evaluation instruments)
    ____interviews
    ____written reports or content papers
    ____oral presentations or reports
    ____supervisor evaluations
    ____other, specify:_____

11. Who evaluates the learning acquired? (Check all that apply.)
    ____ faculty sponsor   ____ a faculty committee
    ____ outside expert(s)   ____ program or course coordinator
    ____ site supervisor   ____ the student
    ____ other, specify:_____

12. How is the program or course funded? (Check all that apply and indicate percentage of each.)
    ____ regular institutional funds (_____%)
    ____ special developmental funds from the institution (_____%)
    ____ grants (_____%)
    ____ other, specify % and nature:_____

13. Which resources are specifically provided for program administration?
    ____ travel funds for site visits
    ____ funds for long-distance telephone calls
    ____ clerical support
    ____ travel funds for professional/faculty development
    ____ other, specify:_____

From *Strengthening Experiential Education in Your Institution*, National Society for Internships and Experiential Education, Raleigh, North Carolina, 1986

	Yes	No
14. Are there formal, written policies at the departmental level?	—	—
At the institutional level?	—	—
15. Is there a faculty committee with oversight or advisory responsibilities for the program?	—	—

16. If there is a faculty committee, what are its functions? Is it elected or appointed? By whom? To whom does it report? What is the academic status of its members? Please respond on a separate page.

17. If there are unique features of the program or course which were not covered in this inventory, please elaborate on a separate page.

Program Plans

1. How was your program or course originally established? By whom? For what purpose? Please respond on a separate page.

2. Has the purpose of the program or course changed over time? How?

3. Of the goals noted under "Program Goals" at the beginning of this inventory, which is a goal that should be given more priority in the future?

Name of person completing inventory _____

Title _____

Date completed _____

From *Strengthening Experiential Education in Your Institution*, National Society for Internships and Experiential Education, Raleigh, North Carolina, 1986

After you have made a list of all the experiential education activities offered, then complete an "Inventory of Experiential Education Programs and Courses" (Figure C) for each program and course. Next, tally the responses from this inventory to help you determine the following:

1. The extent to which experiential education is used on campus and by whom. Is it mostly faculty or staff who are involved in delivering the courses and programs? What percentage of academic departments list internships, practica, cooperative education, field experience, or other experiential learning activities?

2. The types of objectives which are being fulfilled, or which are perceived as being fulfilled, by experiential education. Are they mostly academic or non-academic in nature?

3. The status that the experiential courses or programs have in relationship to the curriculum. Does the "currency value" given to these courses and programs encourage students and faculty to become involved?

4. Is there any consistency to the academic policies and practices across campus, or are there any patterns that emerge about the way experiential learning is seen and used in the institution?

Then, based on the inventory, consider the strengths and weaknesses of curricular integration at your institution. Take a look at the distribution of courses and programs among the three major categories of experiential education listed in Figure A. Note the departments and faculty involved as one of the strengths. They can be the foundation for more ambitious integrative efforts in the future.

Where are the weaknesses? Is there disproportionate involvement by non-faculty in any of the experiential education courses and programs? Are the goals and objectives of existing experiential

AN EXAMPLE OF CAMPUS-WIDE COURSE NUMBERS

In 1973, the Campus Senate at the University of Maryland College Park approved the use of two course numbers specifically for field experience; "—386: Field Experience" and "—387: Analysis of Field Experience" are variable credit courses (1 - 3 credits each) for which students must register concurrently. Because these course numbers are available to all departments and are reserved for experiential education, it is easy for students and faculty to find a ready vehicle for their experiential learning needs. It is also easy for administrators to keep track of the level of experiential learning used in particular departments and across the campus.

education courses and programs primarily in the area of career and personal development? This is not to imply that non-faculty involvement should be reduced. Rather, it is an indication that faculty need to be given more information and more opportunities to become involved. It also suggests that the full potential of experiential education has yet to be realized. Are there regular course slots for field experiences in every department?

What about the status of the existing experiential education courses and programs? Are there some that have achieved significant status as part of a curriculum, for example in a major? If so, study them carefully to understand why they have achieved that status. Can they be used as an examples for other courses and programs? What about other programs and courses which have been given some academic recognition? Can they be strengthened by stating the academic values more clearly, by increasing faculty involvement, or by better quality control?

This assessment exercise is intended not only to provide a status report, but to shed light on the factors that have yielded the current status on your campus and to identify the critical issues that require further consideration. By going through the inventory and assessment process, for example, the Westmont College

faculty and staff involved in internships and practica isolated the following concerns for further study:

1. Of the ten courses or programs included in the inventory, nine had as one of their goals the testing and application of knowledge, but only four had "acquisition of knowledge in an academic discipline" as an objective. Because the faculty wanted these internships and practica to

be academic, it was recommended that efforts be made to incorporate the acquisition of specific academic knowledge as a goal in more of the experiential offerings at Westmont.

2. The assessment also revealed variations in the teaching and administrative practices adopted by the experiential courses and programs. The faculty then recommended a decentralized governance and administrative structure for internships and practica but with general policies, similar to a set of principles of good practice in experiential education, set at the college level. Particular requirements and standards would be left to the departments.

3. While internships and practica in different departments varied in many respects, there was already some consensus about guiding principles, which the faculty found to be both comforting and reassuring, especially in light of the central role of faculty in curriculum decisions.

The identification of the specific issues important to your particular institution or department is the first step in formulating a strategy for integrating experiential education more fully into the curriculum.

Academic Validity and Acceptability

For experiential education to be integrated into the curriculum on any meaningful level, it must be academically valid *and* acceptable to the faculty and administration. This section will help you consider the related issues your institution will need to address. The criteria for determining acceptability generally include the following:

1. Are there clearly stated goals which are well articulated with the overall educational goals of the college or university?

2. Do academic policies and guidelines exist for experiential learning? Are they sound in the eyes of the faculty?

3. Is there an established faculty committee for oversight and advocacy?

4. Is there a policy for compensating faculty adequately for involvement in supervising experiential learning?

5. Is a method of quality control clearly established, either by learning outcomes or educational input, or both?

The acceptability of experiential education (and thereby its integration into the curriculum) is largely dependent on how the faculty and administration perceive the process of assuring that college-level learning is taking place and that it is worthy of the credit being granted. The chapter of this sourcebook entitled "Ensuring Quality in Experiential Education" provides a thorough discussion of the issue of quality controls. We will look briefly here, however, at the

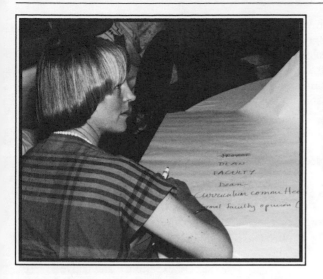

Kristen Murtaugh, Director of Cooperative Education at Manhattan College, talks about seminars and other vehicles for stimulating active reflection on field experiences. Dr. Murtaugh also teaches a Dante course at Manhattan College.

it's very good to make the students reflect on the experience. In our study of an organizational development course, we recommended that an internship be connected to a seminar in which they would all come back and talk about what they were learning. Because if you don't ask students 'What did you learn, and what did it mean to you?', then the internship is going to be like so many other experiences — unarticulated and not as meaningful."

 -Kristen Murtaugh
 Director
 Cooperative Education
 Manhattan College,
 New York

following three concerns that are critical for the academic acceptability of experiential education:

1. **Is learning taking place?** This is generally assured in one of two ways. The most common practice is through a course description or syllabus that clearly specifies what the student will have to do in the field experience: the books and articles to be read; the type, number and length of papers and reports to be written and when they are due; and the basis on which grades are given. The effort here is to continue the classroom practice of rigorous and sustained exposure to scholarly work in the field, insisting on participation in structured learning opportunities and holding students responsible for fulfilling the course requirements. A course description of this kind quickly makes clear to those familiar with the discipline the intellectual rigor being required. What such a course description does not do is tell what learning the student will be expected to acquire. This approach, assuring that learning takes place by controlling the educational input, is one which faculty members feel at home with and, when used, generally reassures them that learning is taking place.

The weakness of this approach is that it concentrates on what the faculty member provides and tends to ignore the unique and distinctive learning opportunities of the placement site as well as the actual learning the student acquires or could acquire through the placement itself.

The second method of assuring that learning takes place is to identify specific educational outcomes that the student must demonstrate to receive credit or attain a specific grade in the course. These outcomes are usually described prior to the beginning of the field experience, and the descriptions contain a clear definition of the skill or knowledge the student will be expected to demonstrate and the conditions under which that demonstration will take place. This kind of documented evidence of learning is more reliable than the previous method but is usually not as readily accepted by most faculty members as an indication of the intellectual rigor and demanding nature of the course. Faculty members of many institutions will need to be educated as to the legitimacy and value of learning that is identified and mastered through the use of learning objectives.

"When our students finish the internship that is credit bearing, one of the things they have to do is to write a summary of the intern experience and answer questions such as 'What did you learn that you wouldn't have learned in school?'. They take those and sit down with their advisors and discuss them. Some of the faculty are learning what's happening because the students have to tell them, and the faculty have to follow up and ask those questions. I think

The establishment of college-wide guidelines for program development and management can help in reassuring faculty that learning is taking place in experiential learning settings. The Curriculum Committee at Michigan State University has used these three guidelines that have proved useful in reviewing proposals for new experiential courses or programs: (1) the course or program should have a carefully spelled out design from recruitment through evaluation, (2) provision must be made for monitoring the learning during the field experience, and (3) there must be a well-designed method of evaluation at the end of the internship. Some such set of guidelines helps to make curriculum integration possible.

There is a faulty notion throughout higher education, based on the "credit hour" syndrome, that the amount of credit granted should be tied to the number of hours in the classroom. This is not and never has been a good measure of learning acquired.

2. Is it college-level learning? See the chapter of this book entitled "Ensuring Quality in Experiential Education" for a discussion of "college-level" learning.

3. Is the learning acquired worthy of the amount of credit being granted? There is a faulty notion throughout higher education, based on the "credit hour syndrome," that the amount of credit granted should be tied to the number of hours in the classroom. This is not and has never been a good measure of learning acquired. It is therefore a mistake to try, as many institutions do, to transfer that method of legitimizing the amount of credit earned to field placements. This method for crediting field experiences is usually based on a similar formula to the one used in reference to classroom instruction. It might be assumed that for each hour spent in class, for example, students should devote 2 - 3 hours to work outside of the classroom. Therefore 3 - 4 hours of involvement for each lecture session per week for the term is worth 1 academic credit. When translated to field experiences, a full-time, 40-hour work week is usually viewed as equivalent to the credit load required for being a full-time student. Credit in situations of less than full-time employment is usually given based on a formula in which 10 - 12 hours of involvement in an internship per week is the equivalent of one course.

A more appropriate measure would be to compare the amount of learning acquired in the placement with that in classroom courses. This is easier if you use educational outcomes as the measure of learning acquired, but unfortunately few classroom courses measure learning outcomes as the way to make sure learning is taking place. If you are using learning outcomes in your experiential courses or programs, the way to assure their acceptability by other faculty and administrators is to do an excellent job of documenting the learning acquired and sharing this documentation with colleagues. The criteria for judging this aspect of acceptability could be:

a. Is the learning well documented?

b. Is the documentation shared with colleagues?

c. Does it compare favorably with the amount of learning acquired in other courses offered for the same amount of credit?

d. Is there consistency between experiential and traditional course offerings in the grades being given and the amount of credit being awarded? This is an important factor. If every student who does an internship gets an "A," then faculty in other programs will naturally be suspicious of the validity of the program. There must be ways provided to distinguish between various levels of learning performance and therefore between the grades to be granted. Do not be surprised, though, if students' grades follow different patterns from those in lecture courses. Some students learn more effectively through concrete experience and active experimentation and may surprise the faculty with their achievements.

Where to Go from Here?

THREE PRINCIPLES. How much experiential education should be a part of the curriculum is a question which each institution must answer with its own faculty. As your institution sets its goals for this integration process, the following three principles may be helpful. First, experiential education should not dominate an entire curriculum any more than any other type of learning opportunity does. Secondly, experiential education lends itself to certain curricular goals better than to others.

"I think the ethical values and moral arena is one area to which experiential education lends itself very well. So when you're talking about philosophy faculty, there is lots of room for hands-on experiences."
-Jane Szutu Permaul
Director
Field Studies
Development, UCLA

"Boston University has a very active program in medical ethics for their philosophy majors. They send them to all of the hospitals in metropolitan Boston to deal with the life support/death issues in working with the physicians, the ethics team of the hospitals, and so on. The faculty really understand the role of experience in grasping the concepts of philosophy."
-Bob McCaffery,
Manager
Field Experience
University of New
Hampshire

"Critical thinking is another example. All of our students who do field studies have to complete a paper, and the paper has to be more than 'I did this and that and that and this.' We want them to say, 'So what?' and come up with some thesis at the conclusion of their experience, to draw upon the experience. The students constantly ask for assistance: 'I've got all of this, but I don't know what it means. Where do I pick up this piece?' One of our approaches at the beginning was, 'How do you do a research paper? You go to the library and you pick out books.' Students would respond, 'Well, I know how to pick

First, experiential education should not dominate an entire curriculum any more than any other type of learning opportunity does. Secondly, experiential education lends itself to certain goals better than to others.

out books and articles, and they are pretty well organized, but my experience is not coming to me in an organized fashion or in any sequential way.' Knowing how to put the pieces together is a skill that is part of critical analysis, critical thinking, and the formulation of concepts. A number of authors, including Paul Breen and Urban Whitaker, have developed lists of the kinds of liberal arts skills that are applicable to all types of professional employment and that lend themselves to being taught experientially. In addition, several internships programs, including Scripps College's Humanities Internship Program, have the goal of expanding students' liberal arts skills.

-Jane Szutu Permaul
    Director
    Field Studies
        Development, UCLA

"It doesn't always need to be 'out there' either. Doing a Greek play in

class might also be a way to do something experientially."
-Doug Boyce, Dean
    King College
    Bristol, Tennessee

"I can think of some ways in which some of my history colleagues could use experiential learning. You could ask, 'Why is the strip development on Highway 29 such a mess? Why does it look the way it does?'. The student could do some actual historical research using papers of thirty years ago when the shopping centers were first built, trying to find out how the zoning laws in fact came into being. There could be some practical and exciting history that could be done on the basis of going out into the community to see why it looks the way it does. . . . On the other hand, there are other colleagues who teach subjects for which I, at present, simply have to throw up my hands and say 'Right, the best I can

hope from you is some tolerance of the people who do find this useful.'"
-H.C. Erik Midelfort
    Associate Dean
    College of Arts
        and Sciences, and
    Professor of History
    University of Virginia

The danger, of course, in accepting these first two principles is to use them as excuses for not incorporating experiential education. So beware, but be reasonable.

The third principle is the importance of meshing the values of experiential education with the objectives of the institution and those of each curriculum. Figure D depicts one possibility for how these three sets of values and objectives can be interwoven. For specific ideas, read the chapter of this sourcebook entitled "Building Experiential Education into the Mission and Values of the Institution."

Figure D

CONTRIBUTIONS OF EXPERIENTIAL EDUCATION:	+	BASIC CURRICULAR OBJECTIVES:	=	INTEGRATION OF EXPERIENTIAL EDUCATION INTO THE CURRICULUM
Academic knowledge		Academic knowledge		
Generic liberal arts competence		Generic liberal arts competence		
Moral-ethical development		Moral-ethical development		
Career development				
Student empowerment, self-confidence, and motivation				
Public service				
Institutional stability and status (admissions, retention, community and alumni relations, development)				
Research opportunities				

IT CAN HAPPEN IN THE CLASSROOM, TOO

"I have a friend, Barbara Altman, who teaches a 300-student class, 'Introduction to Sociology,' at the University of Maryland. She has tried to make that class experiential, which is not easy. But she uses volunteers, people who represent the entire class. Everybody who wants to volunteer can do so at least once. You put your name in a hat and you get extra points if your name is pulled to volunteer. You can turn down a volunteer assignment once, but if you turn it down twice, you're out of the pool. Lots of people volunteer.

"Let me give you an example of how the volunteer system works. On the first day of a discussion of norms and deviance, there was a lot of theoretical information and then some work on what the norms should be for behavior in this class. In large classes people do behave differently than they do in small classes. They come in late, they leave early, they read newspapers, they listen to radios, they shuffle things around. (Most students tell me they don't hear any of that and they don't notice any of it.) So the class listed desirable norms for be-havior in this classroom, and they wrote them all down. My friend then picked out four students who volunteered without knowing what their assignment was going to be. After class she said to them, 'Okay, we've got norms for this class. I want you to come in on Tuesday and sit down and observe the class as if you were a field researcher and tell me at the end of the class in what ways the class' actual behavior differs from what the class thinks its norma-tive behavior should be. Where is the deviance that the class doesn't perceive?'

"So these four researchers looked at the class and wrote down what they saw. They came up with wonderful exam-ples. They met after class, and the teacher said, 'Fine, on Thurs-day you're going to report on this to the class, and then we're going to discuss the class norms and deviance.' Well, the four people got up and reported this, and the class went bana-nas. The students said, 'You didn't really see us. You were looking at us, but you didn't really understand what was going on. But, how dare you do research on us without ask-ing permission?'.

"Then Barbara led the same discussion she would normally lead on the ethics of doing social science research. But people wouldn't leave. They wanted to discuss this. They were furious. The next day they spent the whole hour and a half class period discussing whether you should do research on somebody without permission and what the ethical implications were. The whole class kept coming back to it all semester. That meant some-thing to them because they felt they had been violated. So, those students were engaged in discussing ethical implications in a way that they never would have under normal circum-stances. There were 300 stu-dents in the class. Most of them had something to say and were determined to be heard. They even talked about it outside of class. That was a transforming event for most of those students. I call that experiential learning."

-Sharon Rubin
Assistant Dean
Undergraduate Studies
University of Maryland
(at NSIEE Workshop,
June 1985)

FOUR STRATEGIES. After you have set the target for curricular inte-gration, there are four general strate-gies that will be helpful in realizing your goals:

1. Do your homework and know the territory, especially in three areas—
   a. The goals and objectives of the institution and the curriculum, and the effectiveness of current courses and programs in fulfilling these goals and objectives;
   b. The factors important in developing good experiential courses and programs that effectively speak to the goals and objectives of the insti-tution and the curriculum; and
   c. The enabling factors that are essential when introducing innova-tions and changes.

Get faculty involved in the entire process of integration, from contemplation to implementation and evaluation.

2. Identify or create a need or opportunity for curricular change.
3. Get faculty involved in the entire process of integration, from contemplation to implementation and evaluation.
4. Let go and give the ownership of everything accomplished to the faculty and the academic dean.

Know the Territory

Not only does one need to become an expert in the area for which one has been given responsibility, one

needs to be able to utilize that knowledge in a manner which is valued and respected by the academic community. That means that in gathering knowledge about experiential education and its relationship to higher education, adopt an "academic posture," eloquently described by David P. Gardner, President of the University of California, as ". . . patient inquiry; the sequential development of ideas; the emphasis on reasoned discussion and criticism; and the continued reference to evidence."[3]

You can get most of the information you need about goals and objectives by following the "Mission and Values" chapter of this sourcebook and by doing the institutional assessment suggested previously. Some additional research and evaluation on the effectiveness of existing experiential education programs and courses in fulfilling the established goals may be helpful. Another source of information is the minutes from faculty meetings on matters related to curricular concerns both at the institutional level as well as at the departmental level. This provides the "faculty perspective" on the effectiveness of the existing curriculum as well as on areas of concern which may become "opportunities" for the introduction of experiential education.

In terms of knowing more about the design and development of courses and programs to fulfill specific curricular objectives, no one can be expected to be an expert in all areas. There are, however, some basic areas of knowledge which are essential. Knowledge about cognitive development and experiential education theories and their application in curricular design is essential, not so much to teach the

faculty but to use in the actual design of courses and programs. Here is an opportunity to work collaboratively with a faculty member; you might provide the pedagogy while the faculty colleague provides the curricular substance. Secondly, knowledge about national trends and practices, exemplary courses and programs is important. These lend substance and creativity to discussions about curriculum. Selected sources for more information are noted in the bibliography at the end of the chapter. You will need to know about the design of effective prefield preparation, practices for monitoring and supporting the learning during the experience, evaluation, and relations with work supervisors. NSIEE offers publications and conferences to help faculty and administrators learn these basic elements of effective experiential learning.

The best and most suitable pro-

gram cannot get off the ground without faculty commitment and an academic structure that has room for it. These are essential to ENABLE a course or program to be realized in the curriculum. Besides the faculty who already practice experiential education, the other most obvious candidates for involvement are (1) those who are genuinely interested in teaching or who are good teachers, and (2) those who have the responsibility to assure that the curriculum indeed meets the curricular objectives and the needs of students. The completed institutional assessment can help you to identify these people on campus. For several important strategies for building faculty support and involvement, see the chapter of this sourcebook that focuses on the faculty role in experiential education.

The second enabling element — or stumbling block — for the development of experiential education courses and programs is the academic calendar. The calendar dictates the duration of any experience. In addition, the school's scheduling practices may dictate the time available each week for fieldwork. For example, an economics professor at Guilford College wants to build in substantial fieldwork, but she has really been curtailed because there is no provision in the class schedule to

Mary Brewer, right, a double major in Studio Art and Art History at Scripps College, assists with art exhibits at Security Pacific Bank in Los Angeles. Ms. Brewer participated in Scripps College's Humanities Internship Program. At left is Tressa Miller, Vice President and Director of Cultural Affairs for Security Pacific.

allow her enough time to do field-work with the students as a group. The challenge is whether the students can do the fieldwork individually and then assimilate their experiences during the regular class meetings. Or does the overall academic calendar need to be reviewed?

The third enabling factor is the development of a course numbering system that allows for experiential learning. While using the course slot for independent study may solve the short-range problem of where to record the credit for off-campus learning, it is a short-sighted solution if faculty are not systematically compensated for sponsoring students on independent study. It is very important for departments to "own" their field experience courses so these courses can be a regular part of their degree requirements.

"Most colleges and universities that are sophisticated in their use of experiential learning have a set of reserved course numbers for field experience that are used uniformly in all departments. Although these courses sometimes vary by credit level or by grading option, they signal the institution's commitment to the idea of field experience and the department's use of experiential education as a usual part of the curriculum."
-Sharon Rubin
Assistant Dean
Undergraduate Studies
University of Maryland

Create A Need And Look For Opportunities

The best conceived program or strategy goes nowhere unless those

who are affected feel a need to act differently. Even if the feeling is just to try something new for the fun of it, a need must be there before one can get the attention necessary for change. As an academic dean observed:

"This is where I think the leadership comes in. Somebody has

HOW IT HAPPENED AT THE UNIVERSITY OF COLORADO

"Though individual faculty members supported the academic validity of experiential education and were willing to award independent-study credit for internships, there were no formal endorsements of experiential education in any of the University's major colleges. In order for the College of Arts and Sciences to endorse experiential learning and promote the development of internship opportunities, we needed:

(a) a faculty committee to discuss the issues and submit recommendations for awarding academic credit,

(b) the Arts and Sciences (A & S) Committee on Courses to approve and accept these recommendations, and

(c) the Dean of the College to accept these recommendations and approve these changes in the academic policy.

I worked with Dean Charles Middleton to establish the faculty committee and served as an ex-officio on the committee. I provided them with resource materials to help substantiate their recommendations in support of experiential learning. The faculty submitted their recommendations to the Committee on Courses, which in turn accepted the recommendations and secured the Dean's approval. The Dean then announced that the College of Arts and Sciences will establish a college-wide program for internships and cooperative education. A&S students will be able to receive academic credit via departmental courses sponsoring internship work for major credit, or via upper-division A&S courses offering general elective credit for the

internship experience.

Our next steps are to:

1. Finalize operational procedures for registering students for these credits,

2. Identify a specific faculty member in each department who will serve as a liaison for the program,

3. Establish a faculty advisory board or network system to support faculty initiatives and the development of new internship courses, and

4. Use this progress in the College of Arts and Sciences as a model for initiating similar activities in the Colleges of Business and Engineering."

-Mary Jo White
Assistant Director, Internships & Cooperative Education
Career Planning and Placement
University of Colorado

The best and most suitable program cannot get off the ground without faculty commitment and an academic structure that has room for it.

to say, 'Look what's not happening' or 'Look where our problems are.'"
-Douglas Boyce, Dean
King College
Bristol, Tennessee

Formally, the institutional leadership must come from the academic dean or from someone whose perspective at least crosses more than one department. If you are aiming for changes in one department, obviously the chair or somebody at that level must take the formal lead. In reality, the leadership must originate with the person or persons who discovered the "need" and then be communicated through the dean or the chair. Listen to these comments:

"I have become much broader in my own definition of what I want to aid and abet. And I have decided that my office is what I say it is. One thing that's been very helpful since I've realized that is to begin to tap into faculty who by virtue of their own training have validated the value of experience. These are the people that can get the ball rolling."
-Jim Keith, Director
Experiential Learning
Guilford College
Greensboro, North
Carolina

"I think the most attractive feature of just getting a packet of materials about what happens somewhere else is that it isn't very threatening. You can look at it and say, 'Well that's very interesting.' But its great drawback is that without some discussion of what it is you're trying to do, you can say, 'Well, it is very interesting that Manhattan is doing that, but I'm pretty happy with what I'm doing. And it's not what

they're doing.' But, unless you feel some need to change, some sense that whatever curriculum you have is not meeting some need, then the information about what does go on somewhere else just gets filed in the circular file."
-H.C. Erik Midelfort
Associate Dean
College of Arts
and Sciences, and
Professor of History
University of Virginia

There are many opportunities to entertain changes in curriculum without necessarily "pointing fingers" at anyone or any department within the institution. The newly appointed

academic dean at King College notes one opportunity:

"We are at a point where we are doing institutional planning in serious ways for the first time. One of the things we've done this past year is a very broad-based analysis of strengths and weaknesses and opportunities that we might have. Each department has gone through that process. It has identified strengths and weaknesses in its own areas and within the general education curriculum as well. Right now I'm in the process of developing a survey instrument that will pull out of those analyses a series of statements. I'm

Margaret Schramm, right, English professor at Hartwick College, talks with Laurie Allison about what she is learning in her internship. Dr. Schramm chairs Hartwick College's Faculty Advisory Committee on Internships. *Photograph by A. Blake Gardner*

going to circulate those to the whole faculty and give them a chance to rate their level of agreement with each of these statements. Once the faculty responses come back I'll put them together, pull the faculty together, and we'll see if we can build some consensus of the nature of the problems with the curriculum. And at that point in the planning stage, I'm hoping to highlight experiential education opportunities as some of the methods that we might want to look at. I think it will come very naturally in the course of this planning phase."

-Douglas Boyce, Dean
King College
Bristol, Tennessee

The Dean of Students from the College of Wooster saw another way:

"Since 1945 we have had a required independent study program for all seniors. It is a two-semester thesis that students research and write. It is one thing that many of our students fear. They approach it with all kinds of anxiety. I have begun to realize that maybe some kinds of internship experiences would assist students in focusing their independent study projects. This makes sense because one of the things that is most difficult is the decision about 'What am I going to write? What am I going to research?'. If they had an experience that was related to their majors during the sophomore and junior years and that gave them some alternatives to look at in terms of research, I think we could strengthen the independent study, which we say is the hallmark of our program."

-Ken Plusquellec
Dean of Students
College of Wooster
Wooster, Ohio

Integrating
The Community
and the
Classroom:
A Sampler of
Postsecondary
Courses

Carol Murphy
Lynn Jenks

General education courses and discussions of the goals of general education can present yet another significant opportunity:

"General education is something that experiential educators tend to ignore, but it has an incredible potential. We are used to connecting everything to majors. And every college (except Brown and maybe a couple of others) has a general education program. Students have to take those courses. Those courses are the ones that best represent the liberal learning values of the institution. Where is experiential learning in relation to those values? We don't do enough with general education. Whenever we talk about credit, we say, 'Is it useful for the major?' or, 'Can we give students the work experience that will be helpful to them after graduation?' We might say instead, 'Let's take an introductory sociology course and use

an internship as the basis for understanding sociological concepts.' We tend to think of sociology fieldwork as something just for juniors and seniors.

You can also work with faculty who are interested in putting short-term experiential components into a course, maybe a set of projects for students to do out of class in groups or something like that. To use the work environment. To use what students call the real world — ours isn't? — to use that other environment as a laboratory for the development of liberal arts competence.

One particularly exciting example of the way in which general education has been enhanced by experiential learning was developed by Robert Sexton at the University of Kentucky. The program, which placed students in government internships, was designed to help them think through the ethical implications of decision-making about public policy, and about their own decision-making, as well." [4]

-Sharon Rubin
Assistant Dean
Undergraduate Studies
University of Maryland

In addition to institutional opportunities, there are at least three national phenomena which could prompt a reconsideration of the curriculum at any college or university. First, recent reports by the National Institute of Education, National Endowment for the Humanities, and Association of American Colleges[5] are all pointing to the need for greater attention to undergraduate education. All three reports support experiential education in significant ways. Even the most prestigious higher education institutions are not taking these reports lightly. Use these reports as

Recent reports by the National Institute of Education, National Endowment for the Humanities, and Association of American Colleges are all pointing to the need for greater attention to undergraduate education. All three reports support experiential education in significant ways.

[The coming changes in demographics] can set the stage for a review of the curriculum in order to assure its attractiveness to prospective students and its ability to retain students already at the institution.

the impetus for discussion on curricular changes (references provided at the end of this chapter).

The second national phenomenon that is developing is a change in demographics. The decrease in 18 to 22 year olds will create enrollment pressures, and most institutions are already planning how they will deal with these changes. This phenomenon can set the stage for a review of the curriculum in order to ensure its attractiveness to prospective students and its ability to retain students already at the institution. This rationale for change, however, can be misinterpreted as a "marketing gimmick" and can backfire unless it is accompanied by a substantive educational rationale.

A third reality nationally is the reduction of federal support, putting greater pressure on higher education to look to corporations for assistance. Sooner or later, this will affect the curriculum as institutions have to be more responsive to the needs of private enterprise. The private sector has been critical of recent college graduates in several areas, but especially in generic liberal arts skills, from the inability to write to the lack of general knowledge about the work world. These can all be turned into opportunities for serious consideration of the curriculum and experiential education.

Faculty Involvement

If there is only one area in which faculty can get involved, curriculum is the area. A separate chapter of this sourcebook focuses on getting faculty

involved. Here, only two points will be stressed. One is that INVOLVEMENT ONLY COMES WITH A SENSE OF NEED. THAT NEED MUST BE CLEARLY STATED AND BY A RESPECTABLE SOURCE. Faculty have enough to do; the last thing they want is to serve on another committee which leads to nothing.

Second, involvement requires a sense that one is making a contribution to the cause. To contribute to experiential education, faculty need to know more about it. Faculty can then really contribute to discussion and to ultimate implementation of experiential education as part of the curriculum. See the chapter of this sourcebook entitled "Increasing Faculty Involvement in Experiential Education."

A third reality nationally is the reduction of federal support.

Letting Go

When experiential education finally has its place in the curriculum, let go and give ownership to the rightful owners, the faculty and academic departments. The initiative and efforts may have been shared by many, but the control must reside where the curriculum resides. If the effort has been successful, then experiential courses and programs have become a part of the curriculum and must be treated and viewed as that. To do anything else would be to regress, to bring experiential education back to something other than a part of the curriculum.

"There are so many good examples of the ways in which field experiences can be integrated into curricula. From Scripps College's Humanities Internship Program to Illinois State University's Professional Practice Program in Criminology, exciting models are available to be shared. NSIEE can provide help

to faculty wanting to make use of discipline-based materials."
-Sharon Rubin
Assistant Dean
Undergraduate Studies
University of Maryland

FOOTNOTES

[1] Timothy Stanton and Michele Whitham, "Prefield Preparation: What, Why, How?", PANEL Resource Paper No. 4, National Society for Internships and Experiential Education, Raleigh, North Carolina, 1979.

[2] Carren O. Kaston with James M. Heffernan, *Preparing Humanists for Work: A National Study of Undergraduate Internship Programs in the Humanities*, The Washington Center with the support of the National Endowment for the Humanities, Washington, D.C., 1984.

[3] David P. Gardner, President of the University of California, in comments made to the Board of Regents of the University of California on June 21, 1985, as printed in the *University Bulletin* (a publication for faculty and staff of the University of California), 34:1, July 1 - 5, 1985.

[4] Robert F. Sexton, "The Promise of Experiential Education for the Liberal Arts," *Dimensions of Experiential Education*, ed. by Robert F. Sexton, National Center for Public Service Internship Programs (now NSIEE), Raleigh, North Carolina, 1976, p. 35 .

[5] Association of American Colleges, *Integrity in the College Curriculum*, Project on Redefining the Meaning and Purpose of Baccalaureate Degrees, Washington, D.C., 1985.

When experiential education finally has its place in the curriculum, let go and give ownership to the rightful owners, the faculty and academic departments.

RECOMMENDED RESOURCES

Gamson, Zelda F. and Associates, *Liberating Education*. Jossey-Bass Publishers, San Francisco, California, 1984. This book shows how learning communities can create a strong sense of identity that motivates faculty as well as students. It describes ways to improve education through structures that foster greater faculty and student interaction. The authors also explain the most crucial factors affecting the success of innovative programs and describe ways of obtaining funding, developing consensus and dealing with political rivalries.

Kaston, Carren O., with James M. Heffernan, *Preparing Humanists for Work: A National Study of Undergraduate Internships in the Humanities*. Study supported by the National Endowment for the Humanities and conducted by the Washington Center, Washington, D.C., November, 1984. Available for $10 from the National Society for Internships and Experiential Education, 122 St. Mary's Street, Raleigh, North Carolina, 27605. The companion directory of institutions and departments that offer humanities internships is available for $12 from the Modern Language Association, Customer Service, 62 Fifth Avenue, New York, New York, 10011.

Kolb, David A., *Experiential Learning: Experience as the Source of Learning Development*. Prentice-Hall, Inc., Englewood Cliffs, New Jersey, 1984. This is the latest of Kolb's work in refining his theory of experiential learning. In addition, he discusses several other prominent theories on cognition, development and learning. An informative source on the theoretical basis of experiential learning.

Murphy, Carol, and Lynn, Jenks, *Integrating the Community and the Classroom: A Sampler of Postsecondary Courses*. Far West Laboratory for Educational Research and Development, San Francisco, California, 1981. Available for $15 from NSIEE, 122 St. Mary's Street, Raleigh, North Carolina, 27605. This is a compilation of experiential course descriptions with firsthand comments from the faculty involved about their respective strengths and weaknesses. The book was developed to stimulate new ideas about experience-based courses and to serve as a reference for those who would like to know more about the use of experience as part of an undergraduate curriculum, particularly in the social sciences and humanities. It contains samples of learning contracts, evaluation forms, journal formats, and other helpful tools.

National Institute of Education, *Involvement in Learning: Realizing the Potential of American Higher Education*. Washington, D.C., Superintendent of Documents, U.S. Government Printing Office (Stock No. 065-000-00213-2), October, 1984, $4.50. This is the final report of the Study Group on the Conditions of Excellence in American Higher Education, presented to the Secretary of Education and the Director of the National Institute of Education. The study examines the values and long-term goals for American higher education, offers its analysis of the current status and makes recommendations on needed improvements in undergraduate education. It recommends both curricular and teaching innovations which include experiential education.

Peer Assistance Network in Experiential Learning (PANEL), National Society for Internships and Experiential Education, 122 St. Mary's Street, Raleigh, NC, 27605. PANEL is a clearinghouse and a talent bank which can assist individuals and institutions that are seeking specific information about experiential learning. PANEL has a large collection of resources on all aspects of curriculum design with experiential components. In addition, it has published several monographs related to the design of experience-based courses and curricula. Of special interest for this topic are PANEL Resource Papers Nos. 4, 5, 6, 7, 8, 9, 11, and 12. The PANEL talent bank contains the names, phone numbers and addresses of over 1,300 faculty and administrators who are knowledgeable about experiential education and who are available to provide information to interested institutions or individuals. Contact NSIEE for details about how to use PANEL.

3

Increasing Faculty
Involvement
in
Experiential Education

" . . . the principle of continuity of experience means that every experience both takes up something from those which have gone before and modifies in some way the quality of those which come after. . . . As an individual passes from one situation to another, his world, his environment, expands or contracts. He does not find himself living in another world but in a different part or aspect of one and the same world. What he has learned in the way of knowledge and skill in one situation becomes an instrument of understanding and dealing effectively with the situations that follow. The process goes on as long as life and learning continue."
-John Dewey[1]

"The faculty has been extremely negative. Not all faculty, of course, but the general reaction has been, 'This isn't any of our business. Students aren't here to get into these frivolous things like learning citizenship and becoming able to function in American society. Students are here to learn mathematics or sociology. That's why they come to my class. The real issue is whether they learn the methods of sociology I am teaching them.' When you ask about the

question of other values, they say, 'None of that ideological indoctrination in my class.' And people really have said to me over and over again, 'This isn't a function for higher education' —forgetting that the original function of education in this country was the development of civic leadership. We have a major task on our hands to convince the faculties of this country that they've got to change their ways on this issue. I think it's absolutely at the core of our problems."
-Frank Newman[2]

Ever since John Dewey challenged traditional notions of the relationship between experience, work, and education, faculty members have been reassessing their roles as supervisors of how and where learning takes place. The assumption of most traditional educators is that "information comes from experts and authoritative sources through the media of books, lectures, audio-visual presentations. . . . Learning takes place in settings designated for the purpose, e.g., classrooms and libraries . . . . Problems are defined and posed to the learner by experts and authorities. . . . The emphasis is on solutions to known problems. . . .

Favorable evaluation by experts and authorities of the quality of the individual's intellectual productions, primarily written work" are used as criteria of successful learning.[3]

In contrast, experiential educators assume that "information sources must be developed by the learner from the social environment. Information-gathering methods include observation and questioning of associates, other learners, and chance acquaintances." Learning settings are everywhere, and "every human encounter provides relevant information. In order to solve problems, the learner has to define the problems, generate hypotheses, collect information," and develop problem-solving approaches on the spot.[4] Criteria for evaluation of learning are frequently individualized and may be based on anything from work products to the perceptions of peers in the learning environment. In brief, traditional faculty see themselves as responsible for their students' ability to learn, while experiential educators see learning as student-centered.

The dichotomy between traditional and experiential learning is more apparent than real. Every good teacher knows that while the content presented is important, if the way in which it is presented does not make sense to students — if they cannot identify its relevance and application — no real learning will take place. They also know that students must be self-motivated in order to master any subject matter. Students, on the other hand, like the comfort of cer-

tainty that comes from expert presentation of content, but they know they must integrate it with what they already know and believe and figure out how to apply it if they are to understand it. Therefore, it is not surprising that faculty struggle to understand what the balance between traditional and experiential learning should be.

and therefore communicate the value of experiential learning to their students, the students are much more likely to participate in experiential learning opportunities. Faculty can help students see such experiences as part of the way learning ordinarily occurs.

5. Faculty members are significant role models for students. If faculty adopt the stance of active, self-directed learners themselves, they are more likely to motivate their students to take the initiative to learn experientially. The students will then be better able to incorporate active learning and reflection into their usual styles of approaching problems.

Why Active Faculty Involvement is Critical

"In retrospect, faculty ownership of the internship program was the most important issue we faced. The program had been established in a centralized office under the direction of a full-time administrator. Prior to that time, internships had been arranged on an ad hoc basis through academic departments whose policies ranged from non-existent to formal, written guidelines. The centralized office created concerns about faculty control and departmental autonomy."

-Barbara Lilly
Internship Coordinator
Hartwick College
Oneonta, NY

There are five reasons that active faculty awareness of, support of, and involvement in experiential education is *absolutely* critical for a vital and ongoing institutional commitment to this style of teaching and learning. These reasons are as follows:

1. The faculty is the primary group responsible for teaching. Experiential education is a method of teaching and learning, and it is a necessary component of a complete learning cycle. (See Chapters 1 and 2 of this sourcebook.) Without faculty support and active involvement, experiential education will simply not be part of the primary teaching mission of the institution. Faculty are not the *only* group whose involvement is valuable and appropriate, but faculty participation is critical for a fully institutionalized program.

2. Faculty are needed in order to integrate experiential education into the curriculum.

See the chapter of this sourcebook on curriculum for the many faculty roles that are part of this integration process.

3. Faculty are needed for quality control. Faculty are one of the important parties in the eight tasks in experiential education and are the only group that can take full responsibility for evaluating what students learn on field experiences.

4. Students listen to faculty. If faculty are central actors in the experiential learning process

"Students very much want to have faculty involved in their experiential learning. Several told me that they would have appreciated site visits very much. Others told me that they were uncertain what their work sites would be like, and they would have appreciated the tutoring of faculty to help them be

"What could I have done in the past year that would have made our cooperative education program stronger? I wish I had spent more time on faculty involvement earlier in the process. I concentrated on the job placement functions."

-Kristen Murtaugh, Cooperative Education Director
Manhattan College, New York

Sharon Rubin, Assistant Dean for Undergraduate Studies, University of Maryland. Dr. Rubin also serves as an NSIEE Peer Expert.

more assured in their first days on the job. All of them wanted to share what they felt was important learning — their growth of self-confidence, their new ability to take risks, their socialization within their chosen professions, their changes of career plans, their feelings of personal mastery.

"Although some students felt that faculty were not as interested in these outcomes as in the more 'academic' outcomes, none was disdainful of those academic outcomes. One student reported, 'The internship will make you into a much more well-rounded person, but it will make the college community more well-rounded, too. You use your experience in your courses.' Another said, 'My background from Skidmore made my experience richer. What I learned was application of theory. You've got to use both and you've got to bring the application back into the classroom.' If faculty make systematic use of students' experiences to enrich classroom learning, if students are encouraged to teach other students, and if students and faculty alike take seriously the kind of growth students say they experience as a result of the internships, the entire Skidmore community will benefit."
  -Sharon Rubin
   Consultant Report to
   Skidmore College
   Spring 1985

"Originally we had in mind to try to centralize all the internship functions in one place. After our NSIEE Consultant came and key leaders on campus met to discuss our approach, we are convinced that we have to involve the faculty in a very major way."
  -Edwin Potts
   Assistant to the President
   Westmont College
   Santa Barbara, California

What Faculty Gain from Experiential Education

Most of this sourcebook discusses why experiential education is part of good teaching and how various types of learning can be fostered by direct, active engagement in the phenomena being studied. These educational goals are certainly a big part of why faculty support experiential learning. Faculty who are dedicated to effective teaching and who understand the importance of active engagement in the learning process will support experiential learning. If you are trying to motivate faculty to become involved or if you want to be supportive of faculty colleagues who are already involved, it is also important to understand what faculty gain from experiential education on a more personal level.

When we have asked faculty what they gain, we have gotten a variety of different kinds of answers. For some, it has been the pleasure of taking on new roles — as facilitator of learning rather than expert, of listener as well as speaker, as consultant rather than authority. For others, it has been a sense of new clarity in their expectations of students. For still others, it has been the development of a new set of skills. For all, it has been the excitement of seeing students become

Without faculty support and active involvement, experiential education will simply not be part of the primary teaching mission of the institution.

less passive, more motivated, and empowered as learners and as members of society. Perhaps some of their own best learning was experiential — the semester as an exchange student in Spain, the part-time job working for someone who turned out to be an important intellectual mentor, a stint in the Peace Corps, the volunteer position as chairperson of a community organization. Perhaps they were introduced to personality theory or cognitive development theory, which made a difference in their ability to reach their students. Perhaps they know that they learn best through doing first and conceptualizing later, or they have children who learn best that way.

When the Far West Laboratory for Educational Research and Development asked faculty what they gained from teaching experiential courses, it was clear that faculty developed a number of new skills from their involvement.[5] Of the 42 "new skills" they described, the following ten were mentioned by more than one faculty member in a sample of 48 people:

- Putting control in students' hands
- Developing community contacts
- Dealing with small groups
- Supervising
- Dealing with site supervisors and agencies
- Patience to permit students to proceed at own pace
- Knowledge about agencies
- Facilitating discussions
- Problem solving with students
- Appreciation of curricular problems.

The excitement of seeing students become less passive, more motivated, and empowered as learners and as members of society ...

In the same study, 54 faculty members responded to the question, "Does the amount of personal satisfaction you get from teaching this course differ from other courses?" Of the 36 who responded "yes," 32 said their satisfaction was greater for the field experience courses because of the following:

- More personal contact with students
- One of few ways academic world related to the community
- Opportunity to see students grow and mature
- Contact with a superior group of students
- Seeing students become work-oriented and aware of career opportunities.

As you work to increase faculty involvement in experiential education on your campus or in your department, keep these benefits in mind.

Faculty Concerns and Barriers to Involvement

"The faculty need to become more aware of experiential learning as a pedagogy. Right now, faculty attitudes about experiential learning vary from annoyance that internships exist, to guilt that the faculty do not participate more, to an uneasy tension about the way in which internships are being used for vocational rather than intellectual purposes by most students, to lack of clarity about the appropriate role for faculty in the career development process."
    -Sharon Rubin
    NSIEE Consulting Report

At a discussion on experiential learning this year among faculty at the University of Virginia, they were both excited and anxious about their roles. Opinions ranged from the nervous, "This is great, but someone else ought to be in charge of students wanting experiential learning," to the quizzical, "If experience is the textbook, how do you make up the assignments?" Faculty wanted to know how to bridge the gap between classes and the real world, how to articulate liberal arts values to employers as well as to students, whether the emphasis of experiential learning should be skills or subject matter, whether experiential learning should be used primarily to teach what faculty members cannot teach in the classroom, how to deal with the crises of confidence students may have in unfamiliar learning environments, and "Who controls what?" Most often, they went back to the issue of utmost concern: how to think about experiential learning as an integral part of the curriculum in a course or a department. Such concerns would be voiced at most colleges by most faculty.

In order to encourage faculty involvement in experiential education, you must consider carefully the following concerns and barriers that faculty may experience:

1. **Concern about faculty control of academic quality.** Faculty have an important function that cannot be given over even to the most talented non-faculty coordinator: control of academic quality. It is this control that is most problematic to many faculty. For some, it is, "I don't have the expertise to assess experiential learning. I know about term papers and examinations, but I don't know about evaluating something I cannot see." For others, it is, "I think I know what I am doing with regard to experiential learning, and I think my colleagues do as well, but I'm concerned about all those other departments that are too loose in their standards. They may be giving away credit." The solutions to both of these concerns are trust in faculty and their continued education.

At some point, it is necessary for faculty to trust their peers in other departments, even though some will always be more trustworthy than others when it comes to academic quality. The variety will be extensive. We are used to great diversity in our students. Most faculty have had the experience of reading student examinations and asking themselves, "Were these students all in the same room? What each has gotten out of my lectures has been entirely different." Faculty will be similarly diverse, based on their own backgrounds and skills. Some faculty will take their responsibilities seriously, and some will sign off without using good judgment. Some will have a structured approach, and others will "go with the flow." There is no perfect model that will assure quality where human beings are concerned. However, it is important to understand that if departments have standards for the academic performance of faculty in the classroom, it is possible for them to set standards for nontraditional faculty performance as well. See the chapter in this sourcebook on quality issues for further discussion.

2. **Lack of awareness of experiential education as pedagogy and lack of theoretical knowledge in pedagogy.** As Erik Midelfort observes:

"Many faculty do not really believe that it is possible to learn how to teach. I've heard for 25 years that you can't teach people how to

"The faculty need to become more aware of experiential learning as a pedagogy."

teach because 'Teaching is an art.' But I wonder why we have art schools if you can't teach an art."

-H.C. Erik Midelfort
Professor of History and
Associate Dean, College of
Arts and Sciences
University of Virginia

Faculty received their training in their disciplines. When they served as Teaching Assistants during graduate school and when they applied for teaching positions, the focus was on their knowledge of the discipline. Teaching as a skill received relatively little attention. Again Erik Midelfort makes the point well:

"*Even faculty who want to learn more about good teaching know they don't have a good theoretical base in pedagogy, and that's probably one area where they feel the most lack. Now they don't express it very often, but occasionally they express it. And when they do, it comes from a sense of frustration. . . . I feel that there are a lot of faculty members who are ready to study theory. But they just have not had the opportunity, nor the proper surroundings in which to do it.*"

-H.C. Erik Midelfort

However, an institution *can* increase the chances that faculty will be able to become good experiential educators by giving them as many opportunities as possible to learn from more experienced faculty, and to disuss issues of teaching and learning frequently and with serious intent.

If departments have standards for the academic performance of faculty in the classroom, it is possible for them to set standards for nontraditional faculty performance as well.

Pamela Cox from Suffolk University interns at *The Boston Globe*.

3. Lack of familiarity with techniques for assessing experiential learning. Closely related to the issue of unfamiliarity with pedagogy is the lack of faculty awareness of or commitment to appropriate methods for assessing experiential learning. Most faculty feel particularly vulnerable when asked to evaluate students' understanding of something that the faculty have not organized and presented. A number of helpful works have been written on the topic, including *Efficient Evaluation of Individual Performance in Field Placement* by Stephen Yelon and John Duley.[6] That monograph

contains an excellent chart, adapted from *A Compendium of Assessment Techniques* by Joan Knapp and Amiel Sharon, that lists assessment mode performance tests, illustrations and examples, advantages, indications of appropriate cases for use, problems, and special considerations. Such a chart can be the beginning of a faculty development process that makes faculty confident about their abilities to use assessment methods consistent with the goals of experiential learning and with the maintenance of good academic standards. See also the chapter of this sourcebook on issues of quality in experiential education.

4. Lack of understanding of how experiential learning helps students test the concepts of the discipline.

"I have heard real words of skepticism in the departments that have little contact with the community, like the government department. They send students to Washington for summer internships, but they have never given credit for it. They say people should not get credit for learning how to live away from home or learning how to get around on the subway. They think classroom learning is the only type worthy of academic credit. I think the only way to surmount this attitude is by showing how internships help students apply the concepts of the discipline."
    -A Humanities Professor

5. A belief that application is only useful when it follows theory. Like #2-4 above, this concern of many faculty reflects a lack of familiarity with theories of how people learn and a lack of awareness of multiple learning styles.

"Faculty tell me, 'Look, a student is taking my course. That's the most important thing he could be doing because for the rest of his life he's going to be applying things. But he only has these four years to listen to me. He's not going to get the theoretical/conceptual base anywhere else. In the world it doesn't exist.' I think that's foolish because many students don't learn until the concrete experience stage is completed."
    -An Academic Dean

6. Concern about faculty compensation for sponsoring students in experiential education. At many schools, faculty members may sponsor one or two students a semester in intensive experiential learning activities, so the work load is not particularly heavy. Just as faculty supervise doctoral students, sit on committees, and advise undergraduates in the course of their normal duties, they give stu-

Jeff Chinn, Assistant Provost at Illinois State University, discusses the place of experiential education in the faculty work load.

dents individual attention through independent research opportunities or experiential learning.

However, when a faculty member sponsors several students every term or is in charge of experiential learning for a department, both the administrative work and the academic mentorship can add the equivalent of one or more courses to the ordinary course load. There are several ways around this dilemma. For instance, Mars Hill College has developed a faculty compensation system that attempts to take into consideration the many different kinds of duties faculty have.[7] At other institutions, such as the University of Maryland, faculty who sponsor a number of students may organize a seminar for all students instead of seeing each one

Many faculty have never worked in settings other than classrooms, libraries, and faculty offices.

individually each week. Not only can the seminar then become part of the faculty member's regular course load for the semester, but students can benefit from each others' experiences. However, it is clear that faculty who enjoy the gains their students make from active learning will continue to be involved, and those who are most concerned about the dissemination of particular content will prefer the lecture format. Developing educational models which come closest to compensating faculty adequately for the particular skills they must use as experiential educators should be a matter of concern for all faculty. For more information, see the chapter of this sourcebook on "Supporting Experiential Education in the Financial System of the Institution."

7. Concern about whether involvement in experiential education helps with tenure, promotion, and merit increases. Creative faculty in institutions that value teaching have found ways to include their involvement in experiential education when they present themselves to department chairs and review committees that make decisions about tenure, promotion, and merit increases. Faculty often do not have models for how to present this involvement, however. Therefore they often miss opportunities to use their work in experiential education to show good performance in teaching, in public and community service, and in public relations for the institution. They also miss opportunities to point out how experiential education helped them identify problems that led to research projects and publications. For other ideas, see the chapter of this sourcebook on building experiential education into the institution's financial system.

This concern about tenure and promotion can be especially difficult for young faculty members who are working to get tenure and who feel the pressure to publish and do research. They may feel that just finding time to teach can be a difficult challenge. They need special help to see how experiential education can create research and publish-

"Young faculty members ... need special help to see how experiential education can create research and publishing opportunities as well as substantiate their teaching performance."

ing opportunities as well as substantiate their teaching performance. Jeff Chinn of Illinois State University offers another suggestion:

"We have sometimes offered senior faculty the opportunity to be departmental leaders in the [Professional Practice] program. They often don't have the same time constraints as untenured faculty, and the experience has become an opportunity for professional renewal for them. It can be almost like a new career."
-Jeff Chinn
Assistant Provost
Illinois State University

8. Fear of the world outside the campus. Many faculty have never worked in settings other than classrooms, libraries, and faculty offices. Like anyone facing a completely foreign culture, they may feel unsure of how to talk with work site supervisors, how to assess the learning potential in a work site, how to communicate their expectations and concerns, and even what to wear.

"I can lecture confidently to a room of 200 students, but I came down with an excruciating case of nerves when I called a judge to ask about setting up an internship on ethics in the judicial decision-making process. Fortunately, it was easier the second time."
-A Philosophy Professor
(who now sponsors 15
student interns each semester)

9. Lack of priority on student development. In a 1974 national study of faculty goals and priorities, Richman and Farmer found that "student intellectual development" and "student personal development" came eleventh and fifteenth, respectively.[8] Because experiential education is a methodology for the teaching/learning process, it also falls low on the list of priorities for many faculty. A faculty member who does not value students' intellectual and personal development is not likely to become involved in experiential education.

10. Limitations of the 50-minute class. This problem is seemingly quite simple, but very frustrating. Most class schedules are set up in 50-minute blocks three times a week, or in longer blocks two times a week. Even a professor who wants to integrate experiential learning may be stymied by the lack of time to put it into effect. It is a highly unusual college that attempts to arrange the school day or the school week to encourage experiential learning. Emory and Henry College in Virginia has set aside Wednesdays as a day for field trips and other experiential learning opportunities, extended laboratory research, and other campus activities. Colleges such as the State University of New York at Stony Brook coordinate scheduling of a number of classes so that students participating in Federated Learning Communities can take advantage of blocks of time for special learning activities. By and large, however, the scheduling systems most colleges use make it a great challenge for faculty to extend learning out of short time blocks.

The question of how to proceed once such concerns as these have been voiced is, of course, crucial. Even faculty quite intrigued by the idea of increasing their use of experiential learning processes are tempted to retreat into the comfort of what they already do well. The gains of experiential education are very substantial, however, and the process of becoming better at understanding and encouraging experiential learning can be exhilarating for faculty.

Assessing Faculty Involvement in Experiential Education

Before you consider ways of increasing the faculty role in experiential education, it is important to assess the current degree of faculty involvement. The following list of questions (on page 56) will help you determine whether faculty in your department and on your campus are aware of experiential learning, whether some have a commitment to it and an active involvement in its use, and whether some have the expertise and commitment to ongoing professional development that indicates they can become leaders. Write your responses on a separate sheet of paper. Also ask other interested faculty and administrators on your campus to answer the same questions. After all of you have jotted down your individual perceptions, have a group discussion as an opportunity to pinpoint strengths and weaknesses.

ASSESSING FACULTY INVOLVEMENT ON YOUR CAMPUS

1. Are faculty aware of experiential learning as a learning process and as an option for students? Are they aware of the range of experiential learning varieties, from a set of discreet, short-term, out-of-class activities (like the laboratory of a science course) to an intensive semester of full-time effort (like student teaching)?

2. Are there several key departments on campus that offer experiential learning opportunities, whether for credit or not? How many departments? Are they among the larger, more powerful departments on campus? Using the institutional inventory form in this sourcebook may help you answer this question (see Chapter 2).

3. Within each department, do faculty ever discuss what the role of experiential learning should be? That is, do they consider how experiential learning should be integrated into the curriculum in order to make sense educationally?

4. Do faculty from different departments have opportunities to share their knowledge of various types of experiential learning and exchange information about the practices used in their respective departments?

5. Do faculty, in their roles as academic advisors, advocate experiential learning to students? Do they make efforts to involve students who could particularly benefit from experiential learning?

6. Within the department, do faculty make a conscious effort to determine whether students should become involved in experiential education early in their college programs so they can explore career possibilities, or as a capstone experience so they can "practice" their theoretical expertise in an applied setting?

7. Do faculty discuss possible prerequisites for experiential education and the rationale for these requirements?

8. Have faculty made a conscious decision about the mode of student-faculty interaction in experiential education? For instance, do faculty prefer to work with students on a one-to-one basis for totally individualized attention, or in a seminar so students can share their experiences?

9. Have faculty involved themselves in pre-field preparation of students or in debriefing after the internship experiences? Do they plan and carry out workshops, exercises, or other types of preparation? Do they prepare written materials? Do they expect, and come to, student presentations on their field learning?

10. Do faculty take seriously their responsibilities to students in the field and to work site supervisors? Is there a policy that any faculty member sponsoring a student be required to make a site visit, if at all possible, or at least to communicate with the student and work site supervisor by telephone? Do faculty pre-screen placements, examine job descriptions, or in other ways involve themselves in the actual placement process?

11. Have faculty discussed and made departmental decisions about appropriate methods for evaluating experiential learning? Have they made careful decisions about such assignments as journals, research papers, additional reading, the assessment of work products, or other evaluation materials? Have faculty determined that certain assignments should regularly be given across the board, or do they individualize each student's assignments according to different learning objectives?

12. Have faculty determined how grading options can be established and justified?

13. Within the departments, are there specific faculty who are expected to take major responsibility for working with students involved in experiential learning? Does one faculty member work with all students, or does a coordinator assign each student to an appropriate faculty member? Do faculty members receive pay or release time for their work with students involved in field experiences? Is faculty members' involvement in experiential education integrated with other departmental and committee activities and responsibilities?

14. Does the department have an oversight committee for experiential learning?

15. Is there a college-wide faculty advisory committee for experiential education? What are its functions? To whom does it report? Does it have an official relationship to the main curriculum policy committee?

16. Are there opportunities for faculty to participate in professional development activities related to experiential education on campus or at professional conferences, both as learners and as teachers?

17. Do faculty advocate experiential learning to colleagues across campus and at other colleges, and to administrators? Are there regular opportunities for discussions of experiential education among faculty from different departments?

From *Strengthening Experiential Education in Your Institution*, National Society for Internships and Experiential Education, Raleigh, North Carolina, 1986

Building Faculty Support and Involvement in Experiential Education

There are a number of ways to increase faculty involvement that have been used successfully by the schools in NSIEE's Pilot Project. Consider before you decide on your approaches whether your goals are to increase (1) overall awareness of the value of experiential learning, (2) awareness of what is already happening in your institution or department, (3) attitudinal support, (4) active involvement in using experiential education, (5) commitment to experiential education as an important part of the entire curriculum, (6) the number of faculty who act as advocates and clear leaders for experiential education on campus, or (7) faculty knowledge and skills in utilizing experiential learning. Most likely, your goals include some combination of these levels of participation and commitment.

The following ideas can be successful whether the initiative comes from an individual faculty member, a faculty committee, a director of a departmental or campus-wide program, an academic administrator, or another advocate. We have focused on the institutional level in the wording of these ideas, but most of the principles apply equally to a departmental or divisional effort. Be sure to see also the chapter of this sourcebook on strategies for institutional change.

1. Feed information about experiential learning to the faculty continuously. Do not overlook the campus newspaper and the faculty newsletter as avenues for periodic articles on experiential education.

"You might take as an informal job for the next year the education of faculty about experiential learning. For instance, for liberal arts professors, some information from Paul Breen about the transferability of liberal arts skills might be just

right. For others, syllabi from other institutions would be useful. A speaker like David Kolb or Donald Schon would be impressive enough for any faculty member. If you can't swing the expense, collaborate with another unit on campus that might be interested in co-sponsorship. Introduce faculty to each other, so that people sponsoring students in different departments get a chance to meet informally. Informal lunch discussions are effective."
-Sharon Rubin
Consulting Report to the
University of New
Hampshire

"Feed information about good examples of internships regularly to faculty in various humanities and social sciences departments. This could help them begin to learn about the possibilities. It is important that they see examples and read literature that is geared toward their own disciplines."

To Do

21 Things to Do to Increase Faculty Involvement

1. Feed information about experiential learning to faculty continuously.
2. Act as a catalyst to link faculty from different departments.
3. Organize informal discussions.
4. Find out what people's concerns are.
5. Work through supportive opinion leaders on campus.
6. Establish a faculty committee on experiential education.
7. Let students speak for the value of experiential learning.
8. Conduct workshops or sponsor speakers on campus.
9. Give away money and authority.
10. Reinforce excellence in faculty support of experiential education.
11. Help academic advisors to understand and promote experiential learning as an integral part of the curriculum.
12. Arrange faculty internships.
13. Have a summer study group of faculty focusing on experiential learning.
14. Create a rotating faculty position in the central office for experiential education.
15. Take faculty on site visits.
16. Ask faculty to design and implement research projects related to experiential learning.
17. Help key faculty members arrange sabbaticals that involve experiential learning.
18. Establish "Field Study Coordinatorships" like Teaching Assistantships for graduate students or advanced undergraduates.
19. Offer senior faculty opportunities to take on leadership roles in experiential education as a renewal experience.
20. Establish a library of resources for faculty about using experiential learning in courses.
21. Take faculty to professional meetings for experiential educators.

"It is very important that the faculty here see examples from other prestigious institutions. If a faculty member here reads that Podunk State University is doing a particular program, then that is reason enough not to do it at UVA — no matter how good the program is. The examples need to be from other comparable institutions."
-H.C. Erik Midelfort
  Professor of History and
    Associate Dean, College of
    Arts and Sciences
  University of Virginia

"Help faculty identify others in their own discipline who support experiential learning. If you have a skeptical historian, send him something written by another historian. NSIEE's PANEL talent bank can give you names and publications by discipline."
-Jane Kendall
  Executive Director, NSIEE

"Send around articles telling how particular departments or peer institutions are using experiential learning. The coordinator really has to take responsibility for feeding people good ideas. It doesn't do any good to have this type of information or the literature on the theoretical concepts about experiential learning if you keep it in a file somewhere and don't send it out. Even circulating copies of interesting articles can encourage an environment where the discussion of teaching and learning is legitimate and desirable."
-Sharon Rubin
  Meeting of NSIEE Peer
    Consultants, April 1985

Participants in the NSIEE Pilot Project also caution against depending solely on written communications:

Help faculty identify others in their own discipline who support experiential learning.

"I've learned that I make too many assumptions about the amount of work faculty are willing to do outside of simply coming to meetings to discuss a problem. I also assume that people will read and absorb information I send them, provided it's not too long or complicated. I need to do more face-to-face lobbying and information-gathering to increase awareness among appropriate faculty and staff members."
-Marlene Steiner Suter
  Director of Career Planning
    and Placement
  Otterbein College, Ohio

2. Act as a catalyst to link faculty from different departments.

"I started by researching all the faculty who had sponsored internships over the last eight years. Then I talked with those people and listened to their concerns."

3. Organize informal discussions.

"Have an informal meeting of all the people who you know are supportive of internships. It could even be a brown bag lunch. Find out who else these faculty know (colleagues, neighbors, etc.) who are also supportive. Build on this."
-A faculty member at a large
  university

"We could start by having lunch with 5-10 people that we know are interested. Each of them probably knows one or two others. We could build an informal coalition for mutual support and some work in helping our colleagues see how internships could be used in their departments. We already know the arguments that will be used against the idea. We just need to articulate

Work through supportive opinion leaders on the faculty.

what we know about why internships are valid and useful."
-H.C. Erik Midelfort
  Professor of History and
    Associate Dean, College of
    Arts and Sciences
  University of Virginia

4. Find out what people's concerns are.

"I started by researching all the faculty who had sponsored internships over the last eight years. Then I talked with those people and listened to their concerns."
-Douglas Boyce
  Dean, King College
  Bristol, Tennessee

"One thing I wish I had done early which would have helped me understand the attitudes of key faculty and administrators was to interview the 'key actors' early in the project. Without this, it took a while to get a sense of the scope of the problems with the current structure of the program."
-Marlene Steiner Suter
  Director of Career Planning
    and Placement
  Otterbein College, Ohio

5. Work through supportive opinion leaders on the faculty.

"The faculty have to hear it from people they perceive to be their academic peers."
-An administrator who learned
    this from his own experience

"I could ask the students who the faculty members were who supported their doing internships. This would help us see what others are supportive of the concept. I think our first task is to see what kind of support we really have. Then we need to get the most respected faculty mem-

bers among that group to be vocal about their support of good internships for discipline-based learning. These are the only people that other faculty will listen to."

    -H.C. Erik Midelfort
      Professor of History and
        Associate Dean, College of
        Arts and Sciences
      University of Virginia

"Consolidate the strengths that are already there. Know who your allies are and build on that."

    -Douglas Boyce
      Dean, King College
      Bristol, Tennessee

6. Establish a faculty committee on experiential education. Because of the absolute importance of a faculty committee at some point on almost every campus, an entire section of this chapter is devoted to ideas and examples for a strong, effective faculty committee.

7. Let students speak for the value of experiential learning.

"One [of our most successful approaches] was to plan a meeting at which interns could discuss their experiences with faculty, with other students who have completed internships, and with students interested in doing internships. It was well attended and generated a great deal of interest in internships among faculty and students."

    -Margaret Schramm
      Chairperson
      Internship Advisory
        Committee
        and Professor of English
      Hartwick College
      Oneonta, New York

"The strongest feature of the program is the seminar that pools students together and focuses on what they are actually learning during their internships. Watching those students would soothe any faculty member's objections [about experiential education] very effectively. Those students are really learning how to relate experiences back to theory .

They are learning to articulate things that they observed during their internships that were just fuzzy ideas before. We could possibly invite faculty from other departments to be guest lecturers at those seminars. No, that wouldn't work because then they would not get to hear the students speak. It's hearing the students that is convincing. They could be 'guest facilitators' for the discussions. The trick is how to get them there (No faculty member likes to be invited to 'observe'; they have to think they are being asked because of something they know about.) and yet have them hear the students speak about what they are learning in the field."

    -H.C. Erik Midelfort
      Professor of History and
        Associate Dean, College of
        Arts and Sciences
      University of Virginia

"I have often been surprised at how little faculty know about what really happens to students through experiential education. But then, the kind of publicity that programs put out tends to emphasize how many students we have, where they were

Intern Jay Williamson helps to plan an annual meeting for the alumni office at the State University of New York, Oswego.

'I now know why I'm taking these courses. I now know that there is a relevance to what you're telling me.'

placed, what projects they worked on, what majors they're in, and how many of them are employed by their supervisors after graduation. I admit this nuts and bolts information is important. But what faculty who are not yet involved don't know about is what I would call communication skills. You often find that students don't really lack these skills, they are just so shy and so lacking in confidence that they don't know how to express themselves or they assume that nobody's going to listen to what they say. By the end of an internship, they can often do much more than you ever expected.

What I noticed when I talked with returning interns at Manhattan College, for example, was a change in aspiration. Students there said, 'Something really made me realize that I'm just starting in this field. I think I'm going to work for a year and then go back to graduate school.' Every single student I talked to there said, 'I know now that learning is lifelong. There is so much I want to know more about.' And there are students that say , 'I now know why I'm taking these courses. I now know that there is a relevance to what you're telling me.' So the faculty who participate get to know all these wonderful things. But the other faculty should be told about these successes in learning. And we don't tell them. We don't send those students around. We don't share those stories enough."

    -Sharon Rubin
      NSIEE Consultant
      NSIEE Workshop
      Alexandria, Virginia

Academic advising is a crucial — but often overlooked — link in helping students see experiential learning not merely as practice for a career, but as an alternative method of learning.

8. Conduct workshops or sponsor speakers on campus. Listen to these tips from two consulting reports:

"Workshops run by faculty for other faculty are very effective in the kind of informal 'technology transfer' that needs to occur much more at the University."
    -Sharon Rubin in NSIEE
        Consulting Report to the
            University of New
            Hampshire

"Probably the easiest way for the people to share their goals as experiential educators is through the medium of a workshop on curricular improvement. Many campuses offer a forum for faculty to hear experts from inside or outside the institution discuss good teaching, and it should be easy to arrange a topical workshop on experiential learning. Those faculty who are attracted by the topic may become the nucleus of an informal consortium."
    -Sharon Rubin
        Assistant Dean
        Undergraduate Studies
        University of Maryland

Many of the NSIEE pilot institutions organized faculty workshops. Those schools offer these words of advice:
• Get someone who can communicate well with faculty. The speaker or workshop leader should be an intellectual peer of the participants.
• Publicize it well, not just by putting notices in mailboxes. Get opinion leaders to encourage their colleagues to come. Ask department chairs to bring key faculty members.
• Be sure the faculty want it. Do not expect someone with a briefcase to perform miracles. Workshops or even lectures can help for specific needs — presenting a conceptual overview of experiential education, facilitating an open discussion of related faculty interests and concerns, or working on particular problems that faculty have identified. As with any human beings, if faculty perceive that someone is bringing in an outsider to tell them what to do, the attempt will set you back a year or two.
• Use existing campus series for speakers, faculty lectures, or brown bag lunch discussions. These can all provide a good forum for periodic coverage of topics in experiential education.

9. Give away money and authority. In a time of scarcity, it may be difficult to find the money or the authority to hand out, but there is always some available. For instance, if you can fund a faculty member with a small summer stipend to prepare a handbook on experiential learning for a department, if you can fund a faculty member to prepare a paper on teaching processes for a disciplinary conference, if you can ask faculty members to make policy decisions on experiential learning, informally or through a committee, faculty ownership of experiential learning will increase much more than the amounts given would suggest. The administrative style of Marlyn Lawrentz, who administers the Professional Practice Program at Illinois State University, exemplifies this philosophy. At Illinois State, which has had a large cooperative education grant for several years, the Professional Practice Office is small in terms of staff and functions. Instead, the program funds portions of coordinator positions within departments and colleges, and distributes small grants for materials preparation, job development, travel, and other needs based on proposals made through the coordinators.

10. Reinforce excellence in faculty support of experiential education. Write thank you letters to put in the personnel files of faculty who are effective experiential educators. Offer to write letters when those faculty are considered for tenure, promotion, and merit increases. Issue certificates of appreciation for them to put in their offices. Take them along on the most interesting site visits. Help them establish employer contacts that can support their research and publishing goals. Look for opportunities to give their work visibility among faculty, students, administrators, community leaders, and alumni.

11. Help academic advisors to understand and promote experiential learning as an integral part of the curriculum. Academic advising is a crucial — but often overlooked — link in helping students see experiential learning not merely as practice for a career, but as an alternative method of learning.

12. Arrange faculty internships. Faculty internships are a superb way to help faculty see the value of experiential education, especially if all the elements of a good internship are included — setting learning goals, reflecting on what is learned both during and after the experience, and drawing the experience back to the theoretical base of the discipline. Such experiences also help faculty see the pitfalls and problems they need to address when they sponsor their students on field experiences. A number of schools, including Furman University, have used this method of teaching teachers.

13. Provide other opportunities for faculty development. See the special section of this chapter on faculty enrichment.

Look for opportunities to give their work visibility among faculty, students, administrators, community leaders and alumni.

A Faculty Committee: Important Vehicle for Ownership and Involvement

A subcommittee on experiential learning in a department or an advisory committee to a campus-wide program offers faculty an opportunity to learn and to contribute their own ideas. It is very important for such a committee to have a charge from an administrator and a sense of purpose, or it will soon deteriorate into either a rubber stamp for the ideas of one individual or a group of contentious advocates for their own positions. The experience of the Hartwick College Advisory Committee on Internships (described on right) is instructive in this regard.

Several other significant tasks for faculty committees also deserve attention. A committee can recommend changes in institutional policy to systematize course numbering and crediting throughout the institution. A committee can make sure that the educational role of experiential learning is documented in the catalog, schedule of classes, on transcripts, and in other materials representing the entire institution. Finally, an advisory committee can call representatives of different constituencies together from across the campus to develop consensus on broad policy issues that will then be acceptable to the entire institution. The Internship Committee at Adrian College in Adrian, Michigan, serves several of these functions.

"It is important that those who are affected by change have a part in developing those changes. Change takes a long time! It is important to establish an ongoing committee where issues can be discussed and concerns shared. I would advise other schools to begin working with NSIEE early,

A Case Study

HARTWICK COLLEGE'S ADVISORY COMMITTEE ON INTERNSHIPS

*T*he Hartwick Advisory Committee was instituted by the Dean of the College at the request of Barbara Lilly, the Internship Coordinator, who felt that the faculty had to be responsible for credit-bearing internships. Because the program was new, there were many real issues to discuss, and the Committee was called upon to make a number of policy decisions that would have implications for the entire campus. Many Committee members felt the need to educate themselves about internships in order to be able to make reasonable decisions, and the internship coordinator was able to help them with written materials and other resources. As Barbara Lilly notes:

"The Advisory Committee provided a structure that enabled faculty to share the responsibility and decision-making power needed to strengthen and expand the internship program. The Committee actively addressed and resolved many of the issues raised, including: formulation of a statement of goals for the internship program, approval of an optional abstract on an internship which becomes a permanent part of the student's transcript, listings of internships on pre-registration semester course offerings, assessment and evaluation, faculty rewards for supervising interns, tuition for summer internships, a campus-wide debriefing program for interns, and affirmation of the value of the Internship Learning Agreement which provides the academic structure for internships arranged through all departments."
    -Barbara Lilly, Internship Coordinator
    Hartwick College, Oneonta, NY

The Committee was not set up as a standing committee, but was given several years in which to recommend to the Dean its eventual status. Recently, the Committee decided to retain its appointed status, thereby retaining control over membership. Several members resigned in order to allow new faculty members to become actively engaged in the further institutionalization of the internship program, while some experienced members will remain to provide continuity. The Committee has submitted its recommendations on new members to the Dean with suggestion that the Committee be appointed for two-year terms with the possibility of renewal.
    In evaluating the effectiveness of the Committee, Barbara Lilly notes:

"Not unlike many institutions of higher education, Hartwick is democratic and consequently cautious about implementing change. When issues are near resolution or policies are affected, the democratic process ensures final resolution or reconsideration of implemented changes. ... The Advisory Committee [is] a forum that encourages democratic participation in decisions about policies and procedures, and nurtures ownership of the internship program. It was the Advisory Committee that would not capitulate to those students and departments who viewed the Learning Agreement as superfluous to the experience; it is the Advisory Committee that will not allow the summer tuition issue to go unresolved; and it is the Advisory Committee that may reconsider the issue of a campus-wide faculty reward system sometime in the future. Although membership will change, the Committee will continue to represent the faculty at large and the best interests of our students in determining the future and direction of our institutional internship program."

Barbara Lilly, right, responds to Kristen Murtaugh's questions about the valuable role the Faculty Advisory Committee on Internships plays at Hartwick College.

to seek administrative support as well as faculty support, and to form an advisory committee for the purpose of providing a forum where important issues can be discussed."
-Rose Marie Springer
   Associate Director
   Westmont Urban Program
   Westmont College,
      California

"With a faculty committee, suddenly faculty members realize, 'We own this program. We can make decisions about the policies and standards. We can make decisions about how this relates to our disciplines.'"
-Sharon Rubin
   1984 NSIEE National
      Conference
   San Diego, California

In addition, John Duley points out an opportunity that is often missed with existing committees:

"In order to ground experiential education in the academic base of the institution, you also must use the existing reporting structures for both visibility and communication. For example, Adrian College's Internship Committee reports to the Academic Environment Committee (the major

academic policy body), but until this year had never used this connection as a vehicle for advocacy and support of internships."
-John Duley
   NSIEE Board of Directors'
      meeting
   January 1985
   Washington, DC

"You have to keep after all the committees that relate in any way to the curriculum or to educational policies because all of them relate to experiential education."
-Barbara Buchanan
   Director of Field Education
   College of Public and
      Community Service
   Univ. of Massachusetts
   Boston, Massachusetts

Who is appointed to a faculty committee determines its success or failure. At one college, a skeptical dean appointed mostly opponents of internships to a faculty study committee. The effectiveness of their recommendations was exactly what you would predict. A committee appointed at another institution was not given a clear sense of its responsibilities; it was also a predictable failure. The Dean of Arts and Sciences at the University of Colorado appointed mostly supportive faculty

who were already somewhat involved in internships. Dean Samuel Schuman of Guilford College took the same approach. Doug Boyce of King College shares another idea:

"I included half supporters and half skeptics about internships. I chose opinion leaders in both groups. Their involvement on our ad hoc committee ensured that the committee's recommendations would be accepted when presented to the full faculty."
-Douglas Boyce
   Dean, King College
   Bristol, Tennessee

Finally, we must mention the choice of appointees for Hartwick College's Advisory Committee because of the proven performance record of this group of faculty and administrators:

"Our Advisory Committee on Internships was appointed by the Dean of the College . . . [and] included faculty from the three divisions: two from the Humanities, two from the Physical and Life Sciences, and four from the Social Sciences. The larger representation from the Social Sciences reflected the greater number of internships undertaken through that division. The

Barbara Buchanan, center, explains how she follows the work of several policy committees.

registrar and two students were also appointed.

The charge to the committee was to advise the Dean and the Coordinator of Internships on all matters relating to the internship program, including establishing the goals of the program, defining 'internships,' and developing and modifying policies and procedures for implementing the program. Its function was to provide additional perspective and support to those responsible for the administration of the internship program.

   -Barbara Lilly
     Internship Coordinator
     Hartwick College
     Oneonta, NY

Faculty Enrichment

"Many faculty are not familiar with the pedagogy of experiential learning. Assessment procedures continue to bedevil faculty at most institutions."

   -Sharon Rubin
     NSIEE Consultant
       and Assistant Dean of
       Undergraduate Studies
     University of Maryland

As important as faculty support of experiential education and their active use of it for teaching is their ability to use it effectively. Teaching experientially takes a very different set of skills from traditional classroom teaching. In a classroom setting, faculty are accustomed to having complete control over the subject content to be learned, instructional methods (readings, lectures, papers, etc.), the criteria and methods of evaluation, and the exclusive decision about what valid learning was actually accomplished. The student is a participant observer, and the faculty member alone is in charge.

Experiential education, on the other hand, requires a completely different set of skills and roles.

Objectives and goals are balanced among the student, the professor, and the work supervisor; the content is structured by the nature of the experience; the method of learning is defined by the community's needs and the student's own learning style; the faculty member acts as a facilitator and mentor; the student becomes a self-directed learner; and a business or community person shares the role of supervisor and performance appraiser. The faculty member's relationship to the student is more one-to-one than in the classroom arrangement, and more interpersonal skills are thus required. These are not easy adjustments for faculty who are used to the traditional role. See again the list of skills faculty gain from involvement in experiential education (provided earlier in this chapter). These are the very areas in which faculty often need help. Listen to this discussion among leaders from the NSIEE-FIPSE Pilot Institutions:

Jim Keith (Guilford College): We have a particular focus on new faculty. Just in terms of informal conversations once a week — bringing them together to discuss how they're doing and how their classes are going. There's no chief administrator there to be the heavy. It's almost like a mentoring process with several faculty. It often fluctuates into discussions about teaching, which many faculty had never done until they get into the classroom as the teacher. I've seen some remarkable advancement in faculty over a year's time when they've engaged in this informal process.

Doug Boyce (King College): Furman University in Greenville, South Carolina, has been doing that for about five years. I've talked with several people there who've been very pleased with the results. They had some money to do a new faculty orientation process that included this sort of thing. But they opened it up and said anyone can come. They found that there were all kinds of mid-life faculty who were sneaking in around the edges and listening and participating and benefitting from it. Phil Winstead would be the person to write about it. It's worked very well. It's a very touchy area. Let's face it, these faculty are in many ways very accomplished, and when you hit a slightly vulnerable area, it's difficult to deal with it.

Jim Keith: What gives rise to that with our faculty is that we have a student evaluation system, and the evaluations often point to real places of vulnerability which then can relate to the whole tenure question down the pike. I find often if there is not some medium for intercepting the faculty early and working with them, they feel that the noose has been put around their necks the first year they're in teaching. The series for our new faculty is part of Guilford College's overall program of faculty development. It has also resulted in a faculty colloquium with William Perry. A lot can happen once the lid's off and faculty feel it's legitimate to talk about these things. It works quite well. I think part of what you have to do to begin with is to develop an atmosphere on campus where you discuss teaching.

Erik Midelfort: It's very rare for people to focus on teaching. Many faculty do not really believe that it is possible to learn how to teach. I've heard for 25 years that you can't teach teaching because 'Teaching is an art.' But then I wonder why we have art schools if you can't teach an art.

Kristen Murtaugh (Manhattan College): [During the coming year,] we will help faculty get a theoretical background in experiential education and circulate research that has been done. I am excited that we can use experiential education to draw faculty into discussions of learning in general.

Some of our suggestions for offering opportunities for faculty enrichment in experiential learning are:

• **Have a summer study group** that examines what is known about experiential learning as pedagogy and recommends policy changes based on that knowledge. The group might begin with the works of David Kolb, William Perry, and Donald Schon and continue with discipline-related resources recommended by NSIEE and faculty at other colleges and universities.

• **Establish a rotating faculty position** in the central office for experiential education. Involve faculty from different divisions and departments every year or two. If a faculty member can spend even ten hours a week learning how to administer a program, from finding worksites to helping students prepare learning proposals to speaking to faculty groups about field experiences, that faculty member will go back to his or her teaching refreshed and changed as an educator. This also provides a discipline-based perspective to the central staff and builds a network of knowledgeable faculty advocates in the departments.

• **Take faculty on site visits** to students or potential employers.

"At Illinois State, Bradford College, and several other colleges I visited, many faculty felt inadequate as job developers or evaluators. Because they had spent their professional careers on college campuses, they were often concerned about their ability to speak authoritatively to employers about student learning objectives, and they were hesitant to gain the expertise experientially."
-Sharon Rubin
    NSIEE Consultant and
    Assistant Dean for
    Undergraduate Studies
    University of Maryland

Giving faculty the opportunity informally to learn more about the work world, while making use of their scholarly expertise, is beneficial

"It is important that those who are affected by change have a part in developing those changes. Change takes a long time!"

to students, employers, and program administrators as well as the faculty themselves.

• **Ask faculty to design and implement research projects related to experiential learning.** If one of the primary values of the academic world is that research is important, then research is one of the most compelling reasons for faculty involvement in experiential education

— and one of the best avenues for faculty enrichment. We make many assumptions about what students learn, how they feel about their experiences, the impact of experiential learning on their later academic and work accomplishment, the role of experiential learning in enhancing cognitive and moral development, the relationship of personality type and learning style to learning success, and many other important issues for which rigorous research is needed. At large universities in particular, there are always graduate students searching for dissertation topics and professors in the social sciences and education exploring new research areas. If the administrator of an experiential learning program is seen as a resource on campus, and not a barrier to interest

Doug Boyce, Dean of King College, reviews the departments at his college as he considers their involvement in experiential education. Dr. Boyce is also Professor of Anthropology and Sociology.

To persuade faculty that there is more to experiential learning conceptually than practical work experience takes both deep and broad knowledge of learning theory, cognitive development theory, and group process theory.

in the field, successful collaborations can result in the kinds of publications faculty want to produce and the kinds that are sorely needed in the field of experiential learning.

• **Help key faculty members arrange sabbaticals that involve experiential learning,** perhaps a faculty internship and then a study of field experience as it relates to the discipline.

• **Set up a series of informal discussions** in which faculty can exchange ideas and samples of syllabi, learning proposals, evaluation procedures and journals. But be sure the faculty define their own needs:

"I do not want to mandate to faculty what the issues are. They need to come on their own to the need for more discussion."
　　-Douglas Boyce, Dean
　　King College
　　Bristol, Tennessee

• **Establish a library of resources for faculty** about using experiential learning in courses. Start with the collections of course syllabi and the PANEL Resource Papers published by NSIEE. Include examples of good materials from your own faculty.

"Faculty at one of the small colleges I visited were saying. 'I'm really having a hard time with these learning proposals because I don't sponsor very many students.' Well, there are only 435 students in the whole school, so nobody is going to

become an expert. But faculty could get lots of information just from sharing among themselves. Each faculty member does not have to start from scratch."
　　-Sharon Rubin
　　NSIEE Consultant and
　　　Assistant Dean for
　　　Undergraduate Studies
　　University of Maryland
　　College Park

• **Take faculty to professional meetings in experiential education.** Showcase their work while exposing them to issues, solutions, and practices at other institutions.

"I always take faculty to the regional conferences in experiential education. These provide excellent opportunities for faculty to learn and to have their interest piqued."
　　-Jane Szutu Permaul
　　Director of Field Studies
　　Development, UCLA

• **Establish "Field Study Coordinatorships" like Teaching Assistantships** as is done at UCLA. By creating this new category for graduate student assistantships, you can involve regular faculty in teaching graduate students how to

work with undergraduates by linking field experiences to the discipline. They can monitor and support undergraduate students' learning during internships, recommend readings, review journals and "reflection and analysis tapes," and evaluate what students learn on field experiences. The role of supervising graduate students who are supervising internships can create opportunities for regular faculty to dig into the literature on experiential education, recommend readings, and work with graduate students and faculty colleagues on research studies and publications concerning experiential education in the discipline.

• **Offer senior faculty opportunities to take on leadership roles in experiential education as a renewal experience.** As mentioned previously, Jeff Chinn, Assistant Provost at Illinois State University, reports that the role of departmental or divisional coordinator can create a new career interest for tenured faculty. Illinois State gives release time to a faculty member in each area to help locate appropriate experiential opportunities, publicize them to students and faculty in the department, help faculty design seminars, and help students prepare learning proposals.

Coming Events

November 19, Greenville, NC
Regional Conference co-sponsored by NSIEE and the Cooperative Education Office, East Carolina University. Contact NSIEE, 919-834-7536.

March 2-4, Lake Arrowhead, CA
Third Annual Regional Collaborative Conference of NSIEE, CAEL and NEBCEA. Contact Roger Long, Field Studies Development, UCLA, 213-825-2295.

March 6, Boston, MA
NSIEE Regional Conference in New England, will be held at Suffolk University. Contact John Berg, Government Dept., Suffolk Univ., Boston MA, 02108, 617-723-4700, ext. 126.

Pat Debenham from Brigham Young University teaches at Juaquin Elementary School in Provo, Utah.

Special Considerations for Those Who Are Not Faculty Members

Many people who run internship or cooperative education programs are not faculty members. They may be student affairs professionals, graduate students, or administrative staff who one day find themselves trying to implement programs with significant educational goals from a position outside the departmental structure of the institution. To such staff members, the frustrations may be enormous and the challenges may seem insurmountable. At that point, some people withdraw from trying to reach faculty. They may begin to talk about "us" and "them," those who understand how to administer an experiential learning program and everyone else. Sometimes there is only a "me" rather than an "us" on campus, and isolation and despair can result.

There are a number of particular approaches that non-faculty program administrators can take to reach out to faculty, to find opportunities for collaboration, and to extend the possibilities for institutionalization of experiential education on their campuses. Besides the tips already presented in this chapter, consider the following special advice.

First, non-faculty administrators must redefine their roles. Often they see themselves as advocates for their students rather than advocates for the principles of experiential learning. Program administrators who see themselves as having the broadest possible mandate to extend the practice of experiential learning on their campuses will think of themselves as expert consultants and facilitators for the faculty, and they will seek out opportunities to be helpful to individual faculty members and to departments which have any interest in experiential learning. One way of doing this effectively on a college campus is to become the catalyst for the exchange of information. If you find out what one faculty member is doing as an experiential educator, you can introduce it to another faculty member who might find it useful. Breaking down the barriers between departments and between faculty who do not know each other is one of the best ways of fostering an atmosphere where the discussion of experiential learning can take place. Mary Jo White of the University of Colorado is an excellent example of someone who switched from a focus on administering a large program to the role of a resource person to faculty. See her own description of how she approaches this role in the chapter of this sourcebook on strategies for institutional change.

"Another approach is to assume the posture of a learner, that is to go to the faculty and learn how they manage internships, and then share those ideas with other faculty. So you begin to break down the walls that exist within the institution."
-John Duley
NSIEE Peer Consultant and
Professor Emeritus
Michigan State University

Program administrators who see themselves as having the broadest possible mandate to extend the practice of experiential learning on their campuses will think of themselves as expert consultants and facilitators for the faculty, and they will seek out opportunities to be helpful to individual faculty members and to departments which have any interest in experiential learning.

A FACULTY FANTASY

"On one consulting visit, I asked faculty what their fantasies were for the future of experiential learning on their campus, and they came up with a wonderful list, including cross-cultural experiential learning, experiential learning for graduate students, interdisciplinary programs, research. That made me think about my own fantasy, and I'm afraid I was too selfish to think of my institution. I could only think of my own role as an educator.

I remember the fantasy I once had as I was just finishing my doctoral dissertation. I saw myself as a female Mr. Chips on some beautiful, preferably Gothic-style, liberal arts campus. It would be early summer, and the grass would be wonderfully green. A small class of adoring students would be sitting in a circle on the lawn, and I would be explaining American culture so well that they would be in awe. They would also be very quiet, because I was talking and they were listening.

Today I have a very different fantasy. I am with my students in my kitchen, and we are using the incredible bounty on the kitchen table to prepare a meal. Some of the students are looking at cookbooks and reading recipes to the others, who comment in thoughtful but opinionated ways. One student is on the phone to her grandmother to find out the secret of a family specialty. Others are already at work cutting the vegetables or mixing wonderful-smelling things in bowls. Leaning against the counter, I am busy answering questions, reacting to the recipe suggestions, preparing the work surfaces, and helping people find things in the cupboards. There is a lot of noise — conversations, debate, laughter — and quite a bit of mess.

As we sit down together to enjoy the completed meal, I realize that some of the dishes don't taste at all the way I expected them to, but the creativity of the cooks has resulted in some very interesting combinations. Grandmother's specialty was truly worth the long-distance call, but there are a few dishes for which we had high expectations that haven't turned out very well. I'm a good cook, and I probably could have prepared a very good meal for my students by myself. But what has resulted is quite different and much more exciting than what I would have prepared, even from the same recipes, because I have been cooking for many years with a certain style. Even if this meal wasn't better, our work together has given us the best ingredient — accomplishment. We are very proud of ourselves, and we enjoy the meal much more than the most elegant meal in the best restaurant in town — because it is ours. As we sit around the table after we have finished, we talk about how to make an even better meal next time, and our enthusiasm for our plans compensates us for the knowledge that we have a lot of cleaning up to do.

My new fantasy is very real to me. Somehow, it doesn't seem beyond reach. The best teaching I have done reminds me of this fantasy. As I look around my own campus and the campuses I have visited, I see many faculty bringing students into the kitchen where the real learning, both planned and unintended, gets done. There is a lot more room in the kitchen."

-Sharon Rubin
NSIEE Consultant and
Assistant Dean for
Undergraduate Studies
University of Maryland

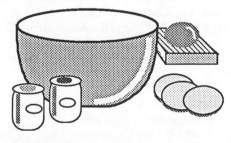

You will either choose to be part of the ongoing academic structure of the institution, or your program will remain on the periphery.

Secondly, working as a consultant to departments gives an important responsibility to non-faculty administrators. If you are going to have the background in pedagogy and the mental file of appropriate examples you will need, continued professional development is a must. Many administrators become stale running their programs because they do not seek out new ways to think about experiential learning. Often, to persuade faculty that there is more to experiential learning conceptually than practical work experience takes both deep and broad knowledge of learning theory, cognitive development theory, and group process theory.

The single most common problem that we observe as we visit campuses and talk with experiential educators who are in central administrative positions is that they do not give away enough power and authority to faculty across the campus. Rather than stimulate and support departmental initiatives to build experiential learning into the regular curriculum, they may become protective of "their program" and unintentionally isolate themselves from the academic mainstream. Program administrators must acknowledge the central role of faculty in the eight tasks of experiential education while they simultaneously explore their own roles as consultant, catalyst, and resource person to faculty. You will either choose to be part of the ongoing academic structure of the institution, or your program will remain on the periphery. As a non-faculty administrator, however, you must adapt to the faculty's culture and way of instituting change. You must also respect the faculty's rightful authority about curricular matters. This puts you in a unique role and one that offers tremendous opportunities and creative challenges *if* you understand the culture and the potential roles of faculty. See the chapters of this sourcebook on curriculum integration, administrative structures, and strategies for institutional change for ideas and concepts to guide you. Also see Jane Kendall's discussion of faculty goals and values in "Values As the Core of Institutional Commitment: Finding a Common Ground" in *Making Sponsored Experiential Learning Standard Practice*. (See Recommended Resources at the end of this chapter.)

FOOTNOTES

[1] John Dewey, *Experience and Education*, 1938, quoted by David Kolb in *Experiential Learning*, Prentice-Hall, Inc., Englewood Cliffs, New Jersey, 1984, p. 27.

[2] Frank Newman, Catherine Milton, and Susan Stroud, "Community Service and Higher Education: Obligations and Opportunities," *AAHE Bulletin*, Vol. 37, No. 10, June 1985, p. 13.

[3] R. Harrison and R. Hopkins, "An Alternative to the University Model," *Journal of Applied Behavioral Science*, Vol. 3, No. 4, 1967, pp. 437-438.

[4] *Ibid.*

[5] Carol Murphy, *Integrating the Community and the Classroom: Instructors Describe the Results*, Far West Laboratory for Educational Research and Development, San Francisco, California, 1981, pp. 7-9.

[6] John S. Duley and Stephen L. Yelon, *Efficient Evaluation of Individual Performance in Field Placement*, Michigan State University, 1978.

[7] Richard L. Hoffman, "Encouraging Faculty to Invest Time in Service Learning," *Synergist*, Vol. 5, No. 1, Spring, 1976, pp. 33-37.

[8] B. M. Richman and R. N. Farmer, *Leadership, Goals, and Power in Higher Education*, Jossey-Bass, San Francisco, California, 1974, pp. 119-120.

RECOMMENDED RESOURCES

Borzak, Lenore, Editor, *Field Study: A Sourcebook for Experiential Learning*, Sage Publications, Beverly Hills, California, 1981. Contains theoretical and practical sections from a variety of points of view. The articles on cognitive development and discipline-based approaches to experiential learning are particularly appropriate for faculty.

Chickering, Arthur W., "Developmental Change as a Major Outcome," in *Experiential Learning*, ed. by Morris Keeton, Jossey-Bass, San Francisco, California, 1976. One of the best discussions of educational outcomes, student learning styles and teaching styles in relation to developmental theory. A good way for faculty to begin to think about their own roles.

Coleman, James S., "Differences Between Experiential and Classroom Learning," in *Experiential Learning*, ed. by Morris Keeton, Jossey-Bass, San Francisco, California, 1976. A very clear distinction between traditional and experiential learning; very basic information for faculty.

Duley, John S., "Service as Learning, Life-Style, and Faculty Function," in *Redefining Service, Research, and Teaching*, ed. by Warren B. Martin, New Directions for Higher Education, No. 18, Jossey-Bass, San Francisco, California, 1977, pp. 23-36. A good rationale for faculty involvement.

Kendall, Jane C., Editor, *PANEL Resource Papers Series*, National Society for Internships and Experiential Education, Raleigh, North Carolina, 1980 to present. This series of monographs presents concise guidelines for faculty who want to establish or improve a course or program for experiential learning.

Little, Thomas C., "Intellectual Passion," *Synergist*, National Center for Service Learning, Vol. 8, No. 1, Spring, 1979, pp. 45-48. An epistomological rationale for experiential learning that would make sense to many faculty.

Little, Thomas C., Editor, *Making Sponsored Experiential Learning Standard Practice*, New Directions for Experiential Learning, No. 20, Jossey-Bass, San Francisco, California, 1983.

Kaston, Carren O., with James Heffernan, *Preparing Humanists for Work: A National Study of Undergraduate Internships in the Humanities*, The Washington Center, 1984 (available from NSIEE), and the companion *Directory of Undergraduate Internships in the Humanities*, 1984 (available from the Modern Language Association, 62 Fifth Avenue, New York, New York, 10011). An extensive exploration of the way in which some liberal arts disciplines use internships. The case studies are particularly meaningful for faculty.

Thorburn, Neil, "Enriching the Liberal Arts," in *Enriching the Liberal Arts through Experiential Learning*, ed. by Stevens E. Brooks and James Althof, New Directions for Experiential Learning, No. 6, Jossey-Bass, San Francisco, California, 1979, pp. 13-22. A chief academic officer's view of the liberal arts faculty's role in experiential learning.

4

Ensuring Quality in Experiential Education

*I*n 1983, Norman Evans, a leader in British higher education, visited a number of American colleges and universities to see what was being done in experiential education on this side of the Atlantic. Each campus visit included conversations with program administrators, students, and faculty sponsors. During his meetings with faculty, the British educator would ask, "What are your standards? How do you know if this experiential education is providing real learning? Is this something colleges should be doing?" Dr. Evans reports that almost invariably, these questions to faculty were answered with blank stares. These stares reflect the different perspectives on standards and quality control in American and British higher education. They also point to a potentially effective strategy for experiential education in winning the mind, heart, and pocketbook of collegiate institutions.

Quality is excellence of character. Simple enough! However, it is difficult in educational endeavors to establish the criteria for excellence and to guarantee the application of these criteria. British higher education persists at both tasks. For a single course to be offered in a British polytechnic institute, the faculty member who is proposing the course must provide pages of documentation. The first question is, "What will the student learn? Describe in detail, including specific behaviors." Then the faculty member must respond to: "How will this be learned? What evidence must a student provide to document the learning? What recognized and authoritative standards will be used for judging this evidence?"

American higher education takes a different approach to quality and quality control. Some would say we take the easy way out. Quality is equated with the type and extent of resources provided for learning activities. Accordingly, we focus on the money expended per student, the size of the library collection, the academic degrees of faculty, and how much faculty are paid. The argument is that if these resources are provided, quality of learning can be reasonably anticipated. The guarantor is each faculty professional who establishes his or her own standards and makes individual judgments on student attainment.

Experiential education has also given relatively limited attention to standards of quality and means of quality control. When it has done so, it has followed the general pattern of American higher education in being concerned with resources which are judged to provide quality of learning activities — faculty time, payment to faculty sponsors, and staff support for experiential education offices.

While this approach to quality and quality control is standard in this country, it may not be the most effective for experiential education. We are the new kid on the block. As an innovation, particularly an innovation which proposes an alternative to the classroom lecture, experiential education must make the case for its quality on the basis of student learning. If this can be done, experiential education can have a relative advantage over the more traditional forms of teaching and learning which claim quality on the basis of longevity, i.e., it must be good because it has been done this way for eight centuries.

These stares ... point to a potentially effective strategy for experiential education in winning the mind, heart, and pocketbook of collegiate institutions.

Defining Quality of Learning for the College Level

*E*xperiential education programs provide an effective means for students to pursue several educational goals important to the student and to the greater society. If student achievement is to be the primary measure of program quality, and it should, it is necessary to identify a particular educational goal or set of goals for any experiential education program or course. In experiential education as in any other endeavor, if you don't know where you are going, any road will get you there.

There are eight particular goals which appear most often in the educational goals statements of all sorts of experiential education programs and courses. These eight common goals for students are:

1. To acquire, apply, integrate and evaluate a body of knowledge or the methodology of an academic discipline,

2. To develop competencies, both knowledge and skills, specific to an occupation, profession or organizational setting,

3. To understand different cultures and environments,

4. To acquire generic academic skills, e.g., analysis, synthesis, stating a problem,

5. To acquire generic living skills, e.g., oral communication, interpersonal interaction, coping with ambiguity, working in groups, goal setting, time management,

6. To acquire skills needed for effective citizenship,

7. To explore career options and acquire documented work experience in an occupation which requires college-level knowledge and skills, and

8. To develop and use an ethical perspective in a complex situation.

Also see Figure B in Chapter 2 for a more extensive list of goals for experiential learning.

"Come, give us a taste of your quality." This challenge to Hamlet is the challenge facing experiential education. The eight goals listed above are laudable. The question is whether they are being met. Faculty have little trouble documenting that the student had an experience, e.g., ten hours per week for a 15-week internship. There is much less evidence presented that it was a learning experience, and even less evidence of specifically what was learned, how much, and at what level.

When asked to document learning, faculty who sponsor experiential education often talk about the quality of the learning environment. A student working at IBM learned a lot because IBM is such a technological leader. Or the student who interned in the governor's office had a great learning experience because the statehouse is the seat of the government. If a faculty colleague responds that the student only operated the postage meter in the governor's mail room, the issue is clear. What did the student learn that deserves academic credit at the college level?

Experiential education needs to show evidence of student learning relative to the specific educational goals of the particular experiential program or course. It is not within the purview of this chapter to provide appropriate criteria for determining quality of learning for each of the eight educational goals listed above. Appropriate criteria are not that difficult to identify. For example, the student in the governor's office might be expected to describe the constitutional powers of the governor, the state's relationship with the federal government in two particular programs, and the primary policy issues in state economic development. Contact NSIEE for referrals to sound programs related to each goal.

It is not sufficient for students to demonstrate that they learned something. It is also necessary for them to demonstrate that the learning is at the college level. Collegiate institutions should only provide academic credit for college-level learning. While the definition of "college-level" is ultimately a matter for each institution's judgment, there are three general criteria for college-level learning listed below that may be helpful as you think about what is appropriate for your school:

1. College-level learning requires a conceptual as well as a practical grasp of the knowledge or skill.[1]

2. College-level learning requires that the learning be applicable outside the specific context in which it was required, i.e., is transferable.[2]

3. College-level learning requires evidence of the higher-level cognitive skills using a standard taxonomy such as Benjamin Bloom's *Taxonomy of Educational Objectives*.[3] For learning which combines the cognitive and affective domains, which is the case for experiential learning, Sydney Fine's taxonomy of skills is useful.[4] The dotted line below suggests a dividing line for college-level cognitive skills:

Data	People
Synthesizing	Mentoring
Coordinating	Negotiating
Analyzing	Instructing
Comparing	Supervising
	Persuading
--------	--------
Compiling	Speaking-Signaling
Computing	Serving
Copying	Taking instructions

"If you're serious about quality control in experiential learning, then you have to focus not on the experience, but on the learning. What you're trying to assure is that college level learning worthy of credit is taking place. Experience can be an instrumentality for learning, but by itself it's not learning. It may be valuable for a person to put on a resume, and it may do a lot of good things in terms of career exploration and so forth, but if there isn't learning taking place, it's not worthy of college credit."

-John Duley
   NSIEE Consultant and
      Professor Emeritus
   Michigan State University

For experiential education programs that focus on community service, Paul Dressel suggests that colleges determine the appropriateness of a particular service-learning experience for academic credit by evaluating the extent to which it (a) strengthens the idea of public service as a value worth passing on to succeeding generations, (b) contributes to the growth, self-development, maturity, and possible career development of the student, and (c) adds the breadth, depth, and integration upon which cognition depends.[5]

Principles of Good Practice

*F*rom experience, observation, and reflection, practitioners of experiential education are reaching some consensus on the issues that must be addressed in the practices which provide quality in experiential programs. From our experience in the NSIEE/FIPSE Project, we have come to believe that several particular principles are critical. Some of the most important issues are discussed below. We offer these to the field as guides deserving serious consideration by any institution, division, or department that utilizes experiential learning on any scale. Each institution must decide its own interpretation and standards for the issues raised here. The issues and principles are organized by the eight tasks required in the management of off-campus experiential education.

We offer these to the field as guides deserving serious consideration by any institution, division, or department that utilizes experiential learning on any scale.

TASK 1: ESTABLISHING GOALS FOR THE PROGRAM OR COURSE

• State the goals of the program or course in a document that has the official sanction of the institution or the sub-unit which sponsors the program.

• Be sure the goals reflect the interests of all three parties in experiential education — the educational institution, the student, and the organization where the student works. Experiential education can provide multiple benefits to these three parties. All outcomes are not of equal importance. Accordingly, the statement of program goals should specifically differentiate between primary and secondary goals for each party. Each of the three parties in the program should be aware of and agree to accept and support the primary goal(s) of the other two parties.

• Establish program goals that translate into measurable objectives. For example, you should be able to derive clear statements of student learning objectives from the educa-

tional goals of the program or course.

"Schools and departments should make conscious decisions about these issues. Sometimes there is a right or wrong answer, and sometimes there's not. If you just fall into program practices, though, you're not dealing with education, you're dealing with chance."

-Sharon Rubin
NSIEE Consultant and
Assistant Dean for
Undergraduate Studies
University of Maryland

Katherine Sirotti of Suffolk University works as a cooperative education student at the U.S. Department of Housing and Urban Development.

TASK 2: IDENTIFYING WORK OR SERVICE SITES FOR EXPERIENTIAL LEARNING

• Give students the primary responsibility for securing the positions for their experiential learning. Faculty, staff, alumni, community organizations, and parents all have natural circles of contacts that can assist students with this task.

• Establish criteria for determining the suitability of particular work or service positions for accomplishing the goals of the program.

• Be sure the organization provides a work supervisor who will help the student adapt to the work environment, direct the work, evaluate the work performance, and support the learning.

• Have an ongoing system for evaluating work positions and individual work supervisors.

• Have an institutional policy to favor paid work positions for students whenever pay can be arranged in work environments that have the potential for meeting the students' learning goals. Outdated policies that prevent students from being paid for their work if they are receiving college credit are discriminatory because they often preclude participation by low-income students. Credit is for what students learn; pay is for work they provide to the field sponsor. The two are neither mutually exclusive nor conflicting.

TASK 3: HELPING STUDENTS ESTABLISH APPROPRIATE EDUCATIONAL OBJECTIVES

• Develop a formal statement of the expected learning to be achieved by each individual student, how this learning is to be accomplished, and how it is to be assessed. Include a description of the work activities, the learning objectives, learning resources (readings, working professionals, faculty, seminars), the criteria to be used for assessing the learning, and the procedure for assessing the learning (who, when, how). The learning plan should include learning objectives consistent with both the goals of the program and the interests of the individual student.

• Establish a system to ensure that the student, faculty sponsor, and work supervisor all agree to this learning plan or contract.

• Have a procedure for making changes in the learning plan to accommodate changes in expectations by the student, the institution, and the host organization.

"The conditions under which particular learning is going to be demonstrated ought to be a part of the learning contract. If the skill to be learned is intake interviewing, for example, you might ask for tapes of two interviews that you could assess when the student gets back. You could then look at the extent to which he or she asked questions that opened up possibilities or questions for which there are only yes or no answers, or whatever criteria you tell that person will be applied to assess the performance when you listen to the tape."

　　-John Duley
　　 NSIEE Consultant
　　　and Professor Emeritus
　　 Michigan State University

TASK 4: RECRUITING, SELECTING, AND ESTABLISHING STUDENTS IN FIELD SITES

• Communicate the goals of the program, the benefits of program participation, the eligibility criteria, and the application procedures widely to all potential student participants.

• Limit the eligibility criteria to only those factors which relate directly to the student's potential for learning and to work performance, e.g., background knowledge, skills, aptitudes. Grade point average is typically not an appropriate work-related criterion.

• Arrange the application process to provide the student experience in securing regular employment — preparing a resume, arranging an employment interview, preparing for the interview, conducting the interview, and negotiating the conditions of employment.

• Develop a procedure to determine whether the student has the knowledge needed to meet the learning objectives and the minimum competence required for effective performance in the field position. Assessment is the key to successful student preparation.

• Establish with the field sponsor the legal conditions for the student's employment, e.g., medical insurance, worker's compensation, accident insurance, social security, liability protection. For information on the legal implications of experiential education, contact NSIEE.

• Require that the field sponsor name a specific supervisor for the student.

TASK 5: PREPARING STUDENTS FOR LEARNING AND WORKING

• Decide with the field sponsor who is responsible for preparing students for effective work and learning as well as how and when this preparation is to be done.

• Include in the prefield preparation information about the program, job-related skills and knowledge (both technical and generic), and an orientation to the work site, the work environment, and to self-directed learning.

"I don't think we recognize often enough the radical nature of the shift from classroom learning to being in charge of your own learning in the field placement. Students will

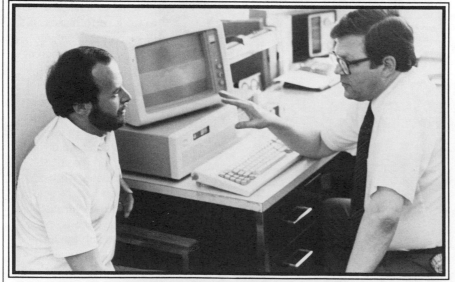

John Morabito, left, is a physically handicapped student who helped develop a computer program to track the needs of handicapped students at SUNY-Oswego. This experience led to a post-graduation position with the Office of Vocational Rehabilitation in Syracuse as a programmer and counselor.

continue to function in the dependency mode unless you somehow reorient them so that they know they're in charge."
    -John Duley
      NSIEE Consultant
        and Professor Emeritus
      Michigan State University

☞ TASK 6: MONITORING AND SUPPORTING THE LEARNING

• Design an intentional support system to assist students to learn from the experience. Without reflection, learning from direct experience cannot be assumed. The school has the primary responsibility for providing this support system. Useful avenues include seminars, telephone visits, written reports, journals, logs, simulation exercises, campus interviews, and work site visits. If possible, include some group activities in the learning support system, since a group process enhances reflection on experience.

"I think the [concurrent] seminars are the strongest thing we have going for us. They are solid, productive learning at its best."
    -H. C. Erik Midelfort
      Assistant Dean, College of
        Arts and Sciences, and
        Professor of History
      University of Virginia

"If I were concerned about observation and interpretation, I'd ask

students to use the left-hand page of the journal to write down their observations and the right-hand page to generate as many possible alternative interpretations for the meaning of that data as they can. They should clearly understand that they're not to interpret as they write their observations, that they need to separate these two processes. And so you've got a documentation of their level of skill in making the distinction. You don't know if what they write down as an observation is accurate or not, but you can tell whether or not they're separating the two processes. The supervisor can judge the accuracy of the observations, and you can judge their interpretation of the data."
    -John Duley

• Require ongoing evaluation of the learning and work performance as a necessary component of the learning support system. Performance appraisal can contribute to student motivation. Distance from the work site does not negate this principle. The problems of good faculty supervision of students at a distance have been confronted recently by Bradford College, Hartwick College, the University of Virginia, and the University of Colorado. Many schools use prefield preparation and debriefing as primary vehicles for conceptualization and analysis, but they also monitor the learning by phone and written communications.

• Clearly establish a policy and procedure whereby each party — student, institution, and organization — can address a complaint with another party.

• Build in enough variety in the components of the learning support system to accommodate the different learning styles of individual students.

"If you're specific about what's expected and the student doesn't do it, the problem may be that the placement doesn't provide the opportunity. That's why you've got to have monitoring throughout the process.

You may need to rewrite the learning contract because that site doesn't provide the opportunity to work on certain skills. That's why it is important to have formative assessment, or monitoring, during the process to make sure that the opportunities to acquire the learning that you and the supervisor and the student agreed upon are really there."
    -John Duley

☞ TASK 7: EVALUATING AND ASSESSING THE LEARNING ACHIEVED

• See the Appendix at the end of this chapter for an extensive statement of good practices in assessing experiential learning.

☞ TASK 8: REPORTING THE LEARNING (TRANSCRIPTS AND STUDENT RECORDS)

• Ensure that academic credits awarded for experiential learning have the same standing as those awarded for classroom-based learning.

• Use letter grades or other standard measures to be sure that the report of the learning achieved provides for different levels of achievement. Alternatives to letter grades such as pass-fail, satisfactory-unsatisfactory, should only be used if this alternative is also used as the standard way of reporting classroom-based learning.

• Include in the student's academic transcript at least a brief description of the experiential education activity, including the name of the organization, the work activities, and the time commitment. For example: "Internship with Central State Hospital, Petersburg, Virginia, as an occupational therapy aid for 120 hours." A copy of the learning contract, evaluations by all three parties (faculty, student, and supervisor), and any final product can also become part of the institutional file.

• If students typically develop placement files for permanent employment, they should be encouraged to include a description of the work activity and the supervisor's evaluation of the work performance.

In addition to these eight tasks related to the quality of students' learning, there are other principles of good practice that are particular to experiential programs that also have the goal of community service. In a classic article, Robert Sigmon summarizes these principles of good

service-learning as:

1. Those being served control the service(s) provided.

2. Those being served become better able to serve and be served by their own actions.

3. Those who serve also are learners and have significant control over what is expected to be learned.[6]

attention to be sure that the principles of good practice specified above are being maintained. At this level, the difficulty with quality control is not from a lack of good intentions. Faculty who provide experiential options to students are typically student-oriented. They want the best learning experiences possible for students. Instead, the difficulty is usually that they are not aware of what constitutes good practice. With the academic orientation toward education as content instead of process, these faculty proponents may not appreciate that experiential education is an eight-step, integrated process with each step interdependent and mutually supportive of the other seven.

Assuring Quality in Experiential Education

"It is ironic that experiential education — considered a suspect practice by many academicians until the last decade — is ahead of classroom teaching in proving its value for students' learning. But then innovations are usually held to a higher standard than traditional practices. This historical 'burden of proof' has put experiential education in a strong position as the public speaks out for greater accountability and more attention to students' learning."

-Jane Kendall
Executive Director
National Society for
Internships and
Experiential Education

Quality control has become the cry of American industry as the key to being competitive in the world economy. Quality control or quality assurance is also being touted as the way to improve the American system of education. Standards of competence for teachers are being established along with all kinds of techniques — from standardized examinations to continuing professional education — to try to assure this competence.

It is not enough to have quality. Quality also has to be maintained and guaranteed. In higher education, "quality assurance" is the collective term for institutional activities, policies, and procedures that provide a measure of confidence that what is done academically is consistent with the institution's goals and is likely to effect learning at levels established by the institution or by external bodies.

For the domain of experiential education, quality assurance might well be considered in terms of who monitors for quality, when this monitoring is done, and how it is accomplished. You have to look at quality assurance at three levels: (1) the individual faculty members, (2) the department, and (3) the institution as a whole. Following is a discussion of each of these levels:

1. As in any educational endeavor, the first line of quality assurance in experiential education is the individual faculty professional. Quality assurance at this level involves ongoing

At this initial level of quality assurance, the task is simply that of communicating what constitutes good practice. This can be done in a variety of ways. Informal faculty discussion groups about quality can provide opportunities to share common experiences regarding experiential education. Some institutions maintain small libraries of literature in the field, provide subscriptions to publications through memberships in professional associations, and make

This historical 'burden of proof' has put experiential education in a strong position as the public speaks out for greater accountability and more attention to students' learning.

-Jane Kendall, Executive Director
National Society for Internships and Experiential Education

A SOAPBOX PLATFORM

"Standards: What They Mean and What They Don't"

by Sharon Rubin
Assistant Dean for
  Undergraduate Studies
University of Maryland

"*In my own institution and in my role as an NSIEE consultant to other schools, I have found a bewildering assortment of requirements for students who wish to participate in internships and other field experience programs. They range from grade-point average and credit level to prefield preparation. When faculty and coordinators discuss these requirements, their usual rationale is that such requirements maintain standards. Let's consider some of these requirements and analyze what standards they are actually maintaining.*

(1) Application to the program — Most programs are not do-it-yourself. They may require students to fill out an application (more or less onerous), to submit to an interview, to document appropriate background, or to conform to the coordinator's expectations for dress and behavior.

While it is certainly useful and responsible to counsel students as they begin to engage in the process of finding an internship or other type of field experience, we always have to ask ourselves whether the real reason we set up some parts of this process is to encourage dependence on the part of the students. Then we are needed to be the wise parents and to assert our own control over students and site supervisors alike.

(2) Major — Many internship programs are run by departments which specify that the opportunities are restricted to their own majors. The rationale is that those internships are directly related to the discipline and that the faculty's expertise is therefore specialized and only accessible to students of a particular background.

While in some cases this may indeed be true, in many cases students with comparable backgrounds and different majors may be equally competent, and faculty may be more accessible than expected. Is the real reason for the requirements a feeling that the department is not there to serve the whole university but should take care of "its own" first and last?

(3) Required courses — A related requirement is that students must complete some basic coursework in a department before they are eligible to participate in internships or other off-campus learning experiences. Although specific background in a discipline seems reasonable, one must ask about the specific relationship between the coursework and preparation for the internship. Will an "Introduction to Sociology" course truly prepare the student to behave as both a participant and reflective observer in an organization? Maybe yes, maybe no.

(4) Credit level — Many programs restrict experiential education to juniors or seniors on the assumption that their maturity or competence will be more assured. Although debates about President Reagan's age remind us that chronological age is not necessarily related to competence, the developmental literature seems to support the notion that seniors are different from freshmen. Still, that provokes more questions than it answers. Can we be sure that the kind of internship experience we are planning is appropriate for the developmental stage of the participant, or are we merely making the numbers of applicants more manageable? What about mature adults who are freshmen?

(5) G.P.A. — Probably the most popular restricting qualification for students is the Grade Point Average. When I talk with experiential educators, they often tell me that a good G.P.A. will assure that students will not "embarrass" the program, department, or institution. Yet the data that relates G.P.A. to competence and accomplishment after college does not support this assumption. There doesn't even seem to be data that proves that 2.3 G.P.A. students tend to embarrass institutions more than 3.5 G.P.A. students. In fact, some of the newest research on high school students suggests that experiential learning can significantly improve the retention and academic performance of marginal students.[7] And of course, we all have lots of anecdotes about the quite ordinary student who was transformed by an internship experience.

If G.P.A. is not related to accomplishment, to what is it related? To gatekeeping — an elite program has more academic respectability than an open-door program. In addition, faculty may feel that the best students won't be harmed — or corrupted — too much by a brush with the real world; if they are wasting time, at least they can afford it more than other students.

Is there any requirement that I would justify? Well, there is one I'll approve — prefield preparation. If the goal is to have program participation by well-trained, well-motivated students who understand the relationship between theory and practice, who have gained reflective observation skills, who have a grounding in professional ethics, and who have a commitment to excellence, prefield preparation is a requirement that really makes sense. Not every program has the funds for, or is set up administratively to be able to offer prefield preparation. But if it does not, a more laissez-faire attitude than we now take about requirements may be indicated. Standards are very much in the eye of the beholder, and we must learn to be honest about them."

-Reprinted from
EXPERIENTIAL EDUCATION
(NSIEE Newsletter)
March-April 1985

available opportunities for faculty to attend meetings of these professional groups. For more ideas, see the last section of the chapter in this sourcebook on faculty involvement in experiential education. Many colleges and universities are looking at experiential education as an important area of faculty development. Institutions of all types are bringing experienced professionals in this field to campuses to share their knowledge and provide information about other schools' models.

2. The second level of quality assurance is the basic academic unit of the institution, typically the academic department. In small institutions the basic unit may be the academic division (e.g., science and mathematics) or even the entire college. The concern at this level is the control exercised by the community of scholars for the integrity of the curriculum and the academic program. What are the educational goals of the experiential programs and courses? Where do they fit in terms of sequence? What are the prerequisites? What are the learning outcomes? What academic offerings can be built

on these outcomes? What academic offerings support the experiential programs? For these concerns of the academic unit, quality assurance is provided in two different ways:

(a) The course approval process. To provide a new academic offering, the department must be able to certify to the community of faculty that the activity can provide quality learning and is integrated with other curricular offerings. The complexity and length of this certification process can vary greatly by institution. If the academic unit approves the new offering through its governance structure, it will likely be approved at other points in the institution's course review process. Accordingly, it is important that academic departments formally consider and establish standards for all their experiential offerings. The statements earlier in this chapter about the practices which provide quality in experiential education might well serve as a beginning point for this task.

(b) The academic review. This is typically a much less formal activity. Faculty usually just report to their peers on their teaching efforts and accomplishments. For these reports, faculty with experiential courses

Many colleges and universities are looking at experiential education as an important area of faculty development.

should be expected to document student learning for the educational goals established for the course. As with more traditional courses, this need not be an exercise in educational research requiring sophisticated statistical methods. It is sufficient to report that students achieved the course's educational goals and to give evidence of this learning for individual students.

"Our first step has been to establish procedures in our own program which enhance learning and require accountability. Requirements include the keeping of journals and logs, the formulation of learning objectives, self-evaluation and an integrative class. We have now begun to talk with other faculty members on campus to share our approach and to incorporate their suggestions and ideas. The results so far are (1) a meeting including all faculty members and administrators involved in experiential education, and (2) a goal of establishing a committee advisory to the Academic Senate and the Academic Dean to attain some unanimity in our approach to experiential education and to provide a forum for sharing and discussing critical issues."
-Rose Marie Springer
Associate Director
Westmont Urban Program
Westmont College,
California

3. The third level for quality assurance in experiential education is the institution itself. Any institution with integrity should have an ongoing concern for any and all educational endeavors pursued in its name. Schools typically heed this responsibility in two ways: (a) internal procedures for the approval of new courses and program

Rose Marie Springer, Associate Director of Westmont College's Urban Program in San Francisco, has helped her college focus attention on its approach to quality and accountability in experiential education.

offerings, usually determined by a curriculum committee, and (b) relationships with external accrediting bodies for the review of all educational activities.

Colleges and universities are just beginning to pay attention to quality assurance in experiential education on an institutional level, usually through faculty committees focused specifically on experiential education. Such committees can have different levels of authority. In most institutions, they are advisory committees for a campus-wide program such as cooperative education or ad hoc committees appointed by academic administrators to develop and review policies for experiential education. These committees can be of great value in institutional quality assurance if they are given enough authority and status. If the experiential education committee is a standing subcommittee of the curriculum and instruction committee, it can establish at least minimum standards for approval of new courses with experiential components and require as a condition of institutional approval that petitioners show how these standards will be met.

Examples of strong faculty committees for experiential education are those at Hartwick College in Oneonta, New York; Adrian College in Adrian, Michigan; Guilford College in Greensboro, North Carolina; and the University of Colorado in Boulder. Westmont College in California and the College of Arts and Sciences at the University of Colorado are good examples of schools that moved recently from individual departmental standards to a broader, college-wide committee to set standards of quality for experiential education. See the chapter of this

It is important that academic departments formally consider and establish standards for all their experiential offerings.

Ann Stone, a student from Vanderbilt University's Center for Health Services, helps children with a preventive health program.

sourcebook entitled "Increasing Faculty Involvement in Experiential Education" for good ideas for establishing a faculty committee.

"Whether it's a curriculum committee, educational policy committee, or an advisory committee for internships, somebody has to be the watchdog, the monitor, and the support system to award kudos to the faculty engaged in it as well as to jack them up a bit."
    -John Duley
     NSIEE Consultant
       and Professor Emeritus
       Michigan State University

External accrediting bodies usually review formally only the experiential learning offered through the professional programs which emphasize practical application, such as nursing, social work, public administration, and teaching. However, accrediting agencies do ask for information about innovative, alternative, and special programs related to instructional improvements. This presents an opportunity to provide information on experiential education at your institution. Nevertheless, accredi-

tation of the total institution by the regional accrediting associations still focuses primarily on resources for instruction, not on the process or the results of instruction. There is a star on the horizon which can be beneficial for experiential education, however. The regional associations are now being challenged to include outcomes, particularly outcomes which focus on a broad set of student competencies. For example, at a conference of the Council on Postsecondary Accreditation, Howard Bowen suggested seven principles for reviewing outcomes.[8] Three of these principles point to a bright future for institutional recognition of experiential education:

a. The study of outcomes should avoid the common confusion of inputs and outcomes .... The only valid tests of outcomes are: What happens in the development of persons? How do persons change and grow as a result of their college experience?

b. Assessment should be linked to all the major goals of education and not be confined just to aspects of human development that can be easily measured or that are related to economic success.

c. Educational outcomes should relate to the development of whole persons .... Colleges should accept individual differences among their students and encourage their students to develop individually along lines consistent with their unique interests and talents. For any individual, such development inevitably means substantial progress along some lines, no change along others, and regression along still others.

Howard Bowen's three-point charge to the accrediting bodies of American higher education constitutes a challenge to the experiential education community as well. As experiential educators, we have placed the student at the center of our attention. More than most of those in higher education, we have recognized students' differences and promoted experiential learning as a way to accommodate these differences. The challenge we now face is to attend to Bowen's first charge. Student learning is the heart of the matter. What is the quality of this learning? How can this learning be enhanced by the ways we administer our programs and courses? What procedures and criteria will we use so we can be confident of this learning? When we have attended to these questions, we are answering the question of quality and quality control. Bowen is right — neither the questions nor the answers are easy. However, unless we speak effectively to the questions of quality and quality control, our concern for students will make only a limited contribution to their development.

In all of the recent commission reports about issues and reforms in higher education, the focus has been on quality. Both the general public and the academic community are increasingly aware of this trend. Experiential education is very much a part of this national movement, and we can respond convincingly to the calls both for better quality assurance and for more active forms of involvement in learning as an integral part of an excellent education. ▫

FOOTNOTES

[1] Warren Willingham, *Principles of Good Practice in Assessing Experiential Learning*, Educational Testing Service, Princeton, New Jersey, 1977, p. 12.

[2] *Ibid*.

[3] Benjamin Bloom, *Taxonomy of Educational Objectives*, D. McKay Company, New York, 1956.

[4] Sydney Fine's taxonomy is used in the *Dictionary of Occupational Titles*, U.S. Department of Labor, and in the *Handbook for Analyzing Jobs*, U.S. Government Printing Office, Washington, D.C., 1972, p. 5.

[5] Paul Dressel, *College and University Curriculum*, McCutchan Publishing Corporation, Berkeley, California, 1971.

[6] Robert Sigmon, "Service-Learning: Three Principles," *Synergist*, National Center for Service-Learning, Vol. 8, No. 1, Spring 1979, p. 10.

[7] Gary Wehlage, Calvin Stone, Nancy Lesko, Craig Newman, and Reba Page, *Effective Programs for the Marginal High School Student*, Wisconsin Center for Educational Research, Madison, Wisconsin, 1982.

[8] Howard Bowen, "Evaluating Educational Quality: A Conference Summary," Annual Conference of the Council on Postsecondary Accreditation, Washington, D.C., 1979.

CHAPTER APPENDIX

Quality in Assessing Experiential Learning

The Council for Adult and Experiential Learning (CAEL), from its perspective that acceptance of experiential education in higher education hinges on the condition of quality assessment, has developed and published *Principles of Good Practice in Assessing Experiential Learning*. This statement of principles has been accepted as the standard for the field by the Council on Postsecondary Accreditation (COPA), the American Association of Collegiate Registrars and Admission Officers, and the Commission on Educational Credit of the American Council on Education. With the endorsement of these principles by the higher education establishment, any experiential education program which abides by these standards can be confident of the quality of its assessment practices. The *Principles* include over 100 statements and extensive commentary on each. The twenty selected statements listed below deserve particular attention:

1. Students should be required to differentiate clearly between learning and experience. College credit is not appropriate for an experience.

2. Prior to the experience itself, students should develop a learning plan that specifies the principle tasks to be performed, learning objectives, how learning objectives will be pursued, and the evidence required to document the learning.

3. Clarity and specificity in describing learning objectives should not be achieved at the expense of relegating learning objectives to trivial skills.

4. There should be formative evaluation of learning. Students should be encouraged to negotiate new learning objectives if their experiences so indicate.

5. Care should be taken to discriminate whether particular documentation describes experience, describes learning, or provides evidence of learning.

6. Assessment of experiential learning should employ measurement methods that fit the character of the learning.

7. In measuring an individual's learning, assessors should use techniques that are appropriate to the background and characteristics of the learner, e.g., learning style.

8. Assessment itself should be a useful learning experience.

9. Institutions are responsible to see that assessment is as reliable

(consistent) as possible to ensure fairness to students.

10. To improve consistency in assessment, more than one sample of learning should be examined, and more than one assessor should be used unless evidence indicates that one is sufficient.

11. Assessors should seek different forms of evidence of learning and use more than one type of assessment.

12. Self-assessment is often very desirable as a means of enhancing personal development and awareness of the implication of acquired skills.

13. Self-assessment is ordinarily not a sufficient basis for granting academic credit.

14. It is highly desirable to assess learning with reference to criterion standards of what the individual should be able to do. In the phrase "criterion standards," "criterion" refers to the content or nature of the performance or knowledge indicated, and "standards" refers to the depth or level of competence expected.

15. In defining criterion standards, the content or nature of the learning or competence should be stated as clearly as possible through the use of references and examples. Useful ways to clarify the content aspects of criterion standards

include references to particular fields and bodies of knowledge, familiar roles or jobs, particular functions the individual can perform, equipment she can operate, and products he can make.

16. In defining standards, several levels of competence should be stated through the use of references and examples.

17. Standards for crediting experiential learning should be the same as or comparable to standards for crediting more traditional forms of learning. Neither should be more or less difficult to attain.

18. It is important to clarify criterion standards before the fact so that students know what is expected and the learning is guided accordingly.

19. Academic credit for experiential learning should be awarded only on the basis of a determination that the student has achieved the learning objectives agreed upon or has achieved alternate learning outcomes clearly satisfactory to the student and the assessor.

20. All standards for awarding credit should be rigorous and reasonable in relation to the goals and character of the institution and the nature of its students.

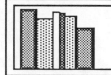

RECOMMENDED RESOURCES

Keeton, Morris T., Editor, *Defining and Assuring Quality in Experiential Learning*, New Directions for Experiential Learning, No. 9, Jossey-Bass, San Francisco, California, 1980. The primary focus of this book is the learning that an individual acquires through experience before matriculating in college. However, Keeton's chapter, "Defining and Assuring Quality: A Framework of Questions," and the chapter by Edwin Kurtz, "A Key to Quality Assurance: Clarifying Learning Outcomes," are particularly useful for experiential education programs provided by colleges for currently enrolled students. The titles are accurate descriptions of the two chapters.

Sigmon, Robert L., "Service-Learning: Three Principles," *Synergist*, National Center for Service-Learning, Vol. 8, No. 1, Spring 1979, pages 9-11. Available from the National Society for Internships and Experiential Education, 122 St. Mary's Street, Raleigh, NC, 27605. An excellent presentation of the principles important for quality in programs that emphasize both learning and community service.

Willingham, Warren, *Principles of Good Practice in Assessing Experiential Learning*, Council for Adult and Experiential Learning (CAEL), Columbia, Maryland, 1977. A statement of standards for assessing experiential learning. Standards for good practices in the other seven tasks (as outlined in this chapter) are also included since quality assessment cannot be done in isolation from other tasks.

For materials or assistance concerning the design of a quality program for experiential education — or the improvement of an existing program — contact the National Society for Internships and Experiential Education, 122 St. Mary's Street, Raleigh, North Carolina, 27605. NSIEE offers resource papers, a national talent bank of faculty and administrators experienced with effective programs and courses, technical assistance materials, publications, and conferences and workshops.

5

Establishing Administrative Structures that Fit the Goals of Experiential Education

*"**P**art of the complexity of where experiential education fits administratively on college and university campuses comes from the unique nature of experiential education. It does not follow any existing structure. Its functions cut across any departmental lines or organizational charts that are found on campuses. So it's really a function that requires alliances regardless of the structure. Of the pilot schools in the NSIEE-FIPSE* *Project, those that have made the most progress have been those that have been the most willing to step outside the traditional ways of looking at organizational charts. The people for whom that is not a problem seem to be the most effective."*

-Jane Kendall
Executive Director
National Society for
Intenships and Experiential
Education

The Dilemma and the Challenge

*D*uring a 1985 conference for the NSIEE-FIPSE pilot schools, representatives of eight different institutions came to a workshop on "Establishing Administrative Structures that Fit the Goals of Experiential Education." At the eight schools, the administrative responsibilities for experiential education are housed in six different types of campus units, and the directors report to six different types of administrators.

And all of the representatives feel that their structures are fairly effective. Even for institutions very similar in size and focus, there is certainly no single magic formula that works for administering experiential education.

Experiential education definitely provides multiple benefits to different units of the institution. For academic affairs, experiential education serves as a powerful instructional tool, a learning source complementing the faculty and the library, and a way to keep the curriculum and faculty in touch with the world beyond the campus. For student affairs, experiential education serves as a tool for career development and community service. Institutionally, it is a means of fostering the town-and-gown relationship, showcasing the institution, serving the larger society, and

making contacts for research and fundraising.

The administration of experiential education involves tasks which also cut across established departments and offices. First, there are developmental tasks such as advocacy, research, development of possible new courses and programs, and general leadership in experiential education on and off campus. These tasks belong in deans' or vice presidents' offices for both academic and student affairs, depending on the specific goals of experiential education. One common characteristic of these tasks is that they are typically performed by administrators rather than faculty. There are exceptions, however, especially in smaller schools.

Then there are coordinating tasks, such as reporting and communicating across courses and programs, coordinating the school's relationships with field work sponsors, networking of all people involved, and ensuring quality control. Where do these tasks belong? Again, they can be in student or academic affairs, but perhaps better in both. What about the faculty? Are these strictly staff functions, or should the faculty be involved when it comes to questions

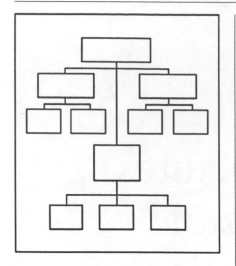

of standards? How should the academic departments be involved?

Finally, there are tasks related to the actual offering of experiential education to students — recruiting, selecting, and monitoring students; developing placements; evaluating the learning; and so on. Whose tasks are these, and should they be under the same pattern of supervision as the other two sets of tasks? How should these three sets of tasks be related? Do they need to be related?

The inability of traditional campus structures to deal with these questions has been reflected at most of the pilot schools in the NSIEE-FIPSE Project. For example:

"While expansion of internships has been a written priority for the College for several years, the administrative mechanisms to implement this priority have not been adequately developed. No one office, individual, or committee has the obvious responsibility, and none has been given a clear mandate and allocated the necessary resources."

-Jim Case, Director
Career Planning and
Placement
College of Wooster
Wooster, Ohio

Further, experiential education as an "entity" has yet to achieve a recognized status in the academic community of most campuses so that it can command a place for itself in the structure. Programs often begin in career development because of the

obvious career link. Sometimes they begin in student activities as part of community service. But as experiential education progresses, the academic values become more visible, desirable, and accepted. Yet, it has been difficult for such programs to straddle the line between academic and student affairs. The cultures of most campus communities still separate student and academic affairs as distinct entities with little common ground. Persons involved in experiential education are often expected to make a choice — be in one or the other, but not both. To "fit" into one or the other by necessity then changes the relative importance of various goals of the program, limiting the value of the program to other units on campus and to the institution as a whole.

"Many people feel that it belongs in career development. Many people in career planning and placement do not know how to 'get there' in terms of academic incorporation. Many are very threatened by the idea of academic integration because this is so different from their own backgrounds and experiences. The administrator of the program is often the very one who has a hard time seeing how the academic part would work. Some realize that they need to be part of the academics because they want a safe,

permanent place — but they may have trouble articulating the educational value."

-John Duley
Professor Emeritus
Michigan State
University

Guilford College resolved the "Student Affairs-Academic Affairs" dilemma by breaking out of the notion that student and academic affairs are distinct and separate:

"Student enrollment in internships has almost tripled since 1981. Faculty sponsors have found themselves less than well equipped for the supervision task and frustrated over the increasing student demand for sponsorship. The barriers were primarily in the awkward situation posed by the fact that direction of the internship program lay in Student Development, and the plethora of issues which needed processing lay in academic affairs. The barriers were overcome ensuing a peer consultant visit which effected greater collaboration between the Academic Dean and the Director of Experiential Learning."

-Jim Keith, Director
Experiential Learning
Guilford College
Greensboro, North
Carolina

Jim Case, right, Director of Career Planning and Placement at the College of Wooster, outlines ideas for administrative structures with Ken Plusquellec, Dean of Students.

Some Principles

While there is no simple solution to experiential education finding an administrative home on college and university campuses, it must and it can. There are some general principles which you can apply in assessing the current administrative status of your program or course and determining whether a new administrative home seems wise:

1. The dominant goals of the experiential program must be compatible with and included in the goals of the administrative unit where the program is placed. If academic learning is the goal of the program, for example, it should be housed in Academic Affairs rather than Student Affairs.

2. Experiential education needs to be among the top priorities and valued by the administrative unit in which it is placed.

3. The administrative unit must enable the program to meet its multi-

---

Check your perceptions with all the people involved.

---

ple goals and perform its varied tasks through collaborative arrangements with other administrative and instructional units on campus and in the community.

"Where the staff perceives its useful and active alliances is more important than whether it is in Student Affairs or Academic Affairs. No program should use its place in the organizational chart as an excuse for limited alliances."
    -Sharon Rubin
    Assistant Dean
    Undergraduate Studies
    University of Maryland

4. The administrative unit must have a status within the institution that facilitates, not jeopardizes, the advocacy and development of experiential education throughout the campus.

Rebecca Dixon, left, Assistant Professor of Business Administration at Otterbein College, and Marlene Steiner Suter, Director of College Planning, struggle with the formal and informal patterns for decision-making at their institution.

Assessing Your Current Administrative Structure

Using the principles just noted, list (in order of importance) the goals of experiential education on your campus. In this case, focus on your existing program(s).

The "Inventory of Experiential Programs and Courses" in Chapter 2 of this sourcebook can help you outline how the experiential offerings on your campus are organized. Then list the goals of the administrative unit in which the program is located, again in order of importance for the unit. Be sure the top person in the administrative unit reviews both lists. Go to the key people responsible whenever you are listing goals. Do not stop with what is in the catalog or in program publicity. Check your perceptions with all the people involved.

Now compare the two lists. Are they compatible? Is experiential education listed anywhere on the goal list of the administrative unit, either as a product or as a means to fulfilling one or more of its goals?

Where are these on the list? On top or at the bottom? Do any of the program's top priorities appear on the administrative unit's goal list, and where? Answers to these questions give some indication of how the first two principles apply to the particular set of circumstances at your institution.

To determine if the current administrative structure lends itself to performing all the necessary tasks, there are several important questions to ask. First, are all the critical tasks being done? Is it clear who is responsible for each task? Are all the people responsible held accountable for their functions? Are the personnel resources and operating budget adequate for each function? Complete the three charts below to indicate the degree of clarity for who is responsible for each function and the adequacy of resources for each. Add other functions that may be important because of the particular goals of your experiential offerings.

"The dominant goals of the experiential program must be compatible with and included in the goals of the administrative unit where the program is placed."

Assessing Your Institution's Administrative Model: Part 1

*P*ut an "X" on each line below to indicate the extent to which each of the following responsibilities related to experiential education is clearly assigned in your institution:

It is unclear who is responsible for this task regarding experiential education.

It is very clear who is responsible for this task regarding experiential education.

a. Advocating experiential learning among faculty, students, and administrators (making the case for experiential education within the institution).

<-->

b. Establishing communication mechanisms for faculty to exchange ideas and techniques with colleagues in other departments and other institutions.

<-->

c. Providing administrative support to the faculty and, if applicable, to the faculty committee on experiential education.

<-->

d. Soliciting input for and making decisions about campus-wide policies.

<-->

e. Establishing quality controls.

<-->

f. Monitoring the quality.

<-->

g. Coordinating the institution's outreach to field supervisors for experiential education.

<-->

h. Reporting on campus-wide trends and needs regarding experiential education.

<-->

i. Conducting research regarding experiential education.

<-->

j. Keeping abreast of the professional literature and other developments in experiential education regionally and nationally.

<-->

From *Strengthening Experiential Education in Your Institution*, National Society for Internships and Experiential Education, Raleigh, North Carolina, 1986

It is unclear who is responsible for this task regarding experiential education.

It is very clear who is reponsible for this task regarding experiential educarion.

k. Arranging professional development opportunities regarding experiential education for faculty and staff.

<-->

l. Representing the institution's experiential education programs outside the institution.

<-->

m. Securing funds for regular program operations.

<-->

n. Securing funds for special projects, research, and development regarding experiential education.

<-->

o. Handling each of the parts of the learning process and the actual program(s) or course(s):

(1) establishing goals for each program or course

<-->

(2) identifying sites for experiential learning

<-->

(3) helping students establish appropriate learning objectives

<-->

(4) recruiting, selecting, and establishing students at field sites

<-->

(5) preparing students for learning and working

<-->

(6) monitoring and supporting the learning

<-->

(7) evaluating and assessing the learning

<-->

(8) reporting the learning (transcripts and student records).

<-->

p. Other, specify:_____
    _____

<-->

From *Strengthening Experiential Education in Your Institution*, National Society for Internships and Experiential Education, Raleigh, North Carolina, 1986

Assessing Your Institution's Administrative Model: Part 2

*P*ut an "X" on each line below to indicate the adequacy of the resources currently provided for each of the following tasks related to experiential education at your institution:

	The resources provided for this function are not adequate to do it well	The resources provided for this function are adequate to do it well
a. Advocating experiential learning among faculty, students, and administrators (making the case for experiential education within the institution).	<-->	
b. Establishing communication mechanisms for faculty to exchange ideas and techniques with colleagues in other departments and other institutions.	<-->	
c. Providing administrative support to the faculty and, if applicable, to the faculty committee on experiential education.	<-->	
d. Soliciting input for and making decisions about campus-wide policies.	<-->	
e. Establishing quality controls.	<-->	
f. Monitoring the quality.	<-->	
g. Coordinating the institution's outreach to field supervisors for experiential education.	<-->	
h. Reporting on campus-wide trends and needs regarding experiential education.	<-->	
i. Conducting research regarding experiential education.	<-->	
j. Keeping abreast of the professional literature and other developments in experiential education regionally and nationally.	<-->	

		The resources provided for this function are not adequate to do it well	The resources provided for this function are adequate to do it well

k. Arranging professional development opportunities regarding experiential education for faculty and staff.

<--->

l. Representing the institution's experiential education programs outside the institution.

<--->

m. Securing funds for regular program operations.

<--->

n. Securing funds for special projects, research, and development regarding experiential education.

<--->

o. Handling each of the parts of the learning process and the actual program(s) or course(s):

(1) establishing goals for each program or course

<--->

(2) identifying sites for experiential learning

<--->

(3) helping students establish appropriate learning objectives

<--->

(4) recruiting, selecting, and establishing students at field sites

<--->

(5) preparing students for learning and working

<--->

(6) monitoring and supporting the learning

<--->

(7) evaluating and assessing the learning

<--->

(8) reporting the learning (transcripts and student records).

<--->

p. Other, specify:_____

<--->
_____

From *Strengthening Experiential Education in Your Institution*, National Society for Internships and Experiential Education, Raleigh, North Carolina, 1986

Responsibilities for Primary Functions of Experiential Education within Your Institution

List the names of the person(s) or group(s) responsible for each of the tasks below. Be as specific as possible. Use extra sheets for clarification if needed.

	Who is responsible for this function in your institution?	Who is responsible for evaluation and long-range planning regarding this function?	Who are the collaborators or other parties with supportive responsibilities related to this function?
a. Advocating experiential learning among faculty, students, and administrators (making the case for experiential education within the institution).			
b. Establishing communication mechanisms for faculty to exchange ideas and techniques with colleagues in other departments and other institutions.			
c. Providing administrative support to the faculty and, if applicable, to the faculty committee on experiential education.			
d. Soliciting input for and making decisions about campus-wide policies.			
e. Establishing quality controls.			
f. Monitoring the quality.			
g. Coordinating the institution's outreach to field supervisors for experiential education.			
h. Reporting on campus-wide trends and needs regarding experiential education.			
i. Conducting research regarding experiential education.			
j. Keeping abreast of the professional literature and other developments in experiential education regionally and nationally.			

From *Strengthening Experiential Education in Your Institution*, National Society for Internships and Experiential Education, Raleigh, North Carolina, 1986

	Who is responsible for this function in your institution?	Who is responsible for evaluation and long-range planning regarding this function?	Who are the collaborators or other parties with supportive responsibilities related to this function?
k. Arranging professional development opportunities regarding experiential education for faculty and staff.			
l. Representing the institution's experiential education programs outside the institution.			
m. Securing funds for regular program operations.			
n. Securing funds for special projects, research, and development regarding experiential education.			
o. Handling each of the parts of the learning process and the actual program(s) or course(s):			
(1) establishing goals for each program or course			
(2) identifying sites for experiential learning			
(3) helping students establish appropriate learning objectives			
(4) recruiting, selecting, and establishing students at field sites			
(5) preparing students for learning and working			
(6) monitoring and supporting the learning			
(7) evaluating and assessing the learning			
(8) reporting the learning (transcripts and student records).			
p. Other, specify:_____			

From *Strengthening Experiential Education in Your Institution*, National Society for Internships and Experiential Education, Raleigh, North Carolina, 1986

Then ask at least two other key persons — the academic dean, a faculty leader, an experiential education director, or others whose perspectives are important to get a complete picture — to fill in the charts also. Where do your responses differ? Is more clarity needed on who is responsible for what? Are there some important tasks that no one is doing? Are there some tasks that need more resources? Are there too many actors or too many resources for any of the functions?

Another important assessment step is to determine if the program staff has access to selected information and contacts on campus on a regular basis. These are people whose thoughts and work may have direct effects on experiential programs and courses.

The following list can help you decide if the communication patterns on your campus are as developed as they should be:

> **Do the program and its director have access to the people responsible for the following functions?**
>
> 1. overall curricular concerns
> 2. academic departmental matters
> 3. faculty welfare
> 4. instructional development and evaluation
> 5. student transcripts
> 6. career development and placement
> 7. community service programs
> 8. student counseling and academic advisement
> 9. financial aid and student employment
> 10. institutional planning and research
> 11. admissions
> 12. alumni affairs
> 13. public relations
> 14. development

This is simply a list of possible campus competitors or collaborators, depending on the relationship the program can foster with them. A lack of easy access, formal or informal, to any of these individuals substantially hinders the operation of experiential programs and courses.

"If you have one program on campus using its resources to compete with another program on the same campus, then you've got some work to do at the upper level of decision-making. Not many institutions can afford this duplication, but I see it happen all the time."
-Jane Kendall
Executive Director
National Society for
Internships and
Experiential Education

Access is critical, but respect, influence and credibility with the entities listed above are equally important. Assessing the extent of these qualities is frequently a subjective process, but there are a few indicators you can use:

1. Are the experiential education program personnel able to relate to these other campus units in the latter's framework and language? Is there a full understanding of their goals, concerns and operating styles?

2. Is the program's administrative unit able to create or provide win-win situations with these units in such a way that all units involved benefit in some fashion?

3. Do the other units consult the experiential education program personnel regarding matters which may affect the program or for expertise on improving their own activities in ways that would support the program's goals?

Also see the questions in "Assessing the Value of the Experiential Educator to the Institution or Department" in Chapter 1 for other indicators of respect and influence. Affirmative responses to these questions are obviously positive indicators of the program's standing among "significant others." Increasing the program's capability in any of these areas strengthens its credibility even more.

There is another set of controlling factors in determining influence, respect and credibility which is based on the "social norms" of higher education as an institution and on the particular environment of the school. Here are some examples of common social norms in relationship to influence and status:

-Academic Affairs has higher status than Student Affairs.
-The administration has more say about resource allocation than faculty do.
-The faculty is more powerful on curricular matters.
-Continuing education is often peripheral to the mission of the institution.
-Traditional liberal arts disciplines are viewed as more academic and scholarly than professional fields of study.

These norms are changing and certainly have varying degrees of influence on different campuses. They nevertheless operate in some fashion on almost all campuses. The placement of the experiential education program in one sector as opposed to another does affect its status in the campus community. Are these social factors affecting your program in a positive way?

Four Basic Institutional Models for Experiential Education

*T*here are four basic administrative models used in the administration of experiential programs — a decentralized model, two types of centralized models, and a model with centralized coordination and decentralized control. Each model has some built-in advantages and disadvantages, and there can be an overlap of two or more models within one institution. But the overall effectiveness of any of the models depends on the program's goals and its placement in the overall administrative structure based on the principles noted earlier. Provided here is a list of some of the advantages and disadvantages for each of the four administrative models. Use this to analyze your current model and to imagine other approaches that could be used.

The Pros and Cons of Four Administrative Models

Model 1:

Decentralized management via academic departments for experiential programs and courses with academic credits

ADVANTAGES

-Enhances quality control unique to the concern of each department if the faculty are familiar with standards of good practice;

-Can ensure academic credibility and provide better integration of experiential learning into the major curriculum of each department;

-Consistent with the prevailing institutional pattern for allocating resources for instruction and for recognition of faculty work load;

-Can be favorable to overall program development and expansion since there are more actors involved.

DISADVANTAGES

-Difficult to accommodate student interests or institutional goals other than those related to credit programs in the academic major (i.e., often does not pay attention to other types of learning that can occur);

-Makes it difficult to bring an institutional focus and attention to experiential learning, including institutional quality controls;

-Inefficient in performing some common tasks, such as policy development and the identification and maintenance of worksite opportunities;

-Can be frustrating and present a disorganized picture to area field work sponsors who are contacted by multiple departments;

-Can decrease the overall availability of experiential education if many departments are slow to take the initiative to offer it.

"While it is beneficial for there to be as many different opportunities for students to engage in experiential learning as possible, and while the presence of more than one program does split the large amount of work among several people, your college is really too small a school (2,500 students) for multiple policies. It is expected that a 38,000-student university with a very heterogeneous student population and very large departments would have a range of policies for student participation in internships or cooperative education, but students at a small college see multiple policies as at best exasperating and at worst unjust."
-Sharon Rubin
 Consulting report to
 a small college

From *Strengthening Experiential Education in Your Institution*, National Society for Internships and Experiential Education, Raleigh, North Carolina, 1986

The Pros and Cons of Four Administrative Models, continued

Model 2:

Institutional central office for credited programs in which a program director and staff assume many of the tasks usually performed by faculty

ADVANTAGES

-Functionally more efficient;

-Allows for standardized policies and procedures in dealing with experiential education;

-Likely to be more responsive to non-disciplinary academic learning, e.g. critical thinking, cross-cultural understanding and other generic liberal arts skills;

-Likely to pay more attention to the process of self-directed learning, i.e., learning how to learn from experience;

-Can provide the impetus for external funding;

-Can serve as a vehicle for revitalizing the curriculum from the perspective of a major division, college, or the institution as a whole.

DISADVANTAGES

-Difficult to maintain adequate financial support in an environment where budgets are departmentally driven;

-More difficult to maintain quality control for discipline-based learning;

-Student recruitment by faculty diminishes as faculty do not see their interest (classroom enrollments) served;

-Lacks academic credibility.

"There are some well established co-op and internship programs within departments at Otterbein, so there is a real issue of turfdom. Among many of the faculty, there is no desire to have standardization or a centralized office to make decisions regarding experiential education. So there are several power issues. Also many of the departments have sought and received external resources, so the programs are real sources of esteem and ownership on the part of some faculty." -Becky Dixon
Assistant Professor
Business Administration
Otterbein College
Otterbein, Ohio

"Often people build their centralized empires, then they lose the faculty involvement. How does a small school keep that initiative from faculty and still have some economy of scale? At too many schools, the faculty say 'It's nice that that central person over there does this, so I don't have to do it any more.'"
-Jane Kendall
Executive Director
National Society for
Internships and
Experiential Education

From *Strengthening Experiential Education in Your Institution,* National Society for Internships and Experiential Education, Raleigh, North Carolina, 1986

The Pros and Cons of Four Administrative Models, continued

Model 3:	ADVANTAGES	DISADVANTAGES
Institutional office for non-credit programs through career development, community service, financial aid or some other student affairs office [NOTE: This model sometimes exists in conjunction with another model for credit programs, but the two need to be viewed in tandem because of the overlaps in function.]	-Functionally efficient; -The limited goal simplifies interpretation and marketing of the program; -Competence of administrator and staff can be fairly focused and developed to a high level of expertise and specialization, effectively addressing the limited goal; -Supports the important non-academic learning that occurs through field experiences — career development, knowledge of the work world, appreciation of community needs, interpersonal skills, money management, etc.	-Non-credit and special programs are contrary to the general movement toward academic and curricular emphasis; -Difficult to maintain quality control for the students' learning; -The full educational potential of experiential education is not being realized or recognized in the instructional program.

Model 4:	ADVANTAGES	DISADVANTAGES
Shared model with centralized coordination and support and departmental control of credited programs and courses From *Strengthening Experiential Education in Your Institution*, National Society for Internships and Experiential Education, Raleigh, North Carolina, 1986	-Combines the advantages and reduces the disadvantages found in the other models; -Provides a focal point for advocacy and expertise about experiential education; -Takes advantage of the discipline-related knowledge of faculty; -Places the curricular responsibility where it should be — with the faculty; -Relieves the faculty and departments from many of the logistical and administrative concerns associated with experiential education; -Lends itself to positive collaboration and cooperation across different departments and offices; -Promotes credibility by assigning responsibilities in a pattern consistent with general institutional and academic practices.	-Deviates from tradition in working across departments; -Can create ambiguity and confusion in the assignment of responsibilities and tasks among the central coordinating office, participating departments, and individual instructors; -Requires a special kind of person to do the coordinating — someone who can relate to students, faculty and administration, someone who is open to change and yet able to provide stability, creditable but not threatening, assertive and yet flexible, enthusiastic but not overpowering, creative but not possessive, i.e., a most competent and self-confident individual.

There are obviously several other possible variations on these four administrative models. The trend of most advanced institutions is to move toward Model 4, the shared model. Listen to the comments from some who have already benefitted from its fruits, including having those very special people coordinating their respective programs:

"From the inception of the formal internship program, the dean of our college has been very supportive of having a coordinator of internships. At first, some faculty were protective of their turf. I think it is to the credit of the coordinator that those feelings are almost non-existent now because we all realize how we benefit from having a coordinator who does

placements for us and who works with us to establish policies. She reports to the Academic Dean, and she wants to keep it that way. Each department has its own internship program, its own prerequisites and policies regarding papers or readings, and its own programs it affiliates with like the Washington Center. The campus-wide faculty committee works on issues like quality control. For example, we have worked on the Learning Agreement . . . on the mid-term and final evaluation forms. We have also planned a workshop on assessment and evaluation. . . . [and] developed the option for faculty members supervising internships to be able to have a written abstract attached to the student's transcript."

-Margaret Schram, Chair
Faculty Advisory Com-
mittee, and Associate
Professor of English
Hartwick College
Oneonta, NY

"The University of Colorado is a rather traditional, residential campus with 20,000 students. Its management structure has three vice-chancellors — administrative, academic affairs and academic services. Career Services is under the Vice Chancellor of Academic Services. In January 1983, the Cooperative Education program was brought under Career Services. So it was assumed under a student affairs structure, but in terms of operation, it is as academically linked as possible (by working through the deans of the academic divisions). From my perspective of managing the career activities on campus, I am very pleased that Internships and Cooperative Education is

Doug Iosue, senior psychology major at the University of Vermont (foreground), one of seven University Year for ACTION interns who work full-time for one year as crisis counselors in the community. *Background:* Valerie Wright, a former UYA intern who is now Assistant Director of the Acute Care Unit of the Alcohol and Substance Abuse counseling and detoxification unit of Howard Mental Health Center in Burlington, Vermont.

associated with career development — because of its integration into the curriculum. It puts the career issues that much closer to the academic end."

-Gordon Gray, Director
Career Services
University of Colorado

Another way of looking at administrative models is to consider the evolutionary stages in the administration of experiential education.

From our work with colleges and universities across the country, we have observed three common stages as experiential education emerges in an institution; these are outlined in the chart below.

For more information and ideas on the administrative models and division of responsibilities between a central office and academic departments, see "A Fly on the Wall" on the following pages.

EVOLUTIONARY STAGES IN THE ADMINISTRATION OF EXPERIENTIAL EDUCATION

Stage 1	Stage 2	Stage 3
Individual faculty respond to students' requests	Increased student interest in experiential learning	Recognition and support of multiple outcomes of experiential learning
Non-credit programs in units related to specific outcomes of experiential learning (Example: career development)	Credit programs within some departments	Movement toward emphasis on academic credit
No institutional policies or programs	More departments and faculty get involved on an ad hoc basis	Institutional and departmental policies to address quality issues
	Coordination becomes an issue, and a central office may be designated or established	Movement toward a model of shared responsibility between a central administrative unit and academic departments

A Fly on the Wall

*Y*ou are invited to be a fly on the wall to listen in during a meeting of the NSIEE Peer Consultants. They have been talking about what staff factors and what organizational factors contribute to a strong program of high quality. But sh-h-h-h-h . . . let's listen . . . .

Jane Permaul: [In considering the effectiveness of the experiential education administrator,] I think about factors like the ability to relate with others in their own lingo and territory . . . and the creation of win-win situations. Do you have the ability to influence without ownership? Are you seen as the center of experiential education expertise, a person to consult when people need to think about experiential education? These are just potential indicators as to whether you're respected on campus.

Tom Little: I think there are some other questions involved that we need to think about. One question is, "Which administrative models allow for certain tasks better than other tasks?" For example, I'm convinced that the quality of learning is best in a highly decentralized model.

The same principle applies to the question of finances. I think you can get a lot more support if everyone puts in a quarter than if you only try to get a big pot of money for a central office. The experiential education model has to fit the other models of activity

and authority in the institution — and the academic model is decentralized. Resource allocation has to fit the administrative model, too. If the administrative model is contrary to the way resources are normally allocated, you've got problems. Same way with quality assurance. The reason that faculty members sometimes don't buy into co-op is that they are often not involved in the learning in a significant way.

I also think schools have a hard time thinking

"I think you can get a lot more support if everybody puts in a quarter than if you only try to get a big pot of money for a central office."

---

about "oddball" models. If a centralized experiential education office is designed as a support unit for the whole campus, the question is whether there are precedents for academic support units — like a reading center — that would have a similar function to an experiential education center. Otherwise it is hard to explain to faculty what an academic support unit does and what it can do for them.

Jane Permaul: I am hesitant to be too hard-lined on this. We could point out in the sourcebook the advantages and disadvantages of a centralized model and a decentralized model, but I think a lot depends on the environment of the particular institution as to what those advantages and disadvantages are.

Jane Kendall: Can we delineate those environmental factors that influence it? There are definite patterns we could outline.

Sharon Rubin: I think that at very small institutions, centralized models make a lot more sense

NSIEE Peer Experts discuss administrative issues important for a coherent program for experiential education. From left, Sharon Rubin, Jane Kendall, and Jane Permaul.

than they do at large institutions.

Tom Little: In terms of learning and teaching, the faculty members in the small institutions trust each other more, and the departments don't rule. The whole school acts more like a unit, so a centralized administrative structure can work more easily.

Jane Permaul: An exception would be Westmont College. That's what they were going to do. It made a lot of sense until they met with all of the faculty and realized that a heavily centralized model would never go .

Tom Little: I think Sharon's point is still true, though. You have a better chance for an effective centralized model at a small school than you do at a large school.

Sharon Rubin: For one thing , you often have a more homogeneous faculty at a small school, so there are more shared assumptions about what good learning is and how you do things. There is a much more intense, shared culture in a small school, so a central office can pick up on that and work with it. It has nothing to do necessarily with cost-effectiveness, but it can represent the values and the culture of the institution. Once you get into larger institutions where the shared values are more minimal, trying to get everybody to march to the same drummer does not work very well.

Tom Little: Also at the large institutions, the faculty member's identification is different. You identify with the discipline more than you do with the institution. I think that makes a difference.

"Schools need to think about all the tasks involved in experiential education and lay them out in a grid with all the people who can handle some of the tasks."

— Tom Little

Jane Kendall: Also in a small school, you've got an economy of scale for certain administrative functions. For example, in the English Dpartment, there may be only five majors doing internships each year. The likelihood of the department having enough students to make it worthwhile to set up all the administrative functions internally is slim. It makes more sense to break out similar tasks and share them across the institution.

Jane Permaul: The English Department would still decide what kind of internship is appropriate, but you can have a central office to help develop the opportunities and do much of the legwork and coordination.

Jane Kendall: That's very different from a centralized program where everything is done through one central staff.

Jane Permaul: Can we conclude that administration should be more centralized in the smaller school; and the larger it gets, the less centralized it should be? I think in the large universities you still have some sort of centralized coordination. Sharon has it at the University of Maryland, and we have it at UCLA.

Tom Little: It depends on what you're coordinating. There's a difference between coordination of information and coordination of a program, like a co-op program.

Jane Permaul: When we're talking about a centralized model even at a small college, we're not talking about running the whole thing, telling the English Department what the internship ought to be, etc.

John Duley: Part of the problem with that model is that a faculty member who has managed internships wonders, "What does that administrator do? Why does he run an internship program if he does not really offer the internships himself? How does he help me as a faculty member? I'm the one doing it. So why do I need him?"

These are real questions that people have on small campuses. If they don't already have a program and somebody wants to start one, they appreciate having someone to turn to. But the problem with justifying some investment of resources in a central office from the faculty's point of view is difficult . At any place where they're cutting back — like at many of the small schools — they wait for faculty to retire and they don't replace them, and department s are losing positions. If you ask for money to coordinate experiential learning, they want to know, "What are we getting that we wouldn't have if we didn't have that person?" You and I know what they're getting — better quality control, professional awareness — but the faculty may not understand that until they see it work. They have to see how someone like Barbara Lilly or Marlene Suter is extremely useful to *them*.

I think experiential educators really have to work

hard to make a case for their role. You have to make your case for justifying the expenditure of institutional resources. I don't think it is self-evident initially.

Sharon Rubin: I really think that one of the few real virtues of the centralized model is in relation to a small community. I think decentralized models in small towns will kill the "whole goose that lays the golden egg." Employers get so irritated when they get calls from seven different people who are tripping over each other and who don't know what's going on in their own school.

John Duley: That is especially true in a non-urban area.

Sharon Rubin: Yes, a small college in Chicago can do whatever it wants, but at the University of Virginia in Charlottesville, there are already irritations among the worksite supervisors who talked with me about how they get called by several different faculty.

Jane Kendall: Central coordination doesn't always solve that problem. It depends on what the central coordinating office does. It can solve the problem if the site development function is done or at least coordinated centrally.

John Duley: I think educationally we do not want to promote job development by somebody other than the students. Really, educationally, we want the student to go out and look for that job and develop it and bring it back to a coordinator or a faculty member.

Sharon Rubin: I disagree. I think you should have a student take it from the referral point. I don't want to be in the computer dating service where I make the match, but I do think there is a lot to be said for having some central place where somebody can call in and say, "I have this opportunity available" and not make a student start from genesis. What the student does to follow up after that is really a matter of student learning and responsibility.

Jane Kendall: One of the best discussions of this issue is in Tom's consulting reports when he talks about tasks and how they might be divided up within the institution. He laid out the tasks and talked about how some of them could be shared, some could be centralized, and how there are different ways of dividing them out.

Tom Little: What I wrote was a type of sort: here are all the characters, and here are all the tasks. Just lay them out against each other. I think the schools just need to think about it and do their own grids. There are about eight tasks in all, from setting goals to transcripts and grades.

Jane Kendall: You also talked about how people tend to leave out the students and the employers completely from the tasks — and that these players could systematically be given more responsibility. [See the chapters of this sourcebook entitled "Ensuring Quality in Education" and "Supporting Experiential Education in the Financial System of the Institution" for more discussion of these tasks.]

Jane Permaul: Aren't there some other administrative tasks, such as faculty development in general, funding, policies, etc.? We need to talk about these *other* tasks here in this chapter. There are really two sets of administrative questions.

John Duley: It is going to be important somewhere to delineate appropriate tasks for the centralized coordinator. In other words, what is the best use of their time? Sharon was making the point that they spend so much time developing placements that they haven't got enough time left to do the important things in terms of the institution. [See the Soapbox Position entitled "The Counseling Model: Is It Harmful to Our Health?" in the financial chapter of this sourcebook.]

What are the important roles? One of them is to serve as an administrative aide to the faculty advisory committee. That's one role that somebody needs to do. It means they're the communication channel, the people who make sure that the committee meets, that they have the materials ready to review, etc. I don't think those functions are ever clearly understood, but these are responsibilities that won't get done without someone who is keeping up with the whole effort. Another role is to offer an institutional view of quality assurance. It would be good for us to spell out some of *those* tasks that must get done if experiential education is going to be an acceptable part of an academic program, even though the experiential education person may not be an academician.

"If we're going to help people see what there is other than only the development of placements, we've got to delineate these other tasks and their importance in terms of the educational quality of the program."

— John Duley

Jane Permaul: Somebody still has to keep the wheel moving.

John Duley: Yes, as well as listing all the opportunities that have been developed in all the departments and having them available in one office. Those are all important tasks that must be done in order to avoid confusion in the institution.

Jane Permaul: Maybe one way to deal with that is to spell out what all of the tasks are, not only the ones that are obvious. What are the important tasks other than working with the students and that kind of programmatic function? We are talking about some of the other tasks — like knowing the faculty. Then the experiential educator can start saying, "This is the better use of my time," and then, "If I'm going to do these, then what kind of administrative or organizational unit do I need to be in so that I can function well?"

John Duley: You need to do that in order to move beyond the counselor model. Otherwise you just fall into that. If we're going to help people see what there is other than only the development of placements, we've got to delineate these other tasks and their importance in terms of the educational quality of the program.

Tom Little: It's a question of who is the advocate, who does the campus-wide reporting, who plays the research and development role, and who looks at experiential education across the institution.

Jane Permaul: And indirectly it's really quality control — making sure all the faculty are doing the kinds of things they should be doing. What are the other tasks of this type?

Sharon Rubin: Communications and reporting.

Tom Little: And representing the institution to the outside world within this area of higher education.

Sharon Rubin: It's really taking leadership professionally in the field and taking leadership professionally on campus.

Jane Permaul: Also building networks on campus.

John Duley: Yes, I think that's an important one by itself. If a central person doesn't make the connections, they don't get made.

Jane Kendall: Then we can begin to look at the administrative structures which either enhance those tasks or do not enhance them. Program administration (or administration of the parts of the learning process) is just *one* task among several that need to be done.

Jane Permaul: Yes, if we list these tasks and talk about what kind of roles the person needs to play, then we can start talking about what kinds of organization will support that within the campus. Suppose someone finds that the current organizational structure does not support these tasks to the extent needed. Then we're talking about change. This is where leadership style comes in.

John Duley: I think it also has to do with the skill to work in the informal networks of the institution, the informal decision-making structures — the

Strategies for Changing Your Administrative Structure for Experiential Education

"Sometimes you just have to be bold. If you don't figure out what structure makes the most sense and then help others see the reasons, you can be sure someone else will decide it. If you are in a good position to see what is needed, you've got to speak up."

-Nancy Gansneder
Director
Undergraduate Internship Program
University of Virginia

Having some notion on both where to place experiential education and what administrative model to use in strengthening experiential education, how do you effect the changes necessary to get there? Once again,

there is no magic formula to follow, but there are a few principles which have been gained experientially through the NSIEE-FIPSE Pilot Project and that are consistent with the literature and theories on organizational development. If you are not already familiar with theories on organizational change, you will find that they provide valuable tips for your approach. See the resources listed at the end of this chapter. Here are a few principles for consideration.

KNOW WHAT IT IS AND WHAT NEEDS CHANGING. Walter Sikes, a private consultant specializing in organizational development, states one of his seven principles as "A change agent must have a sound, internalized understanding not only of

the 'facts' but also the feelings important to the change process. Thus, data collection and feedback are essential to initiating either personal or organizational change. A thorough understanding of the particular dynamics of a system that is to be changed will allow one to tailor the innovation to the specific situation — and greatly increase the chances for success. '. . . Plan for adaptation, not adoption.' "[1]

"A thorough understanding of the particular dynamics of the system that is to be changed will allow one to tailor the innovation to the specific situation — and greatly increase the chances for success."

awareness of what they are and the ability to work within them. It takes a certain type of person. I was just thinking about two of the colleges I've been working with. At Adrian College, Ruth Gilkey is competent and has the respect of the faculty; she was able to relate to them in such a way that they would do things that they wouldn't have done if she didn't have that kind of standing.

The same thing is true in a different way with Marlene Suter at Otterbein College. She has that kind of standing because she took on herself the responsibility that other people were not paying attention to yet. Then people thought, "Here's a person who takes this institution seriously. She isn't building an empire, but she is trying to make sure we don't lose something." So I think a lot depends on whether you have a good leadership style.

Jane Permaul: I agree with you, John. That's why I think it's important to ask: If the individuals involved find themselves lacking in respect and influence in other units, how can they increase their respect and influence? I think we need to come out with suggestions on how to do that. Or what if they're isolated? A great case was made in Sharon's Soapbox that she called "Ask and Ye Shall Receive." A lot of times people just don't go out. And they get so stuck with the counseling of students that they don't go and learn about what's going on around the campus.

Jane Kendall: Sharon's first two consulting reports on the NSIEE/FIPSE project, the ones to Hartwick College and the University of Virginia, were both full of those kinds of things — how you get visibility, the advocacy role, and a lot of down-to-earth ideas on those tasks that are not just the administration of a program.

Sharon Rubin: I concentrate a lot on those tasks in all of my consulting reports, simply because they are amazingly neglected.

John Duley: Too often you accept the position that's been assigned you by the culture — a position or a judgment that is not necessarily true. You view yourself as "off there" in a corner because you think other people do. I think it may be a misperception. If you allow yourself to be left there, that's where you'll stay. You have to work the informal networks.

Jane Kendall: Part of what we are saying is that if people don't know that these other activities are legitimate, they'll fall naturally into the one-on-one counseling. Or into just what comes across the desk.

Sharon Rubin: Yesterday at my niece's high school graduation, the chairman of the school board said, "If you really believe you'll succeed or if you really believe you'll fail, it will be true either way." Some people perceive themselves as powerless, so they are.

John Duley: Those people who think they can make a difference do, and those who don't, don't.

INVOLVE THE FACULTY AND OTHERS WHO ARE LIKELY TO BE AFFECTED BY THE CHANGE, INCLUDING ONE'S IMMEDIATE OR PROSPECTIVE SUPERVISOR. This is based on two general theories about change. First, people tend to support those changes which will lead to benefits for themselves and their units. Thus, if central coordination would reduce faculty load without taking away faculty teaching prerogative, faculty will most likely be receptive. If collaborative work with faculty would raise the general status of student affairs, then the student affairs dean may not feel as territorially protective. The key is to create win-win conditions. Second, persons who are expected to implement the change must be involved in the decision process leading to the change. Such involvement allows the participants to feel a sense of contribution and ownership, which in turn reduces resistance to change and encourages active advocacy for change.

ASSERT LEADERSHIP.
Change implies the need for movement, and someone has to get the action started. John Duley, NSIEE Peer Consultant, observed, "We tend to get stuck in boxes. We are where we are because that's where we happen to be. So, how do we get out of it?" It may sound too simple, but the answer may well be "Do something!" There are many styles of leadership, but they all include initiative, action, and energy. A leader does not wait for someone else to start or to tell him or her to get started. A leader starts when the needs are evident. Also, action speaks louder than words. If a problem needs attention, rhetoric can only go so far before people tune it out. Expansion of energy helps as it conveys a sense of urgency and impor-

tance in addressing a need.

Beyond these characteristics, the most appropriate style of leadership depends very much on the personality of the leader(s) and the situation. For more information, consult the Myers Briggs Type Indicator on personality and Hersey and Blanchard's ideas on situational leadership.

Finally, who should be the leader? The most obvious candidates are those directly responsible for experiential education or those who are strongly committed to having experiential education as an element of higher education.

Following are some examples of how many of the principles discussed here apply to strengthening the administration of experiential education. They are based on reports and observations about selected pilot schools that participated in the NSIEE-FIPSE Project.

"Designing an appropriate admin-

istrative model can be a real problem if there is a strong prior program and an entrenched view of what a program should look like."

-John Duley
NSIEE Peer Consultant
and Professor Emeritus
Michigan State
University

"Lewis Sullivan told us 'Form follows function.' American architectural history was transformed when form began to follow function. Unfortunately, most of us in higher education seem to be stuck with the idea that the function follows the form. We say we are in a particular form. We came into a position that was already in that form, or our form depends on who we happen to report to. There's nothing wrong with where you are if the form matches the function. But where it is no match, where there is an incongruence between your structure and your functions, then it's up to you to take action."

-Sharon Rubin
NSIEE Peer Consultant
and Assistant Dean for
Undergraduate Studies
University of Maryland

"The form alone won't give you what you want. You need to pay attention to both the decision-making process and the form."

-Barbara Buchanan
Director of Field
Education
College of Public and
Community Service
Univ. of Massachusetts
Boston, Massachusetts

"Unfortunately, most of us in higher education seem to be stuck with the idea that function follows the form."

THE PARTIAL MYTH OF EFFICIENCY

"*In* order to be successful as an experiential educator, you have to be able to tolerate models that do not fit organizational charts. They may be messy and inefficient, and often they do not make a lot of sense at first glance. I've watched people trying to draw charts to explain their complex maze of collaborative relationships across the campus, and they can get very complicated. You have to be able to live in that type of environment, or else you have to get out of the field pretty quickly. And people do get out of the field because they cannot tolerate the ambiguity.

"When I first started as a director of experiential learning, I thought very highly of efficiency. I said, 'Why does every department do this differently?' We did have course numbers for the entire campus, but we also had other departmental numbers that some departments used for their majors. And internships in one department were quite different from internships in another department. One department said you had to be a senior, and another said you had to have a 3.0 and take 'Introduction to Whatever.' My office was a clearinghouse, but we had faculty who kept their own lists of people they talked to. I kept saying, 'What a mess! Can't we get organized?' That's where I was. But now I say, 'Look, if the goal is to give as many students as possible the opportunity to be involved in experiential learning, then we could all be doing it, and there still wouldn't be enough of us.'

"The mess shows that the responsibility is shared. People have different policies because they have different goals. In a small institution, it makes sense to have one pattern for experiential learning, because students are generally homogeneous and a small faculty can usually agree to a single model. In a large institution, however, a single model usually does not work effectively to fit students' varied needs or the curricular models of many different departments. For example, some sort of field work may be mandatory in some of the applied fields, and the number of hours a student is expected to work might be very high. In another department, an internship might be project-centered and might demand fewer hours. A freshman might benefit from a service-learning experience to investigate a potential field of interest for further study, but credit may not be needed or appropriate for that student. On the other hand, a senior might develop a full-time, academically intensive practicum, and what she learns deserves a larger number of credits.

"An overlap model can be very strange and delicate to maintain creatively because you don't know who you report to, or you are trying to balance several different reporting structures. However, a model in which a number of programs and courses co-exist in a messy way also has a lot of potential."

-Sharon Rubin
NSIEE Peer Consultant
and Assistant Dean for
Undergraduate Studies
University of Maryland

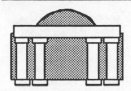

A Case Study

Westmont College:

Perceived Problems:
- No advisory or oversight committee
- No formal written policies
- Lack of uniformity in evaluation
- Lack of control
- Sense of independence among various units, which makes solutions difficult

Initial Proposed Change:
- Centralize administration under the President's Office.
- Create oversight committee at the college level composed of appointed faculty.

Actions Taken toward Implementation of Proposed Change:
- Research report on internships at Westmont prepared by the Chair of the Social Science Division, where the program is most active and extensive.
- Report distributed to all academic departments and selected programs.
- Workshop held with the faculty involved in internships and practica to discuss their specific concerns; NSIEE Peer Consultant invited to speak on the rationale for experiential education in liberal arts education.
- Report summarizing the workshop discussion distributed to all departments.
- Discussion was initiated about transferring the Associate Director of Career Center to the Academic Dean's office to serve as the Coordinator of Field Placement.
- Ad hoc committee appointed to advise the Faculty Senate on matters relating to experiential education.

Obstacles Encountered to Change:
- Differences of opinion among faculty concerning the desirability of "controls"
- A perceived difference between practica arranged by faculty and by student life personnel (i.e., career center personnel).

Strategies to Overcome Obstacles:
- The workshop enabled all faculty involved in practica to express their points of view and to come to some consensus on the issues to be addressed.
- The appointment of an ad hoc committee which has only advisory powers helped allay fears of a loss of control by faculty and the departments.
- The initial notion of having a centralized decision-making administration was altered to centralized coordination in the form of a coordinator of field placement reporting not to student life, but to the academic dean.
- Written reports of progress helped and should continue.

Knowledge Gained from the Ongoing Change Experience:
- The experience has impressed upon administrators that centralized decision-making regarding experiential courses and programs will not be very effective. All affected persons and departments need to participate in the discussion and the decisions.
- It is also not as certain that centralized "control" is the primary need. Probably centralized "coordination" is a better way to look at the need.
- The conviction that it is important to discuss the nature and benefits of experiential education on a faculty-wide basis is stronger as a result of the experience.
- "Face obstacles and disagreements frankly."
- "Welcome faculty initiative and leadership."
- "Work through opinion leaders."
- "Stress good communication."
- "Try out innovations on a small scale, but establish a good feedback mechanism."
- "Expect resistance."
- "Expect to work around resistance (if it cannot be overcome)."

Prognosis:
- Excellent in successfully resolving the initial concerns.

Leadership:
- The Director of Westmont College's San Francisco Urban Program first approached his supervisor because he felt that the educational values of the Urban Program were not being fully realized for Westmont students. His supervisor, the Director of Off-Campus Programs, then took on the leadership.

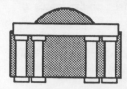

A Case Study

Hartwick College:

Perceived Problems:
-Faculty ownership. The program had been established (one and a half years before the need for change was realized) in a centralized office under the direction of a full-time administrator. Prior to that time, internships had been arranged on an ad hoc basis through academic departments whose policies ranged from non-existent to formal, written guidelines. The centralized office created concerns about faculty control and departmental autonomy.

Change Strategy:
-Creation of an advisory committee with due representation from faculty, staff, and students who would advise the coordinator and the dean on all matters related to experiential education at Hartwick.

Actions Taken toward Making the Change:
-Advisory Committee on Internships appointed by the Dean of the College. Membership included faculty from the three divisions (two from the Humanities, two from the Physical and Life Sciences, and four from the Social Sciences. The larger representation from the Social Sciences reflected the greater number of internships undertaken through that division.), the registrar, and two students. The committee was charged to advise the Dean and the Coordinator of Internships on all matters relating to the internship program of the College, including establishing the goals of the program, defining "internships," and developing and modifying policies and procedures for implementing the program. Its function was to provide additional perspective and support to those responsible for the administration of the internship program.

Obstacles Encountered to Change:
-None since the Advisory Committee provided a structure that enabled the faculty to share the responsibility and decision making power needed to strengthen and expand the internship program.

Knowledge Gained from the Change:
-The centralized internship program model now works well at Hartwick. Its success rests primarily with (1) the Advisory Committee, a forum that encourages democratic participation in policy and procedural decisions, and nurtures faculty ownership of the program, and (2) a coordinator who has the skills in administration, collaboration, and consulting needed to be successful. Although membership will change, the faculty is confident that the committee will continue to represent the faculty at large and the best interests of students in determining the future direction of the program.

Prognosis:
-It looks like Hartwick has resolved its problem.

Leadership:
-The Coordinator of Internships initiated and actively participated in the process which led to the change. The Dean was supportive from the beginning, and the faculty on the advisory committee did the work it took to establish the policies and standards needed.

In conclusion, every campus has its own characteristics and dynamics, painted by the people involved — faculty, students and staff — plus the outsiders. To find a place in this environment, a program, course, or person must be able to contribute to the welfare of the environment, to conform to the norms of the community, and to be in harmony with other parts of the environment. These rules frequently discourage innovations and anything which does not exactly fit the mold. This is one reason that experiential education can encounter resistance on particularly traditional campuses. However, campuses are dynamic entities which are capable of change. The challenge for experiential educators is to articulate the values of experiential education in the framework of higher education in general and to be effective change agents, rocking the boat gently so that the people on it can actually enjoy the ride rather than become frightened by the sensation. ▢

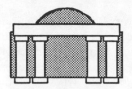

A Case Study

Illinois State University:

Perceived Problems or Needs:
-Recognition of the experiential education program and evidence to support that recognition. For nearly eight years, the program was viewed as a stepchild administratively. Consequently, there was little internal support and virtually no leadership from top-level administration. The program director reported to six different top-level administrators during a nine-year period and was reassigned to eight different office locations during that period. The academic value of the program to the University was not clearly articulated.

Proposed Change:
-Alignment of the program under an administrative unit that has goals compatible with experiential education and that appreciates and values the program as an integral part of the University.

Strategy for Proposed Change:
-Conducted a university-wide study of the program under the direction of the Provost to point out needs of the program. The study involved input from a range of administrators and faculty across the campus.

Obstacles Encountered:
-None, as the Provost both had the power to request such a study and saw the potential for how the program could enhance the quality of the University's curriculum, his major goal and responsibility.

Results:
-Administratively the program has become a part of the Provost's office.
-Other programmatic problems related to instruction are being addressed now since the Provost's office has prime responsibility for dealing with these problems.

Prognosis:
-With this new alignment, the academic value of the program should receive much more attention and clarity. This articulation is bringing increased status for the program among faculty and in the campus community in general. It should no longer be a stepchild.

Leadership:
-The program director seized the opportunity to invite the newly appointed Provost to conduct the study.

FOOTNOTE

[1] Jack Lindquist, as quoted by Walter Sikes, "Some Principles of Personal and Organizational Change," *NTL Connections*, NTL Institute, Arlington, Virginia, March 1985, p. 5.

The challenge ... is to articulate the values of experiential education in the framework of higher education in general and to be effective change agents, rocking the boat gently so that the people on it can actually enjoy the ride rather than become frightened by the sensation.

RECOMMENDED RESOURCES

Agor, Weston H., *Intuitive Management: Integrating Left and Right Brain Management Skills*, Prentice-Hall, Englewood Cliffs, New Jersey, 1984. From a study of over 2,000 managers in a variety of organizational settings, the author concludes that the use of intuition along with "other brain skills" are critical to effective management and leadership. The settings where the use of integrated left and right brain management skills are most effective are similar to the environments of experiential education programs in higher education. Further, the author relates some of his theories and findings to the personality types described by the Myers Briggs Type Indicator.

Bonoma, Thomas V., and Zaltman, Gerald, *Psychology for Management*, Kent Publishing Company, Boston, 1981. Of particular interest is the synthesis model of the "organizational adoption process" which is helpful in guiding managers in designing and implementing change.

Hersey, Paul, and Blanchard, Kenneth H., *Management of Organizational Behavior: Utilizing Human Resources*, 4th Ed., Prentice-Hall, Englewood Cliffs, New Jersey, 1982. This book describes the use of situational leadership in managing organizational behavior and change. In the formulation of appropriate leadership styles for change, the theory takes into consideration the characteristics of the people involved and affected by the change as well as the setting in which the change takes place.

Kotter, John P., and Schlesinger, Leonard A., "Choosing Strategies for Change," *Harvard Business Review*, March-April, 1979. This article suggests four "most common" reasons for resisting change, six strategies to overcome resistance, and four "situational factors" to consider in choosing the right strategy.

Myers, Isabel Briggs, *The Myers Briggs Type Indicator: Manual 1962*, Consulting Psychologists Press, Palo Alto, California, 1962; and Myers, Isabel Briggs, *Introduction to Type*, Consulting Psychologists Press, 1980. These two publications introduce various personality types based on a modified version of the Jungian theory of personality. Four major variables are considered: judgment-perception, thinking-feeling, sensation-intuition, and extroversion-introversion. It is believed that certain types function more effectively in certain environments. Consequently, certain personality types may be more compatible with the characteristics needed to be an effective change agent.

6

Supporting Experiential Education in the Financial System of Your Institution

"I see faculty getting release time, overload payments, funding for professional activities, exposure to good applications in the world off campus, consulting opportunities, and many personal satisfactions from sponsoring students on internships. The reward systems that will sustain experiential education in the long run are regular course teaching credits and extra consideration for tenure and promotion."
    -Tom Little
    NSIEE Consultant and
    CAEL Regional
    Manager

When an NSIEE consultant visits a campus to review and assist the institution with experiential education programs, the program administrators invariably report that financial resources are a problem. In addition, the faculty who sponsor students in the various programs almost always complain they are not compensated or are inadequately compensated for their work. These two patterns reveal *two critical problems in integrating experiential education into the economic framework of the institution:*

1. Like much of the higher education enterprise, experiential education is faced with se- curing financial support from **ever-diminishing resources.**
The changing demographics of the student population are influencing higher education in powerful ways. In states with declining student populations, institutions are faced with economic retrenchment and underutilized facilities. It is difficult to secure resources for instructional innovations such as experiential education when there is pressure within the school to maintain existing programs. In areas with increasing student enrollments, the resources are often not sufficient for what are considered to be the necessary, if traditional, educational programs. It is difficult to secure resources for alternatives when the traditional is not being adequately supported.

In addition, higher education is receiving closer scrutiny at both the national and state levels, and the assessment is not positive. Graduates lack basic academic competencies, the skills needed for such critical professions as teaching, and even a minimal appreciation of their culture. Higher education is responding to this criticism with traditionalism, e.g., expanding core curricula and foreign language requirements.

Anything which has even the appearance of the non-traditional, such as experiential education, is at a relative economic disadvantage in this climate.

2. Whatever support might be available for experiential education is difficult to access because the system for allocating financial resources at the institution was not developed with experiential education in mind. Even in the best of times, experiential education has difficulty getting institutional support because the rules and procedures for allocating resouces assume a different mode of teaching and learning. The system for allocating resources generally assumes an instructional model of a single instructor lecturing to students in a classroom of desks, blackboards, and visual aids. Faculty are usually compensated by the number of classes taught during an academic term. Public institutions receive resources according to the number of students taught, the physical dimensions of the classroom, and the number of hours the classroom is used each day. Even in private colleges, the number of classroom contact hours is the basis for dividing tuition funds within the school.

Experiential education, on the other hand, is done quite differently. The student is off-campus. The work setting in the community becomes the classroom. The work supervisor is also a teacher. The professor on campus has the role of mentor and counselor. It is hard for an economic system which assumes a mode of on-campus, classroom-based instruction to recognize these different characteristics of experiential education.

It is difficult enough to secure institutional resources using the rules for another game, but sometimes experiential educators themselves make it harder by trying to challenge the system. The graveyard of experiential education contains many examples. Some experiential programs, such as cooperative educa-

Until experiential education is an integral part of the ongoing economic system of your campus, it will remain on the periphery of the real educational mission of the institution.

tion, are initiated with the luxury of external financial support. Grant funds may be used to purchase services which cannot, by any stretch of the fiscal imagination at most schools, be expected to be continued from institutional resources simply because the system does not allow this level of service. It is hard, for example, to find institutional precedents or support for having faculty without teaching responsibilities, full-time job developers, or several secretaries for one office. Other experiential educators write their own death warrants in the administrative or curricular models they choose. A common example is an institution-wide internship program which provides academic credit via an independent study arrangement when there is not an institutional policy for

compensating faculty for sponsoring students on independent study.

Until experiential education is an integral part of the ongoing *economic* system of your campus, however, it will remain on the periphery of the real educational mission of the institution. This means it must become part of the faculty compensation and promotion system. It means generating credits that count toward the degree. And it means allocating institutional resources (not grant funds) for the primary activities required for experiential education. (See Chapter Two for a discussion of the credit and curriculum issues.)

Organizational Characteristics of Higher Education that Influence Where the Resources Go

Colleges and universities have several unique organizational characteristics which powerfully influence the process and rules by which resources are distributed. To design experiential education programs and courses that have a chance of securing a fair share of institutional resources, be aware of these five characteristics of most campuses:

1. **Administrative segmentation** — Colleges and universities do not generally act as whole units.

A Threefold Strategy — So what can you do? Start with these three basic tasks:

• Appreciate fully the unique characteristics of universities and colleges as organizations and the implications of these characteristics for making experiential education programs economically viable.

• Design experiential education programs and courses that are consistent with the dominant model for allocating your institution's instructional resources.

• Actively pursue cost savings to realize the most benefit from the financial resources available.

Some say that "A university is many kingdoms which share the same steam plant and telephone switchboard."

2. **Emphasis on inputs rather than results** — Most institutions in our society focus on outcomes. How much profit was realized, how many people got well, and what percentage of clients became self-sufficient or psychologically rehabilitated? In higher education, the orientation is on inputs — the

Joan Marie Korinek is a senior majoring in news editorials in the School of Journalism at the University of Nebraska, Lincoln. She has minors in marketing, speech communications and sociology. Here she is writing a brochure for the Nebraska Department of Environmental Control, where she is an intern in the public information division.

number of students enrolled, courses taught, books in the library, faculty with doctoral degrees. There is relatively less emphasis on results — what students learn. While there is increased discussion now about outcomes, the inputs still get the most attention.

3. The conflict of institutional and professional goals — Students, parents, and legislators see teaching as the primary goal of higher education. Tax resources are allocated to the institution based on this assumption. However, faculty in the institutions add scholarship, research, and publication to their teaching responsibilities. These three additions are necessary for tenure and promotion at most institutions. Along with consulting, these activities can also provide professional stimulation and supplement lagging faculty salaries. As a result, the internal system for allocating resources for teaching is made to accommodate these interests of academic professionals. This accommodation exacts a price, and time for teaching is usually stretched thin.

4. A voluntary association of academic professionals — "Professionalism" signifies the ownership of unique competence. A professional directs his or her own work and is accountable only to other professionals. Colleges and universities often see themselves as voluntary associations of academic professionals. In exercising this prerogative, each faculty member decides how he or she will allocate the time available for instruction. In the classroom, each professor is the ruler, with great discretion in what is taught and almost total freedom in how it will be taught.

5. Collegial governance — As associations of professionals, colleges and universities make decisions about allocating instructional resources through faculty committees operating in a collegial manner. This system of governance has great economic significance. Academic administrators have very limited power when compared to administrators in corporations or government. We could even say that while academic administrators are managers and accountants of faculty resources, they have limited discretion in directing faculty resources. Their influence is often a measure of their ability to free up resources through exceptional management.

FIVE IMPLICATIONS FOR EXPERIENTIAL EDUCATION — What are the implications of these organizational characteristics of higher education for securing institutional support for experiential education? Five are significant:

1. The organizational segmentation of higher education is especially problematic because experiential education is part of several segments. Experiential education provides valid formal education (academic affairs). It also enhances admissions and retention (student enrollment and records) and aids student career development and personal growth (student affairs). This contribution of experiential learning to several aspects of the student's educational experience is difficult for the school to recognize financially because of its own style of administrative segmentation.

The fact that experiential education contributes to the goals of several units within the institution

Jane Permaul, Director of Field Studies Development at UCLA, works with all parts of the University to coordinate the support for field programs and courses.

can also be a tremendous advantage. It can draw on the economic resources of Academic Affairs, Student Affairs, and Public/Community Affairs because it crosses the lines that typically separate these functions. At UCLA, for example, the support for field studies comes from four major sources of "hard" money — student fees intended for student services, instructional fees for instructional purposes, community funds, and instructional development funds.

"We use faculty development funds to help faculty enhance their skills in sponsoring students on internships."
    -Jim Keith, Director
    Experiential Learning
    Guilford College
    Greensboro,
    North Carolina

"It took us eight years to realize that the Instructional Development Center is a source we could tap for faculty who sponsor students on field experiences."
    -A Department
    Chairperson

2. Faculty time, the primary institutional resource, is not allocated on the basis of output, i.e., student learning.

Design experiential education programs and courses that are consistent with the dominant model for allocating your institution's instructional resources.

Therefore, experiential education will not receive any special economic consideration because of its educational effectiveness when compared with the norm of classroom-based instruction.

3. Faculty time for teaching is at a premium. Experiential education needs to look at other institutional resources that it can secure in order to compare favorably with classroom-based instruction in terms of faculty costs.

4. Any faculty who teach experientially should have a reasonable expectation that they will receive fair and equitable compensation for their work. There are numerous professional and personal rewards for faculty who support experiential education (See Chapter Three for an outline of these), but these are usually not adequate to sustain faculty members year after year. An institution cannot reasonably expect uncompensated work to reflect any degree of institutional commitment to experiential education.

"The negotiations to build experiential education into the faculty work load and compensation system need to follow the same lines as regular budget and contract negotiations for that school. It is hard to work out release time on a divisional basis if faculty contracts are usually done by department or individually with the dean."
-Jane Kendall
Executive Director
National Society for
Internships and
Experiential Education

5. Because of their limited discretion in directing major institutional resources, **academic administrators find it difficult to allocate long-term funds for academic support services such as an office for experiential education.**

Realistic Models for Experiential Education

*O*nce you appreciate the unique organizational characteristics of higher education and their implications for experiential learning, how can your school design (or re-design) experiential education in a way that is consistent with the dominant model for allocating instructional resources? Start with the unit currency of higher education resources — the fifty-minute hour of classroom instruction. Faculty work load is generally measured by the number of fifty-minute units provided during a week. Allocating institutional resources by such a simple time measure may be questionable, but it is unlikely that experiential education can change the system to secure recognition of another currency. The quantification of public higher education by management experts in state agencies, acting under a mandate to provide equitable allocation across institutions, is simply too powerful a trend to challenge successfully. While private schools have more flexibility, they have generally adopted a similar measure by time or tuition credits.

"I am concerned that we always feel the pressure of trying to support an alternative program in a traditional system. You have to make some decisions. Are you going to try to contest that system — and probably lose? Or are you going to try to develop a model that can accommodate that system? It works better for a longer time if you try to make it work within the system instead of trying to turn the system on its head so you can have a little piece of it. It's a matter of either being part of the institution or trying to exist in spite of the institution. You know which approach will succeed over time. If it's not part of the culture,

it won't be part of the institution's resources for long."
-Tom Little
NSIEE Consultant and
CAEL Regional
Manager

In this situation, *alternatives to classroom-based instruction such as experiential education have to seek positive accommodations within the current system for allocating resources.* Experiential education programs and courses that follow the principles described below successfully meet this challenge because they emphasize the unit currency — faculty work load in terms of credit courses taught — and make minimum claims on other types of institutional resources. The principles are:

1. Experiential education programs and courses should be credit bearing. Public institutions receive state allocations according to the number of instructional hours provided for academic credit courses. In private institutions, where student tuition provides much of the instructional budget, academic credit for experiential education is usually critical.

2. Experiential education should provide academic credits which have real value to students. Students are usually not as attracted to experiential programs which do not provide academic credits toward degree requirements. Programs which provide academic credits in the academic major are the most attractive because students increasingly concentrate on the major for improving their chances for employability or graduate school admission.

3. The amount of academic credit from experiential education should accurately reflect the learning achieved. Except in applied programs where experiential education is traditional, the tendency is to treat experience-based learning as an inefficient learning mode, deserving only minimum academic credit. Actually, theories of learning

"It's a matter of either being part of the institution or trying to exist in spite of the institution."

EXAMPLES OF POLICIES FOR FACULTY COMPENSATION

Throughout the work of the National Society for Internships and Experiential Education, questions about faculty work load and compensation have been constant. For this reason, we describe here examples of ways that schools have developed equitable arrangements for compensating faculty when they supervise learning in the field rather than in the classroom.

• *Most schools that have a policy for compensating faculty for supervising students in experiential learning go by a normal student/teacher ratio* since the amount of time it takes to supervise students on internships is approximately the same as in normal classroom teaching. At Rhode Island College and Westmont College, for example, supervising students in experiential education is part of a faculty member's regular credit load. Often the ratio is presented in terms of average class size. The average number of upper division students might be 12-15 per course, for example, and the average number of lower division students might be 15-18. At many institutions, such as the University of Maryland, faculty who sponsor a number of students may organize a seminar for all their students rather than seeing each one individually.

• *At some schools, faculty get credit "after the fact."* For example, a professor may sponsor 12 students on internships this spring, then get released time in the fall for the equivalent of one course. In this case 12 students form an average class size. This is the policy at Grinnell College and George Mason University. At small colleges where it may be difficult for one department to have enough students on field experiences at one time to make up a course, there are several creative solutions possible. At Guilford College, faculty members accrue credits for sponsoring students on internships until they build up enough for released time from one course. In many small colleges, some departments sponsor enough interns each semester to provide one course for one faculty member as the coordinator and sponsor. This is the case in the Psychology Department at Hartwick College, for example, and in several departments at Westmont College. Guilford College and Westmont are also examples of colleges that group different majors into one course as a way to offer field experiences to majors from several departments. Such groupings also pave the way for excellent interdisciplinary seminars concurrent with the students' field experiences.

• *At some schools, faculty are compensated on an overload basis for each student supervised.* This is the practice at the University of Maryland's University College, Mary Washington College, and Flint Community College. The range quoted by these and other institutions is $50-250 per student. Some schools use this overload model only for summer internships.

• *Some schools pay faculty on a per-student basis, but not as an overload.* At Sinclair Community College in Dayton, Ohio, for example, a faculty member gets .2 credit hour for each student supervised for a quarter. Because Sinclair has 15 credit hours per quarter as the average faculty load (3 credit hours = 1 course), supervision of 15 students on internships is the equivalent of teaching one course (15 x .2 credit hours = 3 credit hours). This credit is recorded on the faculty member's payroll form, and the faculty member is compensated accordingly during the same quarter. Faculty can therefore be paid proportionally for supervising fewer than 15 students on field experiences during particular quarter. Madonna College has a similar policy. Faculty supervising students in the field receive .1 - .3 semeser hours per student (.1 semester hour requires one visit and evaluation; .2 semester hour requires two visits and evaluation, etc.). This is the equivalent of a regular course for 10-30 students.

• *Professional schools programs often have a smaller student/teacher ratio for supervision.* When the faculty spend more time on field supervision, such as in social work or other programs involving licensure, the policies often allow for a smaller number of students for the equivalent of one course.

suggest that complete, effective learning requires an experiential component. Accordingly, this component should receive due recognition in terms of academic credit.

4. The variety of learning which can be effectively pursued experientially should be recognized. Although at least eight different types of learning that result from experiential education have been identified, most faculty consider only one or two possibilities. Recognition of the multiple outcomes of experiential education provides a basis for greater institutional support. See the chapter of this sourcebook entitled "Ensuring Quality in Experiential Education" for the eight learning outcomes.

5. Experiential education should emphasize and document student learning in areas which are seen as academically important and consistent with the institution's mission. It is unrealistic for experiential education to expect instructional resources for learning outcomes, such as student career development, which have minimum academic standing. See the chapter of this sourcebook entitled "Integrating Experiential Education into the Curriculum."

6. Experiential education is best recognized within the institution as a course — i.e., at least the minimum number of students as required by the institution, learning under the supervision of an instructor, and during a specified academic term. It should be understood, however, that the work tasks of the instructor in experiential courses will differ greatly from those of a classroom lecturer. For examples of how schools and departments make these arrangements, see SAMPLES OF POLICIES FOR FACULTY COMPENSATION in this section.

"The administration has to provide the leadership on experiential education. Faculty need the reward system that only the administration can offer."

— Sandra Kanter
   Academic Dean
   College of Public and
      Community Service
   University of
      Massachusetts
   Boston

"Field Education: Faculty serve as liaisons for College/agency agreements. Duties include curriculum development, agency linkage, instruction. Time spent in the activity varies, but is substantial. College regulations permit the assignment of instructional load equivalent to one scheduled course for each agency agreement that includes ten or more students."

-Faculty Work Load
   Policy
   College of Public and
      Community Service
   University of
      Massachusetts
   Boston, Massachusetts

7. Faculty involvement in experiential education is best recognized in terms of teaching responsibility for a course. A course taught experientially should have the same standing in determining faculty work load as one taught in a classroom.

8. Academic administrative support for experiential programs other than provided by faculty should be kept at a minimum. Comparison studies of the time required of faculty for class-

room-based and experience-based instruction indicate that the work load is roughly equivalent for up to twenty students. Sinclair Community College, for example, did a time-and-motion study comparing the work requirements of faculty in credited experiential courses and traditional lecture courses. While the tasks were different, the time required was the same.

9. Support services for experiential education should come whenever possible from existing (i.e., already budgeted) institutional resources. For example, experiential education programs and courses can use the capacities of career planning centers to teach job search skills, placement and student employment offices for referrals to possible positions in the community, learning resource centers for instructional materials for student preparation, and counseling centers to help students with work-related interpersonal skills. Such cooperation requires an understanding of the goals of experiential education by all these actors and an institutional commitment to a carefully coordinated effort.

"At the University of Maryland College Park, the Experiential Learn-

ing Programs office does not provide information on resume writing or general interviewing skills. Students are urged to meet with the retired professionals who voluntarily staff the Career Development Center's resume development program. These volunteers provide intensive help to students preparing resumes and in role-playing interviews."

-Sharon Rubin
   NSIEE Consultant
   and Assistant Dean for
   Undergraduate Studies
   University of Maryland

10. A separate administrative support unit for experiential education, such as a cooperative education office, should concentrate its efforts on coordinating resources and assisting other parties, such as faculty and students, who are responsible for various aspects of experiential learning. The support unit should not assume responsibility for a program task that can be done by another unit already on campus. If the experiential education office tries to do all the tasks itself, the staffing required will be so great that the office will provide an attractive target for institutional

A claim of outstanding educational benefits is seldom persuasive in a contest for institutional resources.

budget cutters. See the chapter of this sourcebook entitled "Establishing Administrative Structures that Fit the Goals of Experiential Education."

11. The location of any administrative support unit for experiential education should be consistent with the school's system for managing other educational resources. At most institutions, this means experiential education is best located within academic affairs, and at large institutions, this means within academic divisions or schools.

Improving the Cost-Efficiency of Experiential Education

A fair share of your institution's financial support is not the only condition needed for experiential education to be economically viable. It is equally important, perhaps more important, to use whatever resources are provided in the most cost-efficient manner possible. Without cost-efficient program operations, the resources available will never seem sufficient; with cost-efficient operations, limited resources can be adequate for a quality program.

Experiential education, like higher education generally, has given very little attention to the cost-efficient use of instructional resources. You can count on one hand the number of articles on this subject in the field of experiential education. The few articles on the economics of experiential education have focused almost exclusively on its cost-effectiveness, making the claim that the educational benefits of this mode for learning are of such magnitude that its cost, however great, is justified. However, a claim of outstanding educational benefits is seldom persuasive in a contest for institutional resources. As discussed earlier, the allocation of resources in higher education is rarely based on the relative educational merits of different instructional strategies. A more realistic strategy is to seek a fair share by whatever means the institution currently divides its resources, and then get the maximum return from these resources with cost-efficient operations.

IDENTIFY THE TASKS - The first step in becoming more cost-efficient is to consider intentionally the different tasks required in providing any experiential learning opportunity to students. There are other tasks involved in a sound experiential education program (faculty development, policy development and implementation, quality controls, etc.), but the following are eight distinct tasks in the actual delivery of experiential education to students:

1. establish educational goals for the course or program,
2. develop work or service sites for experiential learning,
3. help students establish appropriate educational objectives,
4. recruit, select and establish students into work or service positions,
5. prepare students for working and learning,
6. support the learning during the experience,
7. evaluate and assess the learning achieved, and
8. report the learning (transcripts and student records).

DIVIDE UP THE TASKS - With these tasks identified, the next step is to specify who of the several players is responsible for each task. The principal players include the student, the work supervisor, the faculty sponsor, and the institutional administrator (internship program director, cooperative education program director, or other program administrator). In specifying roles, responsibilities are usually shared by the several players with one player having primary

Barbara Hubert, left, and Sally Snodgrass, both of Skidmore College, explore options for program designs for experiential learning at their liberal arts institution.

Claudia Uriba of Saint Peter's College is learning from Martin Fructman of Square Industries, Inc. Ms. Uriba represents the Cooperative Education Program at St. Peter's College.

experience is required for certifying that students have acquired the skills needed in socially critical professions such as nursing, social work, and medical technology. It may not be an appropriate role in experiential programs and courses which have different educational goals.

USE NON-INSTITUTIONAL PERSONNEL - Two critical players in experiential education programs whose roles have not been taken very seriously in most institutions are the work supervisors and the students. The role of work supervisors is usually limited to directing the work of the students; they typically have not been seen by administrators and faculty as having an important role in assisting the student with educational goals. This perspective dates from a time when higher education had a monopoly on advanced knowledge. How times have changed! In today's complex and technologically advanced society, those who direct the work of others are likely to have advanced degrees. In their areas of professional expertise, student work supervisors often have more current and specialized knowledge than the faculty sponsors on campus. To fail to recognize and take advantage of the expertise of these professionals in the instruction of students is a waste of a valuable resource.

Students themselves are by far the most under-utilized resource in experiential education. In most programs and courses, students have a minimal role in planning and managing their own learning! The passive role of the student in the classroom is transferred to a similar role in off-campus,

responsibility and others having secondary or tertiary responsibility. *In reality, practically none of the eight tasks is done by only one party.*

In specifying primary responsibility for the various program tasks, there is no universal set of appropriate role definitions. Instead, there are many possible configurations. Specifying responsibilities is a matter for each institution to decide, recognizing the institution's governance system, available resources, the location of these resources in administrative units, and the relative interest and expertise of the several parties.

One weakness of many experiential education programs, in terms of economic viability and educational

quality, is that the scarce instructional resource of faculty time is focused primarily on the administrative tasks of developing work positions in the community and placing students in these positions. These are two critical tasks, but they can also be done by students themselves. Scarce faculty time might be better spent in student preparation, supporting the learning during the experience, and assessing the learning achieved. Faculty involvement in developing work positions for students has been traditional since the nineteenth century when experiential education was used for the professional education of teachers and physicians. This role may be appropriate in programs where field

Scarce faculty time might be better spent in student preparation, supporting the learning during the experience, and assessing the learning achieved.

experiential learning. This abrogates the basic educational goal of any experiential program — to aid the transition from passivity to self-directedness and personal responsibility for one's own learning. Examples of this educational paternalism abound in many programs. Students are literally "assigned" to work positions in the community which faculty or administrators have developed. We also intercede for students with the work supervisors when the minimum work behaviors, such as keeping the established work schedule, are not being met. These and other examples could support a claim made by some that experiential education may well be the last bulwark of *in loco parentis* on the American college campus.

"We are so concerned that students in field experiences not reflect negatively on the institution that we send out only our very best, we guide them all the way through, and we try to do everything for them. Some schools arrange the students' transportation, find housing for them, and help them out if they spend their money too fast. We treat them like twelve year olds. That's lousy educationally. It defeats the goal of trying to help students learn to take more responsibility for their own learning."

-Tom Little
NSIEE Workshop,
June 1985
Alexandria, Virginia

Students can have a major responsibility for each of the eight program tasks listed above. They should be primarily responsible for developing their own work or service positions — researching possibilities, establishing contacts with the organization, arranging and having interviews, and establishing the conditions of the arrangement. Students can certainly learn the elements of developing a learning plan — defining the work activities, establishing learning objectives for each activity, identifying the resources needed to support their learning, and negotiating with work supervisors and faculty sponsors the

procedures for assessment of both work performance and learning.

For the other program tasks, students can be important partners. They can help prepare themselves for the work experience using a variety of written guides and self-paced instructional programs. They can take primary responsibility for learning at the work site through reading, interviews of working professionals, and conversations with clients and other students. In the assessment task, they should have primary responsibility for providing the evidence of their learning for faculty to evaluate.

Finally, students are also a signif-

icant resource for the administration of experiential education programs. There is a proud tradition of student management of student volunteer programs. Yet, most experiential education programs do not involve students in any administrative roles, even though the management requirements of student volunteer and experiential programs are similar. In most experiential programs and courses, their role is limited to clerical and secretarial support for faculty and program administrators. How can we claim our graduates are ready to assume professional-level responsibilities in the economy if we

SCHOOLS TO CHECK

• **Cornell University** (Field Studies Office, College of Human Ecology, 607-256-6579). Students are actively involved in managing Cornell's off-campus learning programs.

• **University of Maryland** (Experiential Learning Programs, 301-454-4767). Work-study students and other student workers are trained to act as peer advisors, explaining how to arrange internships, answering questions, and screening potential "special needs" cases for the professional staff.

• **University of Michigan** (Department of Psychology, 313-764-1817). This provides a good model for a department-based program that students help to manage. Experienced students do the field supervision and provide peer counseling support for several hundred other students in a field component of an introductory psychology course.

• **Hartwick College** (Internship Office, 607-432-4200, ext. 597). Parents of students help identify potential work sites for other students.

• **University of Missouri** (Career Planning and Placement, 314-882-6803). Former interns provide program information and guide students through the resume and job search process for internships.

• **University of California**, Los Angeles (Field Studies Development, 213-825-7867). Graduate students acting as Field Studies Coordinators work with undergraduates to link field experiences to the discipline. Paid similarly to Teaching Assistants, these graduate students advise interns, recommend readings, and support and monitor student progress.

• **Skidmore College** (Field Experience Program, 518-584-5000, ext. 2216). The contacts of alumni are used to help identify internship work sites for students.

do not consider them competent to assist with the basic management tasks for experiential education?

REDUCE PERSONALIZED PROGRAM ACTIVITIES - Many experiential educators make the mistake of equating individualized instruction with personalized instruction. Each student, work activity, and work environment is unique. This is the beauty of experiential education — to allow each individual student to pursue particular interests through work responsibilities and in an infinitely rich environment. However, do not mistake the unique opportunity for individualized instruction with a requirement for personalized program administration. Evidence of this personalization of experiential education programs abounds. We spend hours counseling students to determine their career interests when there are a number of interest inventories and computer-assisted guidance systems which are both more effective and cost-efficient. We monitor students' progress and support their learning with visits to the work site when written reports from students and telephone conversations with work supervisors can provide more information and a more accurate reflection of the actual learning. This does not mean that site visits are

always unnecessary, but they are a time-consuming way to monitor and assess learning. See Sharon Rubin's "soapbox" position for further discussion of the trap behind trying to personalize each task.

DO PROGRAM TASKS IN THE AGGREGATE - A corollary of the emphasis on personalized program administration is the tendency to work individually with students rather than in groups. Working on program tasks in groups is both cost-efficient and educationally effective. One basic task that lends itself easily to groups is simply providing information on the program itself. In many programs this is done individually — a faculty member or program administrator talking with a single student. A more cost-efficient method is an orientation meeting for potential student participants. Neumann College, for example, holds an introductory meeting for all eligible students. At larger schools, departments or divisions often hold their own orientation meetings for experiential education.

The task of supporting the student during the experience is also ideal for group work. The collective experiences of several students reported in a seminar provide a much richer basis for learning than the experience of a single student as reported to a faculty

member in an office interview or journal entry. Even the task of assessing and evaluating learning need not be through a one-on-one relationship of student and professor. A group approach to analysis, synthesis, and the demonstration of particular competencies can be most effective. Making meaning is definitely aided by the give and take of Socratic inquiry. Demonstrating key interpersonal skills requires a group setting. How can competence in leadership be shown except as a member of a group? The University of Virginia, Rhode Island College, UCLA, and Guilford College are examples of schools that have developed seminars for student interns that are concurrent with their field experiences.

USE APPROPRIATE TECHNOLOGY - In a world of telecommunications, video discs, and the personal computer revolution, many experiential education programs creep along, bound to the printed word and to speech for their communications. This perspective keeps experiential programs and courses from realizing great cost savings from some very simple and inexpensive technologies. Some programs have developed computer-based management information systems — lists of possible work positions, course credits generated, student participants.

In addition, a number of computer-assisted career guidance systems such as SIGI and DISCOVER can help students identify the kinds of work experiences and work environments which are consistent with their interests. A new computer-assisted instructional program called BRIDGING THE GAP can walk a student through the process of developing and executing a learning plan for experiential education. There are numerous computer simulations such as those designed by Thoughtware which can help students develop work-related management and decision-making skills. Finally, video and audio tapes are valuable technologies for effective communications in many of the eight tasks required for experiential programs. For example, students can do an audio tape log to record and report their learning.

Michele Whitham, center, teaches in the College of Human Ecology at Cornell University. Here she responds to a discussion of student roles in administering field studies programs, along with Robert Sigmon, left, and John Duley, right.

A SOAPBOX PLATFORM

THE COUNSELING MODEL: IS IT HARMFUL TO OUR HEALTH?

by Sharon Rubin
Assistant Dean for
    Undergraduate Studies
University of Maryland

"*It*'s not surprising that most of the experiential education programs I've visited use the counseling model as the basis for student-program interaction. After all, most experiential education programs started from the interest of a particular faculty or staff person, rather than from a considered administrative decision about educational alternatives. Because many internship programs began on a small scale, a career counselor or academic advisor could easily arrange a few excellent placement sites with friends in the community, counsel the few interested students, and cajole a few good-hearted faculty to grant academic credit. But when hundreds of students are going through elaborate placement processes with the same committed but exhausted person, we need to ask some hard questions about why the model hasn't changed to meet new circumstances.

The other side of the coin is that we're burned out.

"Experiential educators' resistance to adopting a less personal model is *fierce*. First, many have come out of counseling backgrounds. We have the kinds of personalities that led us to the field in the first place, and we get lots of positive reinforcement from the gratitude of students we've helped to succeed. Second, we feel we are holding our fingers in the dikes of individualized education. We're afraid that any minute our cozy *gemeinschaft* operation is going to be overwhelmed by the *gesellschaft* educational system, where students will be treated identically, and possibly inhumanely. Third, we see ourselves as guardians of quality. With our fail-safe systems of forms, interviews, careful planning and doublechecks, we can prevent students from taking unnecessary risks as they mismatch themselves with the wrong organizations.

Finally — we keep ourselves busy. If anybody doubts how hard we work, we have the student contact to show that we're indispensable to our schools.

"The other side of the coin is that we're burned out. Often at the busiest time of the semester we feel harassed or even overwhelmed. We can hardly believe our exhaustion, and every time we go through the placement process, it's harder to do it with efficiency, attention to detail, and sensitivity to individual differences.

"*The counseling model keeps us from institutionalizing our programs.* We haven't the time to do the kind of research that will provide compelling

---

In putting such a high value on minimizing student risk, we also sometimes minimize student responsibility.

---

evidence of the educational value of internships, or even that will provide evidence that we need more staff. We don't have time to get to know our institutions inside out, to understand which committees can be used to support our purposes, nor which faculty can help us develop strategies for institutional change.

"We sometimes see ourselves as defenders of students against the institution rather than as integral parts *of* the institution. Our intense contact with students makes us forget that faculty and administrators are our peers.

"We sometimes forget that our final goal is to help students become self-directed learners. In putting such a high value on minimizing student risk, we also sometimes minimize student responsibility. In trying to protect quality, we make students very cynical about paperwork as a substitute for educational meaning. In trying to be supportive, we can stifle initiative and infantilize the very students we hope to help make independent.

"If we cling to a counseling model without considering many other alternatives for sharing our work, our responsibilities, and our many pleasures with other administrators, faculty, and students themselves, we embrace a burden that may prove fatal."

-Reprinted from EXPERIENTIAL EDUCATION
(NSIEE newsletter), May-June 1985

For Cost-Efficient Experiential Education —

1. Identify the tasks.
2. Divide them among faculty, administrators, students, and work supervisors.
3. Use non-institutional personnel for program tasks.
4. Reduce personalized program activities.
5. Do program activities in the aggregate.
6. Use appropriate technology.

Making the Transition

*E*xcept for professional curricula in which experiential learning has become traditional, experiential education is in economic transition at most schools. It is moving from a position of having little or no economic standing in the allocation of institutional resources toward a position of economic equity. The principles for realistic models for experiential education, as described above, suggest useful strategies for securing an equity position. For example, if one characteristic of economically viable experiential programs is that they award academic credit consistent with the learning achieved (principle #3), then the strategy needed is to document the learning achieved, compare the result with that expected from a classroom course, and make a case for equivalent academic credit.

The most critical element of economic equity is the time of your faculty. The desired position of economic equity is to recognize faculty time in experiential courses in the same way as in classroom teaching. This condition has not yet been realized at most institutions. The following strategies may assist with this transition on your campus:

1. Make an assessment of the extent of experiential education at your institution. This assessment will very likely document the contribution that faculty are making to the institution in terms of academic credits for which they are

not being recognized. Use the "Inventory of Experiential Education Programs and Courses" in Chapter Two of this book. Such an inventory helps faculty and deans see the scale of experiential education that is already occurring. Then they can develop responsible work load policies that acknowledge the extent of this activity. They can also then begin to ask important questions about quality. Only when experiential education is recognized in

the economic system can faculty be held responsible for any quality standards.

2. Share the results of the inventory with academic administrators, the curriculum and work load committees, and the faculty union if your faculty are represented in collective bargaining.

3. If you are an administrator for an experiential education program in which faculty have an official role, make an annual report of the extent of faculty involvement, i.e., the number of student participants, the number of academic credits generated, the amount of tuition income to the institution, the number of faculty participants, and how many academic credits each generated.

4. Encourage faculty to include involvement in experiential education in their annual reports to their department or division chairpersons. At several institutions, such as Emory and Henry College in Virginia, faculty make this a regular part of their annual reports to the department chair or the dean.

5. Encourage faculty to include involvement in experiential education

Edward Chin of Suffolk University applied his computer skills at IBM as part of his cooperative education experience there.

116

Only when experiential education is recognized in the economic system can faculty be held responsible for any quality standards.

in their requests for academic promotion and tenure. If there are written guidelines for what faculty should include in their promotion and tenure folders, be sure that sponsorship of students in experiential education is included. At UCLA, for example, the Director of Field Studies Development often writes letters to tenure and promotion committees for faculty who have actively used experiential learning.

"The faculty Personnel Committee should explicitly acknowledge the individual faculty role in developing and sponsoring internships when it comes to matters of promotion and tenure."

-Brendan Furnish
Chair, Social Sciences
Westmont College
Santa Barbara,
California

6. Assist faculty in documenting the value to the institution of their involvement in experiential education. Help them document the service provided to the community by students in experiential education.

7. Consider applying for outside grant funds for special purposes, but be careful that you do not undermine your long-range goal of strengthening the institution's central commitment to experiential education.

Encourage faculty to include involvement in experiential education in their requests for academic promotion and tenure.

$ IF YOU THINK A GRANT IS THE ANSWER ...

Many institutions approach NSIEE with questions like "Should we apply for soft money?" or "What foundations give grants for experiential education programs?" And often the query is more like "Our grant just ended. How are we going to support our program?" Some tips —

Grants can be the kiss of death if you expect grants or outside contracts to fund basic, ongoing program functions indefinitely.

$ Grants can be an excellent way to start something new or "prime the pump" to leverage other sources from the institution on a matching basis. Such funds can motivate people to participate.

$ Grants can be the kiss of death if you expect grants or outside contracts to fund basic, ongoing program functions indefinitely.

$ Use grants, donations, or other special funds as seed money to give the extra push needed at the beginning of a project or program expansion.

$ Be very cautious about seeking any grant funds for student or faculty stipends. Once you, the students, the departments, or the students' work supervisors get used to a model that involves soft money for stipends or release time, it is *very* hard to get the same participants to continue their involvement using their own organizational or individual resources.

$ If you do seek outside funds for program operations, get funds that can be continued on a relatively long-term basis (at least 3-4 years). At one time, for example, the University of Virginia had so many interns in the human service sector that the institution was able to get United Way funding because the school was providing staff to service agencies.

$ If you have a Cooperative Education grant or are thinking of applying for one, plan NOW how the institution will fund the program after the grant ends. Sue Williams from Coker College (a rural institution) suggests, "Do a careful market analysis before applying for a co-op grant. Be sure the area can absorb the number of students you project." Also see the chapter entitled "Case Study: Cooperative Education at Tidewater Community College" by Samuel Lamb in *Making Sponsored Experiential Learning Standard Practice.*

$ If a grant pays for any faculty or staff time, pay for small portions of several persons' time rather than paying for two or three full-time salaries. It is much easier to get several departments to pick up small pieces of salaries later than to try to get new institutional funds for full-time positions.

If you have a Cooperative Education grant or are thinking of applying for one, plan NOW how the institution will fund the program after the grant ends.

$ Do not try to do it alone. Work with the Development Office at your institution and only approach funding sources that have demonstrated serious interest in related efforts. Each grant application or funding source that you approach will require 500% more time than you expect.

A Sample of an Institution's Overview of the Value of Experiential Education

"THE VALUES OF PROFESSIONAL PRACTICE"
Professional Practice Program, Illinois State University

To the Faculty —

- course revision and development
- greater awareness of the field or profession
- interaction with more mature and directed students in the classroom and in research
- professional growth and development
- state-of-the-art education of faculty through students
- a network of colleagues and contacts outside academia
- possibilities for consultantships
- possibilities for leaves or temporary employment

To Academic Departments and Colleges —

- external recognition of students and faculty
- program recognition
- attraction and retention of students
- faculty growth and development
- curriculum development and revision
- state-of-the-art education
- attraction of funds from new sources
- building of alumni loyalty
- building of faculty self-image

To the University —

- faculty growth and development
- attraction and retention of students
- raising of academic standards
- curriculum revision
- relations with business and industry
- enhanced ability to attract funds from the private sector
- better career opportunities for students
- greater access to higher education by a more diverse population
- greater service to the public

ential education.

2. Pursue economic recognition for faculty participation in experiential education in the traditional terms of the "coin of the realm" — courses taught, students enrolled, and academic credits generated in the departments.

3. Decentralize experiential education by academic departments as the best means of securing faculty participation and institutional support. Institutional support is more easily aggregated from hundreds of pebbles of faculty participation than from a single administrative unit that manages all experiential education. Some functions of coordination, faculty development, and policy discussions can benefit from centralized leadership, but the departments or divisions must feel the ownership of (and therefore the commitment to) experiential education as a valid process for teaching and learning in their own fields.

4. Provide for program administrative support by expanding the role of non-faculty personnel. Students are a particularly valuable resource. Greater participation by students is not only educationally valid but can provide the deficit financing needed for economic viability of most programs. Work supervisors and existing student services (career offices, etc.) have significant resources and expertise to contribute also.

5. Reduce costs through appropriate technology and greater use of group processes.

Pursue economic recognition for faculty participation in experiential education in the traditional terms of the "coin of the realm" — courses taught, students enrolled, and academic credits generated in the department.

An Optimistic Conclusion

Experiential education has achieved good standing at colleges and universities as a valued means for teaching and learning. Consistent with this recognition is the movement of experiential education to a balance between a focus on the institution and on individual academic departments. Departmental commitment provides the key to securing institutional financial support for experiential education. With this perspective, this chapter can be summarized in terms of five principles:

1. Put your efforts into securing economic recognition for faculty participation in experiental education. Because the primary commodity of a college or university is the time of its faculty, this is the best way to ensure financial support for experi-

A SOAPBOX PLATFORM

"ASK AND YE SHALL RECEIVE"

by Sharon Rubin
Assistant Dean for Undergraduate Studies
University of Maryland

"As experiential educators, we too often slink around the edges of our institutions. We are in some uncomfortable, never-never land between academic and student affairs. We know we are not a department, so we don't have the clout of Biology or English, but we *do* have a significant impact on the curriculum. We serve students, but we have often little connection with the co-curriculum. In short, we dont fit easily into a box on an organizational chart, and we may not feel at home with faculty, students, or administrators.

"Because of our discomfort, we may see ourselves as marginal people, or perhaps more positively as educational reformers. In either case, we generally don't put ourselves forward. We don't approach the power centers on campus. We don't ask for our due.

"Both at Hartwick College and the University of Virginia, some surprising things happened when the Coordinators of internship-type programs *had* to ask for support from their Deans or Vice Presidents. In order to participate in NSIEE's project on 'institutionalizing' experiential education, some agreements had to be negotiated between these Coordinators and their superiors. In both cases, a monetary commitment had to be sought. And in both cases, the weight of the institution had to stand behind the Coordinator's efforts. Guess what happened? They asked, and they got the kind of response they needed — cooperative, interested, and supportive. A few keys to receiving what you ask for are:

- Be able to document in what ways the increased support will lead to excellence in the program.
- Collaborate with other units on campus and other organizations.
- Arrange some funding from another source to prime the pump (surprisingly little will do).
- Indicate thoughtful planning rather than whining.
- Keep administrators well-informed and involved in the program ceremonially or actually.
- Act with confidence in your mission and its significance to the institution."

-Reprinted from EXPERIENTIAL EDUCATION (NSIEE newsletter), January 1985

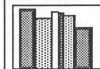 # RECOMMENDED RESOURCES

Breen, Paul, and Whitaker, Urban, *Bridging the Gap: A Learner's Guide to Transferable Skills*, 1984, The Learning Center, Box 27616, San Francisco, CA, 94127. A self-help guide to help students understand their skills.

Stanton, Timothy, and Ali, Kamil, *The Experienced Hand: A Student Manual for Making the Most of an Internship*, sponsored by the National Society for Internships and Experiential Education, 1982. Available from the Carroll Press, P. O. Box 8113, Cranston, RI, 02920. This handbook serves as a self-help guide for students who are seeking an internship. It includes ideas for making the internship a satisfying experience and for reflecting on what one is learning both during and after the field experience.

Thoughtware, Higher Education Management Institute, 924 Talus Drive, Yellow Springs, OH, 45387. Thoughtware provides software for computer simulations that can help students acquire work-related management and decision-making skills. These simulations were originally designed for human resource development programs in the workplace.

Wagner, Jon, "Cost-Effective Design of Sponsored Experiential Education," in *Making Sponsored Experiential Learning Standard Practice*, ed. by Thomas C. Little, New Directions for Experiential Learning, No. 20, 1983, Jossey-Bass, 433 California Street, San Francisco, CA, 94104, pp. 83-97. Addresses a variety of questions about the cost-effectiveness of experiential learning programs: What is essential for the effective and responsible administration of such programs? How can the costs of their benefits be measured and communicated? How can the ratio of benefits to costs be enhanced? Wagner distills some rules for cost savings, both to increase the cost-effectiveness of the institution and to improve the bargaining power of advocates of experiential learning in the contest for institutional resources.

7

Strategies for Institutional Change

*T*his entire sourcebook is a strategy manual. Each chapter suggests approaches for strengthening experiential education within a particular arena of your college or university. This chapter will focus on the *process* of institutional change. It is intended to complement, not summarize, the strategies and tips presented previously. Use it both to clarify your approach and to examine your assumptions about strengthening experiential education in your own school or department.

Systemic changes result from a series of much smaller changes.

The term "institutional change" sounds sweeping, scary, and so difficult that it feels almost silly. We use the term on two levels. First is the level of systemic or structural change, which is indeed infinitely complex. This is the level wherein degree requirements are changed or the expectations for daily faculty use of experiential learning are built. Change at this level almost always takes a long time. And it does not really happen as an identifiable,

planned process in most institutions. Systemic changes result from a series of much smaller changes. Sometimes only after a few years of small adjustments do the scope and nature of the real change become clear. This second level of change — small steps to strengthen experiential education within different arenas of the institution — is the one that will receive most of your attention. Each step contributes to the larger process of "institutionalizing" experiential education within your college or university. If you were just trying to start or improve a particular program for field experiences, the process of change would be much more straightforward — not simple, just more straightforward. It is the very *nature* of the broader goal of institutionalization to be slow and complex because it is reaching to the heart of the academic enterprise — your school's mission, style, curriculum, faculty expectations, quality, administrative structure, and purse strings. We challenge you to plan both your long-range vision and the incremental steps needed to help your school progress toward it. The results will be worth the effort, the time, and the patience because experiential education will in turn strengthen your

institution's capacity to fulfill its multiple missions.

This chapter will draw on the experiences of the NSIEE/FIPSE pilot institutions as they each engaged in a process of planned change to strengthen their use of experiential education. It will also utilize the growing body of literature on how change occurs in organizations in general, and in colleges and universities in particular. By listening to some of the people who have been deeply involved in the process of planned change for two or more years, you can avoid reinventing the wheel. You can at least start with a wheel, and maybe even a wagon. It is a long way from a wagon to a Volvo, though, so get rolling.

Principles of Change in Institutions

*B*efore you plunge into a campaign to strengthen experiential education, consider the *principles* about change in organizations that have been discovered by researchers and by catalysts for change. Students of organization theory and individuals engaged in coaxing institutions toward change report remarkably similar conclusions about what works and what does not. This section divides these principles into four groups. In order to be an effective catalyst or supporter for constructive change, you will need to:

1. Recognize the basic principles of personal and organizational change. After reviewing the voluminous literature on the process of change, we think that the accompanying summary by Walter Sikes will give you the best overview available.

2. Understand the conditions necessary for changes in educational practices to occur. Like all organizations, colleges and universities respond to both internal and external forces to maintain a condition of homeostasis.[1] Therefore, changes in either internal or external needs can initiate change in the college. External forces will always be a strong factor for higher education because it is dependent on external resources. An internal or external perception that an institution is not performing a particular function well is enough to cause a degree of instability in the equilibrium of the college or university as a system. Some such instability or perception of need is thus the first general condition for change to occur. In the words of state legislators, "If it ain't broke, don't fix it."

Secondly, advocates for change are needed. These usually need to be from within the institution. External advocates can have tremendous power in initiating change or creating the level of instability needed for change, but internal advocates are required for the actual process of sustained change.

The third general condition necessary is that of resources for change. This probably does not mean that additional funds are needed. With a change as pervasive as building experiential learning methods into the way the institution teaches students, the necessary resources may come primarily from adjustments in the use of existing resources rather than from new funds.

SOME PRINCIPLES OF PERSONAL AND ORGANIZATIONAL CHANGE

by Walter Sikes

Walter W. Sikes, Ph. D., is the Executive Director of the Center for Creative Change and was formerly program director for the National Training Laboratories Institute and Dean of Students at Antioch College. This summary is reprinted here with the permission of Walter Sikes and the NTL Institute. It appeared in the May 1985 issue of NTL Connections, NTL Institute, Arlington, Virginia.

A few years ago, as I was flying to Memphis to lead a workshop on managing change, I decided to identify what I knew for sure about the principles of change. I could remember lots of research, theories, concepts, and provocative ideas, but they all seemed to be reducible to just four basic generalizations.

This disturbed me because I did not consider four points a sufficient output from a quarter of a century of work as a student and practitioner of change. I later shared my distress with Jack Lindquist, who was presenting the workshop with me, and together we came up with three more generalizations — a thin but possibly more respectable output.

This article presents these seven principles, which I consider the core of what is known about personal and organizational change. Although much more could be said about the various complex processes of change, I feel that the following points represent a good amalgam of the key concepts that persons dealing with change will find helpful.

1. You must know what something is before you try to change it. Diagnosis is the key to effecting planned change. A change agent must have a sound, internalized understanding not only of the "facts" but also the feelings important to the change process. Thus, data collection and feedback are essential to initiating either personal or organizational change. A thorough understanding of the particular dynamics of a system that is to be changed will allow one to tailor the innovation to the specific situation — and greatly increase the chances for success. As Jack Lindquist says, "plan for adaptation, not adoption."

2. Because all human change takes place in systems or organic units, you cannot change just one isolated element. Everything in a system is ultimately connected, so a change in one part affects the whole system. Therefore, one must understand the total impact of the proposed change on all parts of the system so as to reduce the chances of unwanted and unpredicted side effects.

Whether the system constitutes a large, complex organization or a single individual, the person(s) involved probably likes stability and predictability. Kurt Lewin's concept of a field of forces operating to maintain equilibrium presents an accurate image of the tendency of systems to oppose change. When people return from a T Group to their families or work groups, they typically encounter much resistance to their applying their brand-new skills and insights, and much pressure to resume their old behaviors — even if those behaviors were dysfunctional. Partners in architectural firms find it almost impossible to change their functions without involving at least the entire group of partners — and often other members of the firm — in the change process. When designing change, assume that those involved will

— continued next page

probably be reluctant to go along with the new ways of doing things.

3. People resist punishment. Change generally generates discomfort, requiring at the least that one use extra energy to adapt to a new situation. People tend to consider alterations in a system a form of punishment. Even changes that one considers desirable may entail some discomfort. For example, the families of alcoholics frequently become so programmed to deal with the problems of the addict that they resist making changes that would produce more functional behaviors.

We often have difficulty understanding why others consider change so punishing. A parent may wonder, "What does my teenage son consider so painful about reading an additional half hour per day?" Even the son may not be able to give a clear answer — but he knows it feels bad.

4. People are reluctant to undergo current discomfort for long-term gain. Learning a new skill, whether it is technical or behavioral, at the least causes one to undergo the pain of feeling incompetent for a time. We feel more comfortable using familiar behaviors and already-mastered skills, so we prefer to polish, refine, and rely on them rather than develop new, possibly better skills. Even people and organizations taking part in programs to facilitate change tend to depend on the skills developed beforehand and avoid moving into untried areas.

Typically, people will resist changing their lives even on the chance that they will be better off for doing so. When the prospect of future benefit is uncertain, one especially tends to hang onto the current way of doing things. Therefore, people entering a change effort must be provided with support and motivation during the "painful" early stages. They will also find it helpful to experience early rewards.

5. Change generates stress. Studies of the sources of stress have shown that any kind of change induces stress, which is a reaction of a system accommodating new conditions. Changes that we feel we cannot control are the most stressful. Therefore, to reduce the stress of the change process, those affected must, as much as possible, perceive that they can influence the process. They must also have access to devices like support groups that can help them manage their stress.

6. Participation reduces resistance. Probably no principle of social psychology has been studied or confirmed more fully than the concept that one may increase people's acceptance of an innovation by getting them involved in setting goals and devising strategies for achieving these goals.

Such participation, however, requires such preconditions as time in which to consult with those involved, a communications system that allows the parties to reach one another, and sufficient common purposes or values to allow potentially fruitful exchanges to occur. Moreover, those involved must be willing to invest time and energy in the participative process, and those with the most power must be willing to share at least some of that power. These conditions do not always prevail, but frequently they do, and they may often be generated in circumstances in which we assume they are absent. In any event, to the extent that those involved in a changing system can become involved in establishing where the system is going and how it will get there, the movement will occur less stressfully and will likely be more enduring.

7. Behavioral change usually comes in small steps. Few individuals or organizations are willing or able to make dramatic, sweeping changes in a hurry. When we attempt to produce change in another — or ourselves — we usually seek to have it occur right away, especially if the one trying to

---

Typically, people will resist changing their lives even on the chance that they will be better off for doing so.

---

induce the change has more power than the other. When a parent tells a child to stop bouncing on the bed, the parent means "stop now." The child, however, will try to maintain its self-worth and take a few more bounces before stopping. When a boss tells an employee to change her or his way of doing things, the boss usually expects this to occur immediately — but the employee will need some time to make the adjustments requested. This expectation even prevails in T Groups. Despite all of the rules regarding feedback, when a group member expresses a negative reaction to another's behavior, it is usually said in the hope that the behavior will never occur again. Realistically, however, we must realize that abrupt changes in behavior are rare — and probably even unhealthy — and that we must allow adequate time for changes to take place.

These seven points do not represent everything one must know to be an effective change agent. But in my own efforts to bring about or support innovation, I have found that I am more likely to succeed if I can design the effort to take these principles into account.

There are also five more specific conditions necessary for colleges and universities to change their educational practices:

a. What is proposed must be more effective or efficient than current practices in meeting an accepted goal.[2]

b. What is proposed must be consistent with existing values and with what is currently being done in pursuit of these values.[3]

c. What is proposed cannot be perceived as *too* difficult to implement.[4]

d. What is proposed must be dividable into separate components to be introduced across time rather than implemented as a total package at one time.[5]

e. There must be both a mechanism and a language for communicating the benefits of the new practices.

"For any curricular innovation, favorable reception is problematic. Faculty do not see themselves essentially as educators concerned with means and methods. Even in institutions that stress instruction, the emphasis is on content, not process. Where experiential learning is an innovation, communication is even more problematic."[6]

-Tom Little
NSIEE Peer Consultant
and CAEL Regional
Manager

This entire sourcebook is a collection of ideas about mechanisms to communicate the benefits of experiential education. The language and knowledge needed in order for faculty to utilize experiential learning methods has also been developed. The publications of the National Society for Internships and Experiential Education, the Council for Adult and Experiential Learning, and the Cooperative Education Association, and the *New Directions for Experiential Learning* series of Jossey-Bass Publishers can all be used to communicate this knowledge. See the "Recommended Resources" at the end of each chapter and the publications list at the end of this book.

3. Respect the reasons for resistance to change. Walter Sikes' summary suggests several of the most important and valid reasons people and organizations resist change. In addition, a person may discount the value of the proposed change because of a lack of trust in the change agent. Often this lack of trust is not personal, but rather a result of the position the initiator holds in the institution. If you are in a position that is usually held in suspicion or misunderstood by the group who must implement the change you want, then there must be other advocates for the change. In higher education, this means that administrators or other non-faculty personnel almost always *must* work through others if they want to influence the faculty. Faculty as a group are more resistant to change because of their particularly long training in the habits of academe. They observed academicians for years before becoming faculty themselves and thus have especially persistent assumptions and habits.[7]

4. Expect that people will react differently to change. Rogers outlines five types of people in terms of how they deal with innovation in their own social systems:[8]

a. *Innovators* — venturesome, willing to accept risk. Rogers' research suggests that innovators make up 2.5% of the population.

b. *Early Adopters* — respected, regarded by many others in the social system as models (13.5% of the population).

c. *Early Majority* — deliberate, willing to consider innovations only after peers have adopted them (68%).

d. *Late Majority* — skeptical, willing to consider innovation only before adoption occurs (13.5%).

e. *Laggards* — tradition-bound, oriented to the past (2.5%). "While most individuals in a social system

Jane Permaul and Lynn DeMeester listen to a discussion among the NSIEE Peer Consultants about the conditions necessary for changes to take place at a large research university.

are looking for the road to change ahead, the laggard has his attention fixed on the rear view mirror."[9]

Before you read the next section about specific strategies for change, here is one observation about colleges and universities which suggests that the long road to institutionalizing experiential education will be the only road to sustained improvements: "A second ... point concerns the depiction of the pluralistic character of academic institutions and the emphasis on their lack of common goals. Although seemingly a disad-

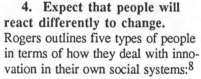

A person may discount the value of the proposed change because of a lack of trust in the change agent.

vantage, this feature of universities does help to ensure that all major issues are widely discussed before decisions are made about how best to deal with them. Despite the anarchical tendencies to reject centrally devised plans, the collegial tradition generally helps in the end to bring about some form of convergence. As a result, the policy that emerges is more likely to reflect the views of those who have to put it into practice than are most hierarchical decisions based upon an imposed consensus."[10]

Specific Strategies You Can Use

As leaders at the NSIEE/FIPSE Pilot Schools used these principles in the process of institutionalizing experiential education on their campuses, they tried quite a variety of strategies. Some worked better than others. Following is our synthesis of the strategies that did work and under what conditions they seem to be most successful.

Know where you want to go. (If you don't know where you're going, any road will get you there.) We cannot stress enough the importance of spending the time needed for a thorough assessment of what is currently happening on your campus and what the needs are. You may have strong feelings about what changes are needed, but a clearer consensus on the current strengths and weaknesses is important for documenting (or altering) your instincts and developing a realistic strategy for strengthening experiential education. This sourcebook contains the following worksheets and guidelines to help with this assessment:

1. "Values of My Institution," Parts 1 and 2, Chapter 1
2. "Values of Experiential Education," Chapter 1
3. "Identifying Student-Centeredness in Learning," Chapter 1
4. "Assessing the Value of the Experiential Educator to the Department or Institution," Chapter 1
5. "Inventory of Experiential Education Programs and Courses," Chapter 2
6. "Assessing Faculty Involvement on Your Campus," Chapter 3
7. "Principles of Good Practice," Chapter 4
8. "Assessing Your Institution's Administrative Model," Parts 1 and 2, Chapter 5

9. "Responsibilities for Primary Functions of Experiential Education Within Your Institution," Chapter 5

Get bottom-up support. Hefferlin's study of curriculum changes in higher education found that "Change is negatively correlated with a feeling of powerlessness defined as domination by administrators and/or senior faculty in decision making."[11] In short, start with input from the people most directly involved. Most colleges and universities have particularly "bottom heavy" power structures because of academic freedom and departmental autonomy. Thus, the general principle of building grassroots support is even more important in colleges than in more hierarchical organizations.

"Negotiate rather than legislate change. Centralized decision making regarding experiential courses and programs will not be very effective. All affected persons and departments need to participate in the discussion and the decisions.... It is important to discuss the nature and benefits of experiential education on a faculty-wide basis. [If we were to start over again, we would] begin with a faculty committee to discuss the issues."

-Edwin Potts
Assistant to the
President
Westmont College
Santa Barbara,
California

If you are in a large institution, you might translate "faculty-wide" to refer to the faculty within your department or division. When asked "What has this work on experiential learning taught you about your own leadership style and about how colleges work?" one academic dean replied:

"First, it has convinced me that an autocratic leadership style will not work in an academic community. I sensed that from the last ten or so years of teaching full-time and from being involved in committees in a college that went through a major curriculum overhaul. As I look back now at the areas where things are not working very well, it seems to me one of the reasons they are not working is that faculty were not adequately involved. Faculty were not invited to be freely involved in the process, in both defining the problems and in identifying solutions.

I see that administrative decisions require listening to the input of a number of people and being sensitive to the concerns of the faculty and others that are directly affected. For example, when I brought Tom Little to campus in February, two of the people that I had him meet with were just not really ready to listen, and it was a waste of time. They perceived my bringing him in as a manipulative power play on my part, to kind of beat them over the head with the expert, the big gun from outside. I

Edwin Potts, Director of Off-Campus Programs and Assistant to the President at Westmont College, has worked closely with his faculty to devise a centrally coordinated, but departmentally controlled field experience program.

The general principle of building grassroots support is even more important in colleges than in more hierarchical situations.

AND NOW, BACK AT THE RANCH!
(Ground Rules For Getting Your Way Against The Odds)

by Morris Keeton

GR 1. Get the People Worried!

Nader couldn't sell safe cars until he had us convinced that ours are "Unsafe at Any Speed!"

a. Have your identified the problem clearly?

b. Is the problem genuine and important? (Surely not bogus?)

c. Do you have enough people worried about it? If not, stop and return to "Start."

GR 2. Finger the Devil! (Or: Market Your Miracle!)

It's all well and good to be concerned about a real need, but can people really visualize the hell it will be without your remedy? Is there any enemy you can get your hands on or at least get your imagination around?

a. Do you have a cogent diagnosis of the problem? No diagnosis means no rationale for your solution. Even if your diagnosis is wrong, you're more likely to find the truth if you at least take a guess.

b. Have you named the problem? How can you exorcise devils, or worship spirits, if you haven't named them?

GR 3. Prepare Your Witches' Brew! (Design a Potent Patent!)

With a real problem and a hateable devil, you still can't get your change without a strategy and a prescription for the ill.

a. Do you have a recipe? Are the ingredients handy? What fuels the fire? Does your prescription fit your diag-

nosis? What if you run out of something? Are your cooks competent? What will you do in an emergency?

GR 4. Mix with Flourish! Surprise the Imps! (Delight the Angels!)

Knowing the chemistry of change as well as the making of good theater will be critical to the outcome of your change process.

a. What do you have for happy surprises? Committed funds are hard to beat.

b. Is there added cause for the initial concern? Solid facts are sure to produce surprise.

c. How will you sustain concern while the brew is brewing? Even if worry is well-grounded, diagnosis sound, and recipe tasty, how are you going to cope with vested interests? Outworn habits? Discouragement and exhaustion?

GR 5. Enlist a Few Demons!

You can't make a significant change all alone. Build some powerful coalitions and disarm the opposition.

a. What's in it for bystanders and opponents? You're outnumbered at the outset. Don't overlook the most unlikely recruits. Let 'em cook, and let 'em eat. You're not Louis XIV!

b. What credits can you give away? Please, not academic credits. But who else gets credit for seeing the problem? Had a hint of the right objective? Had parts of the solution? Your own ego-

— continued next page

really wasn't trying to do that. I had tried to avoid that by not arranging a big workshop when Tom came because I thought that then he would be perceived as someone coming in to tell them all the answers and steamroll the administrative line. In a small sense though, both of these individuals felt that. And if you do that with too many individuals along the line, you just destroy your effectiveness in a leadership capacity.

I've never been comfortable with an autocratic style, and I'm almost relieved to find that it doesn't work. So I can justify my own style, which is much more participatory and laid back. I can look at somebody who is resistant and not immediately see that person as a roadblock, but perhaps as having certain defenses for good reasons. He may have some substantive concerns about the issues, or he may have been so seared by past

encounters with overpowering administrators that he is automatically cautious. My own academic background in anthropology is such that when I come into a new situation (and I've only been at King for two years now), I feel I need to spend some time listening and coming to understand the subculture before I go plunging in like gangbusters anyway. Before I make too many recommendations on some key points, I really

needs are in the way here.

c. How are you drawing on others' priorities? Terminology? Expertise? (Even in hell there's a place for Frank Newman's "enlightened Barnumism," but you don't need to give Frank credit except in Colorado.)

d. How are you cooling the opposition? A few determined devils can outwit a host of indifferent ones. Note the single-issue lobbies and take a hint.

GR 6.   Prepare for Shocks! Be Ready to Improvise!

Remember Murphy's Law. If anything can go wrong, it will. So you must be prepared for unexpected opposition, for discovering mistakes in your basic idea, for treason in your ranks. So when these things happen, be ready both in spirit and with some tricks of your own.

a. What are your strategies for learning as you proceed with your cookery? Remember, you are only guessing at causes and cures. Perhaps the problem as first defined is insolvable. The devils may have surprises for you! But nothing to match your readiness to learn as you go.

b. What are your strategies for improvisation? Can you double the stakes and call? Surrender the leadership without giving up the cause? Improvisation is not indecision, disorganization, planlessness, or incompetence. If you have any of those, you are part of the problem.

GR 7.   Bring to Boil and Serve Hot!

You need to plan for and drive toward consummation of your plan for change. Do not dilly-dally, but also don't lose your nerve and try to finish before the brew is done.

a. Have you a lively timetable and a plan for closure? (When barefoot on hot rocks, keep moving.) Momentum has merits other than avoiding burns.

b. What provisions have you made for the change process itself to be efficient and cost-beneficial?

GR 8.   Hell Hath Its Judgment. Prepare to Meet It!

Every innovation should undergo evaluation, preferably formative (to improve its chances and its outcomes) as you go, but also summative (or is it terminal?) for the benefit of humankind.

a. What are your plans for evaluation of your brew once it has been served? The evil — or good — day can be put off only so far. It may be prudent to schedule it in advance, beginning well before the change is completed, permitting periodic readjustments of the Satanic thermostats.

b. What procedures for response to the evaluation have you provided? (Knowing better is not enough. Next comes doing better.)

GR. 9   Resign Before Fired! (Alternative Scenario: Accept Your Laurels with Modesty, and Don't Let Them Make You Dean!)

Others believe in us. Why shouldn't we?

(Thanks to the formative evaluation of several attempts to develop rules for bringing innovations home to campus. These rules were presented through the Lilly Endowment Workshops on Liberal Education. Special thanks to Frank Newman for his contributions to the rule book.)

---

want to find out more about what's happened here before me so that I can understand people's current reactions and how they're likely to react to new ideas."

-Doug Boyce, Dean
King College
Bristol, Tennessee

Introduce doubt. "Leaders may need to disrupt a comfortable environment in order to make it receptive to change. Few elements disrupt complacent, uncritical environments as much as doubt aimed at the core beliefs of the culture. Challenging these crucial underpinnings can bring old forms of action to a halt, create substantial uncertainty, and heighten receptiveness to change."[12]

Take advantage of changes in the society and in school leadership. As economic shifts, higher tuitions, and questions of cultural values have helped to raise public concern about the quality of college teaching, the outcomes of a college education have received considerable attention. Experiential education is in a strong position because it is premised on what is known about how people learn. Take advantage of the climate of instability (i.e., receptiveness to change) that this and other social developments create. Hefferlin's study found that curriculum changes are positively correlated with shifts in society. As might be expected, the results also show that curriculum changes correlate positively with faculty turnover, institutional growth, and turnover in departmental leadership.[13] The experiences of several of the NSIEE/FIPSE pilot schools confirm this finding.

Use a consultant. A person who is knowledgeable about experiential education *and* about institutionalization issues can be helpful in clarifying your school's (or division's) needs, developing a strategy for addressing those needs, and planning specific next steps in getting started. The National Society for Internships and Experiential Education has developed a small group of such "Peer Experts" who are available for consulting. NSIEE can work with you and your colleagues to determine

---

HOW TO USE AN OUTSIDE CONSULTANT EFFECTIVELY

SOME OPTIONS —

1. *As a co-strategist.* The main role of an outside consultant is to support you and the other "major actors" at your institution to assess and strengthen your strategy for integrating experiential education more fully into the ongoing curriculum, administrative structure, budget, and faculty reward system. Use this person to analyze your goals, your approach, your obstacles, and your tasks.

2. *As an information gatherer.* The consultant can offer you a unique outside perspective by meeting individually or in groups with key faculty, administrators, students, and field sponsors to find out what the hidden strengths and weaknesses of your program(s) are.

3. *As a source of credibility.* By sharing information about successful experiential education programs at other institutions and about the validity of this educational approach, the consultant can help highlight the credibility of your goals. *But* it is equally (or more) important for *you* to be able to articulate the reasons that experiential education fits the mission of your institution. Be *sure* that the consultant helps you with this if you need it.

4. *As an evaluator.* For some institutions, a consultant can be most useful as an assistant in evaluation design. It is unlikely that a thorough evaluation could even be started in one or two days, but the person could help you design your evaluation strategies and give you his or her own assessment of your program's strengths and weaknesses.

5. *As a professional support person.* Feel free to talk with your consultant about your real concerns and needs on the job. Chances are that he or she can suggest several individuals or materials that can help. If the consultant is from NSIEE, he or she *is* a peer and has walked in your shoes before. The consultant can discuss with you ideas for your own professional growth, including suggestions for readings, workshops, and other professional development activities.

6. *As a speaker or trainer.* Training may or may not be the best use of your consultant's time if he or she is only on campus for one or two days. If faculty or staff training is an activity that you feel you need, it is very important that those being "trained" have expressed the need for the type of workshop you are planning. Talk with your consultant about this by phone ahead of time, and be sure you have talked with several people from the recipient group for the prospective training. It may be that a second visit for training related to specific needs expressed during the first visit would be more effective. If you do ask the consultant to do a presentation or provide training, publicize it heavily and be sure there is a turnout that justifies the effort and expense. One faculty member from an NSIEE/FIPSE pilot school recalls, "When our consultant came to campus, announcements were put in faculty members' mailboxes to invite them to come. We had only ten people there. With a few personal calls, we would have had 50-60 people. It was an excellent presentation and very convincing."

7. *As a catalyst.* The consultant's visit is an opportunity for you to put together people whom you'd like to get to know each other. It can also provide a stimulus for the gathering of materials or ideas that are needed to help conceptualize a project or a policy change.

WHAT A CONSULTANT IS NOT!

1. *The Big Gun* — who can come in to wow the dean and get what you cannot get for yourself.
2. *The Mercenary* — to come in and do what you're afraid to do.*
3. *The Magician* — who can transform your program in two days.
4. *The Fan* — to ratify everything you're now doing.
5. *Your Mother-in-Law* — who expects the royal treatment. Simple accommodations and food are fine.
6. *The Godfather* — who is there to settle interpersonal or territorial squabbles.
7. *The Program Planner* — who designs or reshapes your program.

* The consultant can, however, play the role of Visiting Firefighter/starter who can say some things that it is difficult for an inside person to say. The purpose of this may be to get a dialogue started at the institution or in a particular division, or to help in the

— continued next page

rephrasing of the existing dialogue. He or she can even play an unpopular role by saying what no one else wants to say. If this may be appropriate at your institution, be sure that the consultant knows that he or she will be put in this role.

WHAT YOUR CONSULTANT NEEDS AT LEAST A MONTH AHEAD OF THE FIRST VISIT:

1. A catalog
2. A complete organization chart of the college or university
3. Copies of all written materials related to the experiential education program(s) at the institution or in the appropriate unit. This includes brochures, other publicity materials, all relevant written policies, all materials for students and faculty, information for and about site supervisors, questionnaires, application materials, learning contracts, procedures, etc.
4. Samples of several *representative* forms that have been completed. It is important that these not just be your shining examples, but that they represent the work of your strong and weak students, faculty, and site supervisors.
5. Copies of any formal or informal evaluations that have been done by your program or on it; any research that has been conducted for planning or evaluation purposes.
6. Copies of any proposals that have been written for internal or external funding. These are helpful because they often include your basic rationale for your program(s).
7. Vitae of the staff of the program.
8. The name, rank, and department of each faculty member on the faculty committee(s) overseeing or advising the program(s).
9. Alternate dates for the visit in case of snow.

WHAT YOU NEED TO DISCUSS WITH YOUR CONSULTANT AT LEAST TWO WEEKS AHEAD:

1. What you hope to accomplish during the visit. It is very important to focus on the highest priority issues or tasks. What are they?
2. What you can't put in writing, including your complete personal analysis of the situation at your institution and what is needed in order to institutionalize experiential education there.
3. What the consultant's major functions will be. The consultant can only be helpful if you are clear about what you need at this point.
4. How best to use the consultant's time on campus. What format and schedule are you planning? How much "public display" will you need, and how much private time with you and one or two other key individuals? Discuss the individuals and groups with whom the consultant will be meeting. What are the names and positions of each person, and

what are their respective formal and informal roles relevant to experiential education and your program? What is the purpose of each meeting? Unless there is an important reason for a general "courtesy call" with a particular individual or group, it is more effective if each person's specific interests and concerns are clarified ahead of time; this way the consultant can be prepared with the appropriate materials or ideas. Don't make the mistake of telling someone that "So-and-so will be coming by to talk with you at 10:00 about our internship program" without finding out more about what that person would like to discuss. *Work the consultant* and don't just send him or her around to be pleasant to everyone. This does not accomplish much on most campuses.
5. What formal presentations, if any, are expected. What is the purpose? What is the size of the audience, and how do you know? What are the backgrounds of the people who will attend? How long will the presentation last? What format do you want? What kinds of questions are the participants likely to have?
6. What has been tried so far. What has worked, and what has not? Why?
7. Your own personal interest in the institution and how your work there fits into your own career. How long have you been there? How long do you anticipate that you will stay? How secure is your position?
8. If the consultation is about a particular draft policy or materials, provide the consultant with a copy *at least* a week before the visit.

WHAT ELSE?

1. Don't be afraid to schedule the consultant tightly, but do leave time for some relaxed discussion on site with you and other key people.
2. Consider small group discussions with the consultant and selected faculty and administrators rather than having only individual meetings. The stimulus of a group can increase the energy, the range of ideas, and the likelihood of effective follow-up action. Don't use this as a substitute for clarifying the specific responsibilities for each person's follow-through, however.
3. If possible, arrange for the consultant to talk with students who have participated in the program. This is most useful if you include students with different types of experience and different levels of success in the program.
4. What else are you concerned about?

Prepared in 1985 by the National Society for Internships and Experiential Education. If these ideas are utilized by others, we request that you give credit to NSIEE.

whether your institution or division is ready for an outside person and what the most effective roles might be for that person. As Sharon Rubin warns, however, "Such symbolic gestures as bringing in experts can give people the illusion of change while maintaining the status quo."[14] While a consultant can make observations and suggestions, the school has to make its own changes. From our experiences in consulting with many colleges and universities, we

A consultant is not a mercenary to come in and do what you're afraid to do.

have identified some principles for using an outside person effectively. See the preceding shaded area for tips.

Measure what you want to be noticed. "What is measured almost always receives more attention than what is not measured. Hence, moving to quantify an activity can help increase its importance in the way it is regarded within the department"[15] or school.

"Every semester, a faculty member, graduate student or internship coordinator should collect information on the number of student inquiries about internships, the number of students enrolled in experiential courses, [and] the number of agency requests for students. If development of a divisionwide or campuswide program is being considered, an even more comprehensive census is necessary.... However, qualitative benefits must also be assessed. [In addition to the formal assessments of the outcomes of experiential learning,] students, supervisors, and faculty must be polled regularly for anecdotal information on the success of participants. A regular collection of relevant comments from student self-evaluations and from agency and faculty evaluations can also reveal the academic quality inherent in internship experiences. Finally, a collection of student work projects can

help to make decision makers comfortable about extending a program that has obvious academic quality." [16]

-Sharon Rubin
Assistant Dean
for Undergraduate
Studies
University of
Maryland

Use the views of students, alumni, and the community. Students want experiential learning. It engages them in the content of their studies and brings theories to life. Encourage students to voice through all the channels available to them their desire for experiential learning opportunities. Hefferlin found that curriculum change is positively correlated with student participation in educational policy making.[17]

"Much of the pressure for keeping internships at Skidmore has come from students. When we moved away from a 4-1-4 system when internships were done primarily during the January term, students were extremely concerned that internships might be lost. They fought hard. They presented a formal petition at a faculty meeting. They

wrote articles in The Skidmore News. It generated a real furor."

-Barbara Hubert, Director
Career Planning and
Field Experience
Skidmore College

Like students, alumni often have strong views about the value of experiential learning. Most say they wish they had had more opportunities to apply concepts and gain experience while still in school so that they could better understand the relationship between theory and practice. The views of alumni can be influential to policy makers, especially if you make sure the relevant questions are posed to alumni and the results disseminated broadly. Involving alumni as field supervisors and mentors for current students can help to ensure their continued support, both philosophically and financially.

Sometimes even a reluctant liberal arts faculty member will sponsor a student on an internship when the field supervisor is "one of our own." If that student demonstrates valuable liberal arts learning from that experience, the faculty member is more likely to sponsor another student next semester. Also bring respected alumni back to campus to talk to faculty about the value of

Barbara Hubert, right, of Skidmore College discusses with Marlene Steiner Suter of Otterbein College the importance of student input into decisions about experiential education.

what they learned experientially through the curriculum of their alma mater.

Finally, the community can be an ally in your efforts to institutionalize experiential education. If there are potential needs for students to assist with environmental research, opinion surveys, publicity campaigns, computer adaptations, or other projects in your community, bring these to the attention of the appropriate faculty members. If you hear complaints that your school is "disorganized" because employers have to go to a dozen departments for internship

---

To implement the change of a policy or administrative structure, you need top-level support.

---

referrals, raise this problem through a committee or appropriate leaders. Talk with employers about the strengths and weaknesses of your school's graduates. Are there particular competencies — like writing or speaking effectively — that need more attention and that experiential education could help to teach?

Get others to speak for you. Whether you are trying to change attitudes or program structures, those whose support is needed will be more likely to participate if they are approached by their own peers. Faculty like to hear from other faculty. People in Academic Affairs are more likely to listen to others from Academic Affairs than they are to Student Affairs professionals (and vice versa). Potts suggests:

"Work through opinion leaders."
-Edwin Potts
Director of Off-Campus
Programs and Assistant
to the President
Westmont College

Get top-level support. This may sound contrary to the previous advice to "get bottom-up support," but it is not. Support at different levels is needed for different purposes

and at different times. To sell an idea in a college takes grassroots support among faculty. To implement the corresponding change of a policy or administrative structure, you need top-level support.

"[Since we began working toward institutionalizing experiential education,] the need for support for experiential education at the highest administrative level of the College has emerged as essential to the eventual resolution of the issues facing the School of Arts and Sciences."
-Kristen Murtaugh
Director
Cooperative Education
Manhattan College

"We have found that if you ask for help with good information, if you plan instead of whining about how you can't possibly do it, if you prime the pump a little bit (for example, through a university research council which gives funding to faculty for research, some outside money from a co-op grant, collaboration with a couple of units on campus who all want to do the same thing), it takes very little money to get an administrator interested in how to pursue excellence through experiential education. It is really important to involve the highest level of administrators both ceremonially and actually. You not only need to get their permission when you write a grant proposal, but when you give a meeting, invite them to say hello. Then they at least know you exist. When you have an honor to bestow, have the President bestow it to a work site supervisor or to a student whom you are honoring — so that your presence is felt on a continuing and active basis."
-Sharon Rubin
Assistant Dean for
Undergraduate Studies
University of Maryland
Presentation at 1984
NSIEE National
Conference

Plan incremental, not sweeping changes. "Many academics are unwilling to make a five-

year plan, either on the grounds that nothing will change in five years or that they have no power over circumstances. However, in the course of five years, it is possible to introduce a great many changes, a small number at a time, in well-planned stages."[18] Expect the overall process of institutionalizing experiential education to be slow and ongoing. Higher education adheres more closely than almost any other social institution to F. M. Cornford's advice, "Nothing should ever be done for the first time."[19] As Frederick Rudolph succinctly puts it, "Experimentation, which was the life of the university, and innovation, which was its gift to society, were seldom tried upon the colleges and universities themselves."[20]

"Know that it will take time to schedule [opportunities] for input and review."
-Sister Anita Cattafesta
Arts and Sciences
Department
Neumann College
Aston, Pennsylvania

Use other colleges and universities as models. More than most institutions, higher education relies on precedent. While models from within the campus are especially powerful, programs and approaches used at other *peer* institu-

---

It takes very little money to get an administrator interested in how to pursue excellence through experiential education.

---

tions are also good targets for emulation. When advocating for particular programmatic or policy changes, the key is to recommend good models from institutions that are the same as or slightly better than your own in terms of status and academic reputation. As Erik Midelfort says it:

"[At the University of Virginia], it is very important that faculty here

see examples from other prestigious institutions. If a faculty member here reads that Podunk State University is doing a particular program, then that is reason enough not to do it at UVA — no matter how good the program is. The

examples need to be from other comparable institutions."
- H.C. Erik Midelfort
Professor of History and
Associate Dean
College of Arts and Sciences
University of Virginia

Through its Peer Assistance Network in Experiential Learning (PANEL), the National Society for Internships and Experiential Education can provide referrals to different models for various types of administrative structures, faculty

AN INTERVIEW WITH A CATALYST FOR CHANGE

Jim Heffernan conducted this interview with Mary Jo White, Assistant Director of Career Services for the Cooperative Education and Internship Program at the University of Colorado, during a national workshop for the NSIEE/FIPSE pilot schools in June, 1985. Dr. Heffernan is the Vice President for Student Affairs at the SUNY College of Forestry and Environmental Sciences.

Jim Heffernan: What principles of institutional change have you experienced as you participated in this process at your university? You evidently manifested lots of leadership, and it's had an impact.

Mary Jo White: I didn't know that much about the principles of institutional change. What I've experienced in this whole process is just that there *is* a process, and there are certain steps that you have to go through if you want to change anything in a large institution. I never knew before how the committee on courses works. I never knew that the different colleges are so autonomous in deciding what degree requirements their students will have. I always thought that the President or the Vice Chancellor of Academic Affairs sets the policy, but that's not the way it happens. What I learned about this process is that we need support at every level. First of all, it's got to come from faculty because it's *got* to be their initiative that introduces a new process like experiential education. Then you've got to have support from the Committee on Courses or in this case, the Curriculum Committee. You need the support of the dean, first the Associate Dean and then the Dean of the College, because they are the ones who are going to "yea" or "nay" what the committee has to say. Then as you pass things on up the ranks you need support at every single level — the Associate Vice Chancellor, the Vice Chancellor, and then the Chancellor.

JH: And they each have a totally different agenda, and you have to know what these are. You've been a good map maker to have worked through that.

MJW: I was very fortunate in that I had a number of mentors, people in various stages and at different levels of responsibility within the University. On one level I would be introduced to a Vice Chancellor and have to learn how to deal with the Vice Chancellor. On another level I'd be introduced to faculty and I'd have to deal with faculty. And I found that in putting this whole thing together, I had to work on every single layer simultaneously. The only way the changes could happen this quickly was to work on every single layer simultaneously.

JH: So there's a formal structure, and there are informal politics. It sounds like you've got to be a student of both.

MJW: And ask a lot of questions and do it in a meaningful way and ask people for assistance and make sure what you're asking for is realistic. For example, after Associate Dean Charles Middleton of the College of Arts and Sciences and I came back from a visit to the Washington Center, I said, "Okay, now how can we get the University of Colorado to waive the tuition charge to senior students so that they only have to pay tuition for the fall term?" But then I heard, "Wait a minute, wait a minute. We can't do that. First of all we've got to get them to recognize that experiential education is even important and valid." So I had mentors, people who said, "Stop. We have to go back here." And that whole thing was very interesting, very informative, and very frustrating for me at times because I like to see things happen quickly. And I found out more than once that I needed to back up and start again and cover this base before I could go on further. On the question "What did I learn about my leadership style?" I learned that I am a persistent person. If there's something that I feel is worthwhile and that I believe in and that I want to make happen, then I'll do what it takes.

JH: It sounds like a good rule, to back out of a blind alley and not just quit. That persistence really seems to have paid off. We're talking about a lot of progress in two and a half years.

MJW: The other thing I find is that if you really want to win people's respect and their cooperation, then you have to do things. It's one thing when you

— continued next page

compensation systems, and curriculum policies.

"Use papier-mâché instead of concrete."[21] Avoid the tendency to try to anticipate every possible problem in the program or policy by setting rules to address each one. A

Develop policies as they are needed rather than artificially imposing limitations at the beginning.

new approach can sink of its own weight if you load it down with too much structure before it even gets started. Instead, experiment with one department or for a limited time. Develop policies as they are needed rather than artificially imposing

---

ask for something, and they say "Fine." And it's another thing for them to say, "Okay, fine, now you do this and get back to me by next Wednesday with such and such" and knowing that you're going to do it. So you have to be able to follow through and produce results. And you have to do it to their specifications. So you have to play by other people's rules.

JH: And people will tell you their rules?

MJW: Yes, if you ask. Often I will ask what their criteria are, what their standards are, and what they really want to know. How do you want this written? Those kinds of things. You have to learn not to make assumptions because then people are more comfortable dealing with you. In a political model, it's often thought to be out of place to ask what the rules are because "One is supposed to know." Well, if you *don't* know, you'll never get anywhere if you don't ask for help. I found people are very willing to give me guidelines once we have established a personal relationship. I found in this whole process that first of all I had to convince people that I was qualified, that I was somebody who was committed to this cause and that I had some idea of how to go about doing things. It's almost like you have to win them on yourself personally before they're going to listen to your ideas. By establishing that working relationship first, it became very easy to ask questions.

JH: What would you say to someone from another selective, comprehensive research institution who is two years behind you if that person wanted to make the same kind of progress?

Mary Jo White, center, of the University of Colorado discusses the institutional planning process with colleague Gordon Gray. At left is Kaye Sutterer of the Washington Center.

Make sure you're very clear on what your objectives are.

MJW: I would start off by saying to make sure you're very clear on what your objectives are. What kind of program do you really want to have? Do you want a program that just focuses on career development? Well, then maybe it should be in student services. But if you want a program that also focuses on intellectual development and that has the right faculty support, then I would house that program in the academic affairs side of things. I would say to scrutinize the design of your program. Decide whether or not you want a centralized program or a decentralized one. Who's going to run it? Really think of all the administrative structures that will enable you to set up efficient, effective procedures.

The other advice I would give is to know who your supporters are. And make sure you have support at every level where you need it. You don't want to be out talking to a dean about how wonderful this program is and the concept is and how viable it is for them if your own staff is not already sold on the idea. And also, qualify your support. Does that support mean that somebody says, "Yes, yes, yes, you do a great job," or does the support mean, "Here, I'm going to give you $2,000 for this part of the work"? Is it just verbal support, or is it actual participation?

JH: What would you do differently if you could start over?

MJW: I would tie the program closely to Academic Affairs, and I would start with a rather broad definition of experiential education rather than just one model. As I said, we started with cooperative education. So if I could start from scratch, I'd start with a broader definition of my program. What I think is key to our program is faculty support. Now faculty are going to support something that they have a partial interest in. What we do get in being part of career services is the interaction with people who are very well connected to employers. We do need to have a strong employer base in order to offer these field opportunities. Being connected with career services and student services gives us that advantage. There are trade-offs.

limitations at the beginning. A trial approach can be revised during and after the initial period so that the best model emerges over time — in small, incremental steps.

"Try out innovations on a small scale, but establish a good feedback mechanism."
-Edwin Potts
Assistant to the
President
Westmont College

Use outside funding to prime the pump. Grants can stimulate change and offer opportunities for low-risk experimentation. They can also prime the pump for the commitment of institutional funds or other resources. Sometimes it takes very little from a foundation, corporation, or government agency to convince an institution to try something. This can be true for new programs as well as new policies. BEWARE, however, of the *frightfully* common pitfalls of outside funding. These are outlined in "So You Think a Grant Is the Answer" in Chapter 6.

Expect each department or division to react differently. The autonomous nature of most academic departments or other sub-units in colleges and universities means that each has its own culture and priorities. Anticipate that their responses to change will also differ, and respect these differences.

"It always takes twice as long as you think it will to make a decision that involves more than one department."
-Marlene Steiner Suter
Director
Career Planning and
Placement
Otterbein College

"Each basic unit has its own particular type of academic challenge, its own style of operation, its own set of professional practices, its own disciplinary culture. In consequence, solutions to management problems have necessarily to be adapted to the needs of the individual unit rather

than applied globally and without differentiation. The business of implementation ... is best left to the people who know most about how particular policies could be put into effect, and who have to live with their consequences."[22]

Expect resistance. If there were no barriers to overcome, institutionalizing experiential education would not be a process of change. When resistance comes, you have made progress in clarifying what problems need to be addressed. Consider the resistance as an invitation to negotiate. The strength of the resistance will also be a measure of just how big the proposed change is. If it proves to be too big, this is a helpful signal to slow down and break the changes down into smaller steps. If the resistance cannot be overcome and if the proposed change cannot (or should not) be scaled back, work around the resistance. Remember there are five predictable types of responders to innovation — Innovators, Early Adopters, Early Majority, Late Majority, and Laggards.[23] You can expect several of each type on your own campus. It is not productive to spin your wheels trying to convince the Laggards of the need for change or for the particular changes

under consideration. Focus on the Innovators and Early Adaptors first and then on the Early Majority.

Share everything. Look for opportunities to give the visibility and "ownership" of the new policies or programs — and even the strategy for institutionalizing experiential education — to the people who must implement them. With ownership comes commitment. If a strategy for institutionalization or a particular program remains "your baby," it will never gain the commitment needed from others in order for it to work. Like parenting, nurture it and then let it go — or at least bring others into the process — if you want vital and sustained results.

Publicize the progress. Keep as many people as possible aware of proposals and changes as they develop. Then the next incremental step will not seem like a giant leap. This does not mean you should burden people (or make costly political mistakes) by circulating every draft plan or set of brainstorming notes across the campus, but do look for opportunities for broad communication of key developments.

Use rituals or ceremonies. "When a professional sports organization has a losing season, it fires its

Terry Schidoni, SUNY-Oswego intern at Farnham Youth Development Center, says "Counseling young women who are participants in Project Aware has given me a chance to improve my counseling skills. I know now that I want to be a social worker."

coach. The firings don't represent substantive changes so much as symbolic affirmations of the team's commitment to a better future. Inaugurations, ceremonies, and commencements — not to mention receptions, teas, and parties — fulfill analogous symbolic functions at the departmental level and can be used to manage the meanings and interpretations which constitute the groundwork of change."[24] What are the usual ways that changes or special events are recognized on your campus? When you pass a milestone in the institutionalization of experiential education, look for ways to recognize the progress through your school's usual rituals or ceremonies. Have a luncheon for your first group of field sponsors who participated in the newly developed advisory board for community representatives. Plan a faculty reception for the new director of a centralized coordinating office for departmentally controlled experiential learning opportunities. Invite the dean to give the award to the most outstanding faculty sponsor for students doing internships.

Increase your personal effectiveness. Broaden your base in the institution. Become an academic advisor. Sit in on policy committee meetings. Talk to the people in the instructional development center and the office of institutional research. Offer to help with committee assignments through which you could learn about a new area of the institution. Look at the enrollment projections and annual fiscal reports of the institution. In short, learn more about how things work across the campus. If you have not taken the Myers Briggs Type Indicator, you may find this a useful way to understand your own approach to leadership. See the discussion under "Assert Leadership" in Chapter 5. And finally, learn to take risks, there is no way around it: change involves risk.

"Now [all this] sounds drastically like very risky behavior. One of the people at a workshop for the NSIEE/FIPSE schools said to me, 'You know nobody likes to stick his head up and get it shot off.' But you

have to remember that if you put your head down in the sand, the part of your anatomy that is going to get shot off is certainly no better. If you have a strong set of beliefs (as we in experiential education do), and if you have lots of knowledge (which you can get), then it's perfectly acceptable — and will probably work — to take risking behavior."
        -Sharon Rubin
        Assistant Dean
            for Undergraduate
            Studies
        University of Maryland

Assessing Different Strategies

*A*n approach that is right for one problem may be exactly the wrong strategy for another. How do you know if the strategy that you or your committee is considering is the best one? Here are a few questions to ask:

1. Does the strategy fit the culture of your institution? See Chapter 1 for a discussion of institutional values and cultures.

"You have to listen and understand the subculture before you go barging out like gangbusters."
        -Doug Boyce, Dean
        King College

2. Does the strategy fit the size of your institution? For some issues, a successful approach at a small college will be quite different from what will work at a large university. At large schools, the autonomy and strength of the academic departments may dictate a "one at a time" strategy. The presence of graduate programs can present different types of opportunities. There may be more ways to get funds at a large school, and standard course numbers for experiential courses may be even more important than in a small school. Universities are more likely to have precedents for instructional support services that may provide models for centralized support services for experiential education.

3. Does the strategy fit the problem? If you are working to strengthen faculty support for internships, for example, you may find that it is appropriate to spend a year providing relevant publications, information about successful programs at respected institutions, and exposure to a good consultant. If the problem is the lack of compensation for faculty who sponsor experiential learning, on the other hand, information about policies at other institutions may be all that is needed by the faculty on your campus. If you are seeking acceptance of experiential education by top administrators, face-to-face exposure to a knowledgeable source may be useful.

4. Is the strategy better than the alternative(s)? To assess different proposed strategies, answer the following questions about each one and compare your responses:
a. What is the level of risk involved? Am I willing to accept these risks?
b. What will be the result if the strategy is successful? How great a contribution is this result to the

If a strategy for institutionalization of a particular program remains "your baby," it will never gain the commitment needed from others in order for it to work.

overall effort to strengthen experiential education?

c. How likely is the strategy to be successful, and does the likelihood of success make it worth the risk level?

d. How much work will this approach involve? For whom? Is this realistic?

e. How long will it take?

f. What is the cost in non-personnel resources?

g. Does the strategy take into account the short-term needs of the institution as well as the long-term needs?

h. Does the strategy fit the principles of institutional change outlined in this chapter?

For any strategy you devise, the most important challenge will be to help faculty and administrators see the benefits of strengthening experiential education across the institution. If you understand the principles of how change occurs and develop strategies for incremental steps toward the changes needed, you will make a real contribution to the education offered by your institution. Your route will certainly be interesting even if it is a bit unpredictable:

"Scylla is the rock of principle; expediency is Charybdis. Politics being what they are, the ship seldom contrives to steer a straight course between them. Usually, if there is progress, it is achieved by bouncing from one rock to another."[25]

John Duley, Professor Emeritus from Michigan State University, ponders the advantages of various approaches to strengthening experiential education at a liberal arts college.

FOOTNOTES

[1]Thomas C. Little, "Changing Educational Policy," unpublished paper, 1980, p. 7.

[2]Richard I. Evans, *Resistance to Innovation in Higher Education*, Jossey-Bass, San Francisco, California, 1968, pp. 16-17.

[3]*Ibid.*

[4]*Ibid.*

[5]*Ibid.*

[6]Thomas C. Little, Editor, *Making Sponsored Experiential Learning Standard Practice*, New Directions for Experiential Learning, No. 20, Jossey-Bass, San Francisco, California, 1983, p. 23.

[7]Sharon Rubin, "Overcoming Obstacles to Institutionalization of Experiential Learning Programs," in Little, *op. cit.*, 1983, p. 45.

[8]Everett M. Rogers, *Diffusion of Innovation*, Free Press, New York, 1962, p. 155, as quoted by Little, *op. cit.*, 1983, p. 20.

[9]*Ibid.*

[10]Tony Becher, "Principles and Politics: An Interpretative Framework for University Management," *International Journal of Institutional Management in Higher Education*, November 1984, Vol. 8, No. 3, p. 198.

[11]J. B. Lon Hefferlin, *Dynamics of Academic Reform*, Jossey-Bass, San Francisco, California, 1969, as quoted by Little, *op. cit.*, 1980, p. 12.

[12]Kim S. Cameron, "Organizational Adaptation and Higher Education," *Journal of Higher Education*, Vol. 55, No. 2, March-April 1984, as quoted in Academic Leader, Vol. 1, No. 8, September 1985.

[13]Hefferlin, *op. cit.*

[14]Rubin, *op. cit.*, p. 49.

[15]Cameron, *op. cit.*

[16]Rubin, *op. cit.*, pp. 50-51.

[17]Hefferlin, *op. cit.*

[18]Rubin, *op. cit.*, p. 52.

[19]Francis M. Cornford, *Microcosmographia Academia: Being a Guide for the Young Academic Politician*, 5th Edition, Bowers and Bowers, Cambridge, England, 1953, p. 15.

[20]Frederick Rudolph, *The American College and University*, Random House, New York, 1962, p. 492.

[21]Rubin, *op. cit.*, p. 53.

[22]Becher, *op. cit.*, p. 198.

[23]Rogers, *op. cit.*

[24]Cameron, *op. cit.*

[25]F. G. Bailey, *Morality and Expediency*, Blackwell Publishers, Oxford, England, 1977, as quoted in Becher, *op. cit.*, p. 199.

RECOMMENDED RESOURCES

Gross, Edward, and Paul V. Grambsch, *University Goals and Academic Power*, American Council on Education, Washington, D.C., 1968, Chapter 2.

Havelock, Ronald G., *The Change Agent's Guide to Innovation in Education*, Educational Technology Publications, Englewood Cliffs, New Jersey, 1973.

Hefferlin, J. B. Lon, *Dynamics of Academic Reform*, Jossey-Bass, San Francisco, California, 1969.

Little, Thomas C. Editor, *Making Sponsored Experiential Learning Standard Practice*, New Directions for Experiential Learning, No. 20, Jossey-Bass, San Francisco, California, 1983.

Rogers, Everett M., *Diffusion of Innovation*, Free Press, New York, 1962.

Watson, Goodwin B., and Edward M. Glaser, "What We Have Learned About Planning for Change," *Management Review*, November 1965, pp. 44-46.

PARTING RHYME ON NSIEE CONFERENCE
by Lynn DeMeester

Excerpted from a poetic summary at the end of a workshop sponsored by the National Society for Internships and Experiential Education on June 10-12, 1985, in Alexandria, Virginia. Dr. DeMeester is a Program Officer at the Fund for the Improvement of Postsecondary Education (FIPSE).

The purpose today is to be wise and sagacious,
To synthesize meanings without being outrageous;
I considered that goal for a moment or two,
And quickly decided: the following will do!!

The Team:
Little, Permaul, Rubin and Duley
Kendall keeps them from being unruly;
Your peer experts, mentors, colleagues and friends
The outsider could say what inside offends;
They consulted, assisted, prodded, cajoled,
Sometimes low-key, sometimes bold;
Jane formed networks of many and networks of few,
Said, "You'll know your next question before you are
 through!
FIPSE seeks to learn from you,
FIPSE seeks to learn from you!"

The Meeting:
You spoke with peer experts, heard the Dean's
 perspective,
Discussed the sourcebook, played project detective,
Analyzed collegiate decision styles,
Examined barriers and inducements awhile;
You pre-conferenced, post-conferenced, interviewed too,
Did charts and surveys before you were through.
Axioms and pundits were easy to net,
One said: I read and I forget;
Another one, quite fine and grand,
Said: I see and I understand;
A third, like a smouldering ember,
Conveyed: I do and I remember.
For days now you've discussed topics concerning
The design and content of experiential learning,
Pay and credits, administrative concerns,
A central issue is how students best learn;
Psychology, sociology, work is the text,
The content's unleashed, anything's next;
New developments have emerged in learning technique
For pondering the sublime, analyzing the unique.
Journals, work samples, simple observation

Discourse, debate and course simulation;
Avoid parceling learning into discrete compartments
Unless you wish to mimic departments.

Faculty:
Are you feeling suspicious, cautious and slow
Unsure how to measure what students might know?
Unconvinced of the worksite's educational niche
Afraid it's really a well-hyped gliche?

Deans:
Do you find the administrative-academic nexus,
Is the rub and problem that perplexes?
Do you fight tough issues of resource allocation,
Not to mention faculty compensation?
Staffing, equipment, transcripts and space
No wonder you feel in the rats' rat-race.
Do you find that your budget is deeply buried,
Your lives eclectic and slightly harried?

Program Administrators:
Your programs seek validity
In the wasteland of institutional rigidity;
For students, your programs know no dirth
Do you think this is an issue of comparable worth?
Stick out your neck, take a risk
If it doesn't work, cease and desist;
Are you haunted by a ghost — the undercredential,
Perceptions that PhDs are essential?
Perhaps we construct false reality
Creating the we-they duality.
The term marginality was sometimes used,
Transformed to advantage it allows you to fuse,
Cross department ties and use of your roles,
Building networks, thereby advancing your goals;

Building Support:
Essential, of course, are friendly cohorts,
It helps a lot if there's top-level support;
Nurture the advocates, convert the sour
Form advisory committees to amass group power;

Do you know your sources of support?
And have a loyal team cohort ?
Can you build departmentally diverse coalitions
Which then proceed on their own volition?

Really Building Top-Level Support:
Does the program contribute to institutional mission?
Advance others' agendas with new founded vision?
Engage top administrators in community relations
Requiring erstwhile their active participation?

Dissemination and Evaluation:
Does your program need some visibility
Brochures, catalogues, and publicity?
A press release has a central place
As does a well developed case
Of students who were wise and discerning
In applying to studies their worksite learning.
We argue experiential education for students.
It's sound, it's active, it's educationally prudent,
It's inductive, real world, a formative treasure,
It's just slightly elusive and difficult to measure.
What is the meaning of quality control?
A production term for goods that are sold?
Assurance that products are worthy of credit
Instead of tallying a learning debit?
It's your job to quantify and discern
Just how much students really learn
Co-op, work study, experiential learning
Oh those feds are yearning
FIPSE seeks to learn from you
FIPSE seeks to learn from you.
What have you learned of institutional change?

That it's slightly unwieldly, mightily strange?
Smuggled in sideways, top down on occasion,
Is often a ripple, sometimes a sensation?
Do you think that there's a central logic,
In treating your program like a federal project
With concerns of administration, budget and scope
Communication and how to keep it afloat?

Institutionalization:
There seems to me a perverse kind of logic,
If after this we must institutionalize your project
Better your project, however, than you
To be institutionalized before you are through.
You've been through two days of quite an immersion
Perhaps a slight bit of NSIEE conversion,
Quantify, qualify, seize the lead
The process of change is strategic indeed;
Admissions, retention, for new program starts
Discover what tugs at administrators' hearts;
Jump the system if you must,
Be bold, be resourceful and robust;
But treat sacred cows with hallowed reverence
Or your pay may be on the way to severence;
Discover the information nets,
Whom it begats and whom it begets.
May your various programs flourish and abound
With your goals in the sky but your feet on the ground,
May you have a budget, permanent staff and more,
An office with windows on the President's floor!
So on to the Sourcebook, and questions anew,
Remember, FIPSE seeks to learn from you,
Before you are through,
FIPSE seeks to learn from you.

Index

145

Publications of the
National Society for Internships and Experiential Education

nsiee

Order Form

Quantity ordered

Quantity ordered

The National Directory of Internships
by Barbara A. Coluni.

    A directory of over 800 internship opportunities across the country for students and adults of all ages. Divided by type of organization. Contains indexes by field of interest, location, and name of the host organization. 315 pp., $12 NSIEE members, $15 others.

Integrating the Community and the
Classroom: A Sampler of Postsecondary
Courses by Carol Murphy and Lynn Jenks.

    A collection of syllabi for humanities and social sciences courses with field experience components. Useful for faculty and administrators. Includes an extensive bibliography on experiential education and sample forms for learning contracts, applications, and evaluations of both students and the courses. 256 pp., $12 NSIEE members, $15 others.

Preparing Humanists for Work: A
National Study of Undergraduate Internships
in the Humanities by Carren O. Kaston with James M. Heffernan, the Washington Center, sponsored by the National Endowment for the Humanities.

    Results and analysis of a major national study of the internship programs offered by humanities departments across the country. 99 pp., $8 NSIEE members, $9 others.

Strengthening Experiential Education
Within Your Institution by Jane C. Kendall, John S. Duley, Thomas C. Little, Jane S. Permaul, and Sharon Rubin.

    A sourcebook for college and university administrators and faculty who want to help their institutions tap the full benefits of experiential education. Includes chapters on building experiential learning into the institution's mission, curriculum, faculty roles, quality controls, administrative structures, and financial system. $17 NSIEE members, $20 others.

A Guide to Environmental Internships
by Jane C. Kendall.

    A concise handbook about how to utilize internships effectively in any organization. Examples are drawn from environmental organizations. 48 pp., $4 NSIEE members, $5 for others.

PANEL RESOURCE PAPERS —

    Concise papers on major issues to consider in designing, administering, or evaluating programs for experiential learning. $6 each.

    #1 - *History and Rationale for Experiential Learning* by Thomas C. Little

    #2 - *How to Start a Program* by Robert Davis, et. al.

    #3 - *Legal Issues in Experiential Education* by Michael Goldstein

    # 4 - *Prefield Preparation: What, Why, How?* by Timothy Stanton and Michele Whitham

    #5 - *Monitoring and Supporting Experiential Learning* by Jane Szutu Permaul

    #6 - *Learning Outcomes: Measuring and Evaluating Experiential Learning* by John Duley

    #7 - *Performance Appraisal Practices: A Guide to Better Supervisor Evaluation Processes* by Sharon Rubin

    #8 - *Applications of Developmental Theory to the Design and Conduct of Quality Field Experience Programs: Exercises for Educators* by Michele Whitham and Albert Erdynast

    #9 - *Internships in History* by Suellen Hoy, Robert Sexton, Peter Stearns, and Joel Tarr

    #10 - *Research Bibliography in Experiential Learning, Internships, and Field Studies* by Jennifer Anderson with Leslie Smith

    #11 - *Environmental Internships* by R. Rajagopal

    #12 - *Experiential Learning and Cultural Anthropology* by E. L. Cerroni-Long and Sharon Rubin

147

	Quantity Ordered

#13 - *Self-Directed Adult Learners and Learning* by Virginia R. Griffin   ____

#14 - *Research Agenda for Experiential Education in the 80's* by Jennifer Anderson, Linda Hughes, and Jane Szutu Permaul   ____

NSIEE OCCASIONAL PAPERS -

Monograph series on concepts in experiential education and issues of quality. $5 NSIEE members, $7 others.

#1 - *Toward a Comprehensive Model of Clustering Skills* by John W. Munce   ____

#2 - *The Immediate Usefulness of the Liberal Arts: Variations on a Theme* by John M. Bevan   ____

#3 - *Policy Issues in Experiential Education* by Michael B. Goldstein   ____

#4 - *Field Experience and Stage Theories of Development* by Albert Erdynast   ____

#5 - *Students at Work: Identifying Learning in Internship Settings* by David Thornton Moore   ____

#6 - *Life Developmental Tasks and Related Learning Needs and Outcomes* by Judy-Arin Krupp   ____

#7 - *Dimensions of Experiential Education* edited by Robert F. Sexton   ____

#8 - *Public Service Internships and Education in Public Affairs* by Allen Rosenbaum   ____

NSIEE-SPONSORED GUIDES AVAILABLE THROUGH OTHER PUBLISHERS:

The Experienced Hand: A Student Manual for Making the Most of an Internship by Timothy Stanton and Kamil Ali.

Ten steps show students how to get a satisfying internship and how to learn the most from the experience. Includes sample forms for all stages of the internship process as well as tips for evaluating what is learned. Useful as a text book in courses with internship components and for the departmental library. 1982, 96 pp., $6 for NSIEE members, $6.95 for others. Prices include postage and handling. Send check to Carroll Press, P. O. Box 8113, Cranston, RI, 02920.

Field Experience: Expand Your Options edited by John Duley.

Six do-it-yourself modules to help students decide what type of field experience or internship best fits their current learning goals. $5.50 (includes postage and handling). Send check to Instructional Media Center, Michigan State University, East Lansing, MI, 48824.

TOTAL OF BOOKS $ _____

Plus required handling fee:
Up to $20 order - add $2.00
Up to $50 order - add $3.50
Over $50 order - add $5.00   + _____
   Includes 4th Class postage and processing costs. Please allow 4-6 weeks for delivery.

OPTIONAL
For 1st Class delivery add an   + _____
additional $1.50 for first publication and $. 50 for each additional publication.

TOTAL PAYMENT DUE $ _____
Full payment or credit card charge *must* accompany order. Make checks payable to NSIEE. Foreign orders must be paid in U.S. funds. Credit card users complete credit card section. All prices subject to change without notice.

Mail to:
National Society for Internships and Experiential Education
122 St. Mary's Street
Raleigh, NC 27605
(919) 834-7536

Name _____ Title _____

Program/Department _____

Institution _____

Address _____

_____ Zip _____

Area Code and Phone Number _____

Are you a member of NSIEE?   ☐ I would like information
Yes ☐   No ☐   about membership in NSIEE.

Credit Card Section

☐ Visa   ☐ Mastercard   Expiration date _____

Card No. _____

Account name _____

Signature _____

Publications of the

National Society for Internships and Experiential Education

Order Form

Quantity ordered

The National Directory of Internships
by Barbara A. Coluni. ____

A directory of over 800 internship opportunities across the country for students and adults of all ages. Divided by type of organization. Contains indexes by field of interest, location, and name of the host organization. 315 pp., $12 NSIEE members, $15 others.

Integrating the Community and the Classroom: A Sampler of Postsecondary Courses by Carol Murphy and Lynn Jenks. ____

A collection of syllabi for humanities and social sciences courses with field experience components. Useful for faculty and administrators. Includes an extensive bibliography on experiential education and sample forms for learning contracts, applications, and evaluations of both students and the courses. 256 pp., $12 NSIEE members, $15 others.

Preparing Humanists for Work: A National Study of Undergraduate Internships in the Humanities by Carren O. Kaston with James M. Heffernan, the Washington Center, sponsored by the National Endowment for the Humanities. ____

Results and analysis of a major national study of the internship programs offered by humanities departments across the country. 99 pp., $8 NSIEE members, $9 others.

Strengthening Experiential Education Within Your Institution by Jane C. Kendall, John S. Duley, Thomas C. Little, Jane S. Permaul, and Sharon Rubin. ____

A sourcebook for college and university administrators and faculty who want to help their institutions tap the full benefits of experiential education. Includes chapters on building experiential learning into the institution's mission, curriculum, faculty roles, quality controls, administrative structures, and financial system. $17 NSIEE members, $20 others.

Quantity ordered

A Guide to Environmental Internships
by Jane C. Kendall. ____

A concise handbook about how to utilize internships effectively in any organization. Examples are drawn from environmental organizations. 48 pp., $4 NSIEE members, $5 for others.

PANEL RESOURCE PAPERS —
Concise papers on major issues to consider in designing, administering, or evaluating programs for experiential learning. $6 each.

#1 - *History and Rationale for Experiential Learning* by Thomas C. Little ____

#2 - *How to Start a Program* by Robert Davis, et. al. ____

#3 - *Legal Issues in Experiential Education* by Michael Goldstein ____

4 - *Prefield Preparation: What, Why, How?* by Timothy Stanton and Michele Whitham ____

#5 - *Monitoring and Supporting Experiential Learning* by Jane Szutu Permaul ____

#6 - *Learning Outcomes: Measuring and Evaluating Experiential Learning* by John Duley ____

#7 - *Performance Appraisal Practices: A Guide to Better Supervisor Evaluation Processes* by Sharon Rubin ____

#8 - *Applications of Developmental Theory to the Design and Conduct of Quality Field Experience Programs: Exercises for Educators* by Michele Whitham and Albert Erdynast ____

#9 - *Internships in History* by Suellen Hoy, Robert Sexton, Peter Stearns, and Joel Tarr ____

#10 - *Research Bibliography in Experiential Learning, Internships, and Field Studies* by Jennifer Anderson with Leslie Smith ____

#11 - *Environmental Internships* by R. Rajagopal ____

#12 - *Experiential Learning and Cultural Anthropology* by E. L. Cerroni-Long and Sharon Rubin ____

149

	Quantity Ordered

#13 - *Self-Directed Adult Learners and Learning* by Virginia R. Griffin ____

#14 - *Research Agenda for Experiential Education in the 80's* by Jennifer Anderson, Linda Hughes, and Jane Szutu Permaul ____

NSIEE OCCASIONAL PAPERS -

Monograph series on concepts in experiential education and issues of quality. $5 NSIEE members, $7 others.

#1 - *Toward a Comprehensive Model of Clustering Skills* by John W. Munce ____

#2 - *The Immediate Usefulness of the Liberal Arts: Variations on a Theme* by John M. Bevan ____

#3 - *Policy Issues in Experiential Education* by Michael B. Goldstein ____

#4 - *Field Experience and Stage Theories of Development* by Albert Erdynast ____

#5 - *Students at Work: Identifying Learning in Internship Settings* by David Thornton Moore ____

#6 - *Life Developmental Tasks and Related Learning Needs and Outcomes* by Judy-Arin Krupp ____

#7 - *Dimensions of Experiential Education* edited by Robert F. Sexton ____

#8 - *Public Service Internships and Education in Public Affairs* by Allen Rosenbaum ____

NSIEE-SPONSORED GUIDES AVAILABLE THROUGH OTHER PUBLISHERS:

The Experienced Hand: A Student Manual for Making the Most of an Internship by Timothy Stanton and Kamil Ali.

Ten steps show students how to get a satisfying internship and how to learn the most from the experience. Includes sample forms for all stages of the internship process as well as tips for evaluating what is learned. Useful as a text book in courses with internship components and for the departmental library. 1982, 96 pp., $6 for NSIEE members, $6.95 for others. Prices include postage and handling. Send check to Carroll Press, P. O. Box 8113, Cranston, RI, 02920.

Field Experience: Expand Your Options edited by John Duley.

Six do-it-yourself modules to help students decide what type of field experience or internship best fits their current learning goals. $5.50 (includes postage and handling). Send check to Instructional Media Center, Michigan State University, East Lansing, MI, 48824.

TOTAL OF BOOKS $ _____

Plus required handling fee:
Up to $20 order - add $2.00
Up to $50 order - add $3.50
Over $50 order - add $5.00 + _____
Includes 4th Class postage and processing costs. Please allow 4-6 weeks for delivery.

OPTIONAL
For 1st Class delivery add an + _____
additional $1.50 for first publication
and $.50 for each additional publication.

TOTAL PAYMENT DUE $ _____
Full payment or credit card charge *must* accompany order. Make checks payable to NSIEE. Foreign orders must be paid in U.S. funds. Credit card users complete credit card section. All prices subject to change without notice.

Mail to:
National Society for Internships and Experiential Education
122 St. Mary's Street
Raleigh, NC 27605
(919) 834-7536

Name _____ Title _____

Program/Department _____

Institution _____

Address _____

_____ Zip _____

Area Code and Phone Number _____

Are you a member of NSIEE?   ☐ I would like information
Yes ☐   No ☐   about membership in NSIEE.

Credit Card Section

☐ Visa   ☐ Mastercard   Expiration date _____

Card No. _____

Account name _____

Signature _____

Publications of the
National Society for Internships and Experiential Education

Order Form

	Quantity ordered

The National Directory of Internships
by Barbara A. Coluni.

A directory of over 800 internship opportunities across the country for students and adults of all ages. Divided by type of organization. Contains indexes by field of interest, location, and name of the host organization. 315 pp., $12 NSIEE members, $15 others.

Integrating the Community and the Classroom: A Sampler of Postsecondary Courses by Carol Murphy and Lynn Jenks.

A collection of syllabi for humanities and social sciences courses with field experience components. Useful for faculty and administrators. Includes an extensive bibliography on experiential education and sample forms for learning contracts, applications, and evaluations of both students and the courses. 256 pp., $12 NSIEE members, $15 others.

Preparing Humanists for Work: A National Study of Undergraduate Internships in the Humanities by Carren O. Kaston with James M. Heffernan, the Washington Center, sponsored by the National Endowment for the Humanities.

Results and analysis of a major national study of the internship programs offered by humanities departments across the country. 99 pp., $8 NSIEE members, $9 others.

Strengthening Experiential Education Within Your Institution by Jane C. Kendall, John S. Duley, Thomas C. Little, Jane S. Permaul, and Sharon Rubin.

A sourcebook for college and university administrators and faculty who want to help their institutions tap the full benefits of experiential education. Includes chapters on building experiential learning into the institution's mission, curriculum, faculty roles, quality controls, administrative structures, and financial system. $17 NSIEE members, $20 others.

	Quantity ordered

A Guide to Environmental Internships by Jane C. Kendall.

A concise handbook about how to utilize internships effectively in any organization. Examples are drawn from environmental organizations. 48 pp., $4 NSIEE members, $5 for others.

PANEL RESOURCE PAPERS —

Concise papers on major issues to consider in designing, administering, or evaluating programs for experiential learning. $6 each.

#1 - *History and Rationale for Experiential Learning* by Thomas C. Little

#2 - *How to Start a Program* by Robert Davis, et. al.

#3 - *Legal Issues in Experiential Education* by Michael Goldstein

#4 - *Prefield Preparation: What, Why, How?* by Timothy Stanton and Michele Whitham

#5 - *Monitoring and Supporting Experiential Learning* by Jane Szutu Permaul

#6 - *Learning Outcomes: Measuring and Evaluating Experiential Learning* by John Duley

#7 - *Performance Appraisal Practices: A Guide to Better Supervisor Evaluation Processes* by Sharon Rubin

#8 - *Applications of Developmental Theory to the Design and Conduct of Quality Field Experience Programs: Exercises for Educators* by Michele Whitham and Albert Erdynast

#9 - *Internships in History* by Suellen Hoy, Robert Sexton, Peter Stearns, and Joel Tarr

#10 - *Research Bibliography in Experiential Learning, Internships, and Field Studies* by Jennifer Anderson with Leslie Smith

#11 - *Environmental Internships* by R. Rajagopal

#12 - *Experiential Learning and Cultural Anthropology* by E. L. Cerroni-Long and Sharon Rubin

	Quantity Ordered

#13 - *Self-Directed Adult Learners and Learning* by Virginia R. Griffin ____

#14 - *Research Agenda for Experiential Education in the 80's* by Jennifer Anderson, Linda Hughes, and Jane Szutu Permaul ____

NSIEE OCCASIONAL PAPERS -

Monograph series on concepts in experiential education and issues of quality. $5 NSIEE members, $7 others.

#1 - *Toward a Comprehensive Model of Clustering Skills* by John W. Munce ____

#2 - *The Immediate Usefulness of the Liberal Arts: Variations on a Theme* by John M. Bevan ____

#3 - *Policy Issues in Experiential Education* by Michael B. Goldstein ____

#4 - *Field Experience and Stage Theories of Development* by Albert Erdynast ____

#5 - *Students at Work: Identifying Learning in Internship Settings* by David Thornton Moore ____

#6 - *Life Developmental Tasks and Related Learning Needs and Outcomes* by Judy-Arin Krupp ____

#7 - *Dimensions of Experiential Education* edited by Robert F. Sexton ____

#8 - *Public Service Internships and Education in Public Affairs* by Allen Rosenbaum ____

NSIEE-SPONSORED GUIDES AVAILABLE THROUGH OTHER PUBLISHERS:

The Experienced Hand: A Student Manual for Making the Most of an Internship by Timothy Stanton and Kamil Ali.

Ten steps show students how to get a satisfying internship and how to learn the most from the experience. Includes sample forms for all stages of the internship process as well as tips for evaluating what is learned. Useful as a text book in courses with internship components and for the departmental library. 1982, 96 pp., $6 for NSIEE members, $6.95 for others. Prices include postage and handling. Send check to Carroll Press, P. O. Box 8113, Cranston, RI, 02920.

Field Experience: Expand Your Options edited by John Duley.

Six do-it-yourself modules to help students decide what type of field experience or internship best fits their current learning goals. $5.50 (includes postage and handling). Send check to Instructional Media Center, Michigan State University, East Lansing, MI, 48824.

TOTAL OF BOOKS $ _____

Plus required handling fee:
Up to $20 order - add $2.00
Up to $50 order - add $3.50
Over $50 order - add $5.00 + _____
  Includes 4th Class postage and processing costs. Please allow 4-6 weeks for delivery.

OPTIONAL
For lst Class delivery add an + _____ additional $1.50 for first publication and $.50 for each additional publication.

TOTAL PAYMENT DUE $ _____
Full payment or credit card charge *must* accompany order. Make checks payable to NSIEE. Foreign orders must be paid in U.S. funds. Credit card users complete credit card section. All prices subject to change without notice.

Mail to:
National Society for Internships and Experiential Education
122 St. Mary's Street
Raleigh, NC 27605
(919) 834-7536

Name _____ Title _____

Program/Department _____

Institution _____

Address _____

_____ Zip _____

Area Code and Phone Number _____

Are you a member of NSIEE?   ☐ I would like information
Yes ☐   No ☐   about membership in NSIEE.

Credit Card Section

☐ Visa   ☐ Mastercard   Expiration date _____

Card No. _____

Account name _____

Signature _____

Publications of the
National Society for Internships and Experiential Education

Order Form

Quantity ordered

Quantity ordered

The National Directory of Internships by Barbara A. Coluni.

A directory of over 800 internship opportunities across the country for students and adults of all ages. Divided by type of organization. Contains indexes by field of interest, location, and name of the host organization. 315 pp., $12 NSIEE members, $15 others.

Integrating the Community and the Classroom: A Sampler of Postsecondary Courses by Carol Murphy and Lynn Jenks.

A collection of syllabi for humanities and social sciences courses with field experience components. Useful for faculty and administrators. Includes an extensive bibliography on experiential education and sample forms for learning contracts, applications, and evaluations of both students and the courses. 256 pp., $12 NSIEE members, $15 others.

Preparing Humanists for Work: A National Study of Undergraduate Internships in the Humanities by Carren O. Kaston with James M. Heffernan, the Washington Center, sponsored by the National Endowment for the Humanities.

Results and analysis of a major national study of the internship programs offered by humanities departments across the country. 99 pp., $8 NSIEE members, $9 others.

Strengthening Experiential Education Within Your Institution by Jane C. Kendall, John S. Duley, Thomas C. Little, Jane S. Permaul, and Sharon Rubin.

A sourcebook for college and university administrators and faculty who want to help their institutions tap the full benefits of experiential education. Includes chapters on building experiential learning into the institution's mission, curriculum, faculty roles, quality controls, administrative structures, and financial system. $17 NSIEE members, $20 others.

A Guide to Environmental Internships by Jane C. Kendall.

A concise handbook about how to utilize internships effectively in any organization. Examples are drawn from environmental organizations. 48 pp., $4 NSIEE members, $5 for others.

PANEL RESOURCE PAPERS —

Concise papers on major issues to consider in designing, administering, or evaluating programs for experiential learning. $6 each.

#1 - *History and Rationale for Experiential Learning* by Thomas C. Little

#2 - *How to Start a Program* by Robert Davis, et. al.

#3 - *Legal Issues in Experiential Education* by Michael Goldstein

4 - *Prefield Preparation: What, Why, How?* by Timothy Stanton and Michele Whitham

#5 - *Monitoring and Supporting Experiential Learning* by Jane Szutu Permaul

#6 - *Learning Outcomes: Measuring and Evaluating Experiential Learning* by John Duley

#7 - *Performance Appraisal Practices: A Guide to Better Supervisor Evaluation Processes* by Sharon Rubin

#8 - *Applications of Developmental Theory to the Design and Conduct of Quality Field Experience Programs: Exercises for Educators* by Michele Whitham and Albert Erdynast

#9 - *Internships in History* by Suellen Hoy, Robert Sexton, Peter Stearns, and Joel Tarr

#10 - *Research Bibliography in Experiential Learning, Internships, and Field Studies* by Jennifer Anderson with Leslie Smith

#11 - *Environmental Internships* by R. Rajagopal

#12 - *Experiential Learning and Cultural Anthropology* by E. L. Cerroni-Long and Sharon Rubin

	Quantity Ordered

#13 - *Self-Directed Adult Learners and Learning* by Virginia R. Griffin _____

#14 - *Research Agenda for Experiential Education in the 80's* by Jennifer Anderson, Linda Hughes, and Jane Szutu Permaul

NSIEE OCCASIONAL PAPERS -

Monograph series on concepts in experiential education and issues of quality. $5 NSIEE members, $7 others.

#1 - *Toward a Comprehensive Model of Clustering Skills* by John W. Munce _____

#2 - *The Immediate Usefulness of the Liberal Arts: Variations on a Theme* by John M. Bevan _____

#3 - *Policy Issues in Experiential Education* by Michael B. Goldstein _____

#4 - *Field Experience and Stage Theories of Development* by Albert Erdynast _____

#5 - *Students at Work: Identifying Learning in Internship Settings* by David Thornton Moore _____

#6 - *Life Developmental Tasks and Related Learning Needs and Outcomes* by Judy-Arin Krupp _____

#7 - *Dimensions of Experiential Education* edited by Robert F. Sexton _____

#8 - *Public Service Internships and Education in Public Affairs* by Allen Rosenbaum _____

NSIEE-SPONSORED GUIDES AVAILABLE THROUGH OTHER PUBLISHERS:

The Experienced Hand: A Student Manual for Making the Most of an Internship by Timothy Stanton and Kamil Ali.

Ten steps show students how to get a satisfying internship and how to learn the most from the experience. Includes sample forms for all stages of the internship process as well as tips for evaluating what is learned. Useful as a text book in courses with internship components and for the departmental library. 1982, 96 pp., $6 for NSIEE members, $6.95 for others. Prices include postage and handling. Send check to Carroll Press, P. O. Box 8113, Cranston, RI, 02920.

Field Experience: Expand Your Options edited by John Duley.

Six do-it-yourself modules to help students decide what type of field experience or internship best fits their current learning goals. $5.50 (includes postage and handling). Send check to Instructional Media Center, Michigan State University, East Lansing, MI, 48824.

TOTAL OF BOOKS $ _____

Plus required handling fee:
Up to $20 order - add $2.00
Up to $50 order - add $3.50
Over $50 order - add $5.00   + _____
Includes 4th Class postage and processing costs. Please allow 4-6 weeks for delivery.

OPTIONAL
*For lst Class delivery add an   + _____
additional $1.50 for first publication and $. 50 for each additional publication.*

TOTAL PAYMENT DUE $ _____
Full payment or credit card charge *must* accompany order. Make checks payable to NSIEE. Foreign orders must be paid in U.S. funds. Credit card users complete credit card section. All prices subject to change without notice.

Mail to:
National Society for Internships and Experiential Education
122 St. Mary's Street
Raleigh, NC 27605
(919) 834-7536

Name _____ Title _____

Program/Department _____

Institution _____

Address _____

_____ Zip _____

Area Code and Phone Number _____

Are you a member of NSIEE?   ☐ I would like information
Yes ☐   No ☐   about membership in NSIEE.

Credit Card Section

☐ Visa   ☐ Mastercard   Expiration date _____

Card No. _____

Account name _____

Signature __40020066__

DATE DUE

GAYLORD			PRINTED IN U.S.A.